THE
AWAKENED
SELF

Books by Lucien Stryk

Taproot
The Trespasser
Zen: Poems, Prayers, Sermons, Anecdotes, Interviews
Notes for a Guidebook
Heartland: Poets of the Midwest
World of the Buddha: An Introduction to Buddhist Literature
The Pit and Other Poems
Afterimages: Zen Poems of Shinkichi Takahashi
Twelve Death Poems of the Chinese Zen Masters
Zen Poems of China and Japan: The Crane's Bill
Awakening
Heartland II: Poets of the Midwest
Three Zen Poems
Selected Poems
Haiku of the Japanese Masters
The Duckweed Way: Haiku of Issa
The Penguin Book of Zen Poetry
The Duckpond
Prairie Voices: Poets of Illinois
Zen Poems
Encounter with Zen: Writings on Poetry and Zen
Cherries
Bird of Time: Haiku of Basho
Willows
Collected Poems 1953–1983
On Love and Barley: Haiku of Basho
Triumph of the Sparrow: Zen Poems of Shinkichi Takahashi
Bells of Lombardy
Of Pen and Ink and Paper Scraps
The Dumpling Field: Haiku of Issa
The Gift of Great Poetry
Cage of Fireflies: Modern Japanese Haiku
Zen, Poetry, the Art of Lucien Stryk (ed. by Susan Porterfield)
Zen Poetry: Let the Spring Breeze Enter
Where We Are: Selected Poems and Zen Translations

THE AWAKENED SELF

Encounters with Zen

Lucien Stryk

KODANSHA INTERNATIONAL
New York • Tokyo • London

Kodansha America, Inc.
114 Fifth Avenue, New York, New York 10011, U.S.A.

Kodansha International Ltd.
17-14 Otowa 1-chome, Bunkyo-ku, Tokyo 112, Japan

Published in 1995 by Kodansha America, Inc.
by arrangement with Ohio University Press.

This is a revised edition of *Encounter with Zen*, published in 1981
by Swallow Press, Inc., Ohio University Press, Athens, Ohio.

This is a Kodansha Globe book.

Acknowledgments appear on pp. 353–54.

ISBN 1-56836-046-0
LC 95-79553

Printed in the United States of America

95 96 97 98 99   RRD/H   10 9 8 7 6 5 4 3 2 1

To Lucy and Leslie
with affection and gratitude

Contents

PART II   ENCOUNTERS

PART III   ENCOUNTERS WITH LUCIEN STRYK

THE
AWAKENED
SELF

Introduction

I   Last summer, strolling in deep serenity through daisy-lacing
grass, by sky-blue iris, whopping scarlet poppies, dark-plum
snapdragons, dusk-rose and shocking-pink lupins, the
breeze-stirred fluff of ducklings sparking ideas in the sun,
I saw an old park-bencher, squirrel sniffing at his boot, as he sat unaware of both of us, elbows on knees, chin deep in hands, eyes open
but unseeing. Was he, I wondered, caught up in the inner music of
this lovely day? Perhaps reflecting on a personal loss, or into a serenity,
hard won and fleeting, of his own? Passing, I saw the headphones
clamped over his ears, and left him to the boom box by his side. Serenity,
rare as it is precious, delicate as flake on flake of snow, is necessary as
the air I breathe, in a world grown weary of senseless violence, intol-
erance, the daily sweat and stew. Even Marcus Aurelius, in his *Medi-
tations*, spoke of a serene hour as the only hour worth counting. As
most leaders of his time, he found fame a mixed blessing: so much
demanded of one, intrigues to unravel, battles to fight. Even the most
spartan was bound to lose control, and the miracle of calm—for so it
must have seemed—was greatly treasured.

In the Far East, life was just as difficult. For centuries China had
been bristling with cruel despots constantly at war with each other. Six
hundred years before the birth of Christ, Confucius emerged as some-

one capable of imposing humane order on chaos, yet his rigidly patterned ethical system, governing all aspects of life, was hardly conducive to serenity. Indeed to the Taoists of his day the Confucian orthodoxies and imperatives, however well meant and socially productive, were nothing less than shackles. The Taoists hungered for the freedom which only a tranquil mind could know. Several centuries after the Taoism of Lao Tzu and Chuang Tzu had won over the important artists and intellectuals, it merged with the reigning Buddhism of the day into Zen, which had as its chief goal the achievement of inviolable serenity. And that in our own time is still the goal of Zen.

While the few on the path, through meditation and spiritual exercises, may find some form of tranquility, the world as a whole has a low opinion of such pursuits. I confront with dismay a view, often vehemently expressed, that so-called quietism is retrograde, if not immoral, that the wage of pointless un-ambition is bound to be failure. How manifestly inferior such "softness" appears to the dynamic everquesting power of the modern spirit, with its global networking and instant communication. Man has shot so far ahead of his nervous system, not to speak of his mind, that there is real and imminent danger of self-destruction. When finding myself a participant in the day's hectic ritual, I think back to Zen masters and laymen I have met, especially the great Zen poet Shinkichi Takahashi. A poem of his:

The Pipe

While I slept it was all over,
Everything. My eyes, squashed white,
Flowed off toward dawn.

There was a noise,
Which, like all else, spread and disappeared:
There's nothing worth seeing, listening for.

When I woke, everything seemed cut off.
I was a pipe, still smoking,
Which daylight would knock empty once again.

Very much involved with the piece since first wrestling with its translation, I asked the poet: Must it be read as sheer nihilism? Or was it like so many of his poems an expression of some special Zen insight? He laughed for a while before explaining the poem should be taken quite literally, that he often felt like a pipe, filled, knocked empty, filled again, and he supposed he had been made to feel that way by the thrusts of modern life. He was especially troubled by its speed, would have loved to see the mailman not more than once a week, and the outlawing of most telephones. Shinkichi Takahashi died in 1987, and thus was spared some of the notorious suffocations of the spirit, fax machines, cellular phones, sundry beepers, all making it virtually impossible to shield oneself from importunate, and often painful, intrusions, so bombarded are we by them. Are we reaching the perilous point of no return? Surely it is fit time to step back, far back, to a pace more natural, an air less noxious.

How can we find serenity of the kind offered by Zen in such frantically botched-up times, when even the seemingly fortunate confess anxieties of all sorts? How much sun can they safely absorb, how much rich food consume? It is as true today as it was for Marcus Aurelius and all seekers of true peace and awakening that the serene hour, tranquil life, is hard-earned, more likely to be won doing the work of the world, in the realm of action, thought, or creativity.

There is neither East nor West in the need for tranquility. Some of the finest pages devoted to its quest are found in essayists of the past, among them William Hazlitt (1778–1830), who distinguished himself as a great stylist and for a very modern sensibility. Though sorely troubled in life, everything he wrote has the intensity and assurance of a master. No one more avidly sought relief from common tensions, and in order to find it he would take long walking tours, escaping London, editors, abrasive reviewers. In the essay "On Going a Journey" he gives an altogether memorable image of serenity:

> It was on the 10th April 1798 that I sat down to a volume of the *New Eloise* . . . over a bottle of sherry and a cold chicken. The letter I chose was that in which St Preux describes his feelings as he first caught a glimpse . . . of the Pays de Vaud, which I had brought with me as a *bonne bouche* to crown the evening with. It was my birthday, and I had for the first time [visited] this delightful spot. . . . But besides the prospect . . . another also opened to my inward sight, a heavenly vision. . . .

One thousand years before those heartening words, on the other side of the globe, the Chinese monk Ryuge (835–923) found an equal measure of contentment in mountains and valleys:

> A vegetarian in shabby robe, my spirit's
> Like the harvest moon—free, life through.

> Asked where I dwell, I'll say:
> In green water, on the blue mountain.

So did his contemporary Zengetsu (833–912):

> Mind, mind, mind—above the Path.
> Here on my mountain, gray hair down,
> I cherish bamboo sprouts, brush carefully
> By pine twigs. Burning incense,
> I open a book: mist over flagstones.
> Rolling the blind, I contemplate:
> Moon in the pond. Of my old friends,
> How many know the Way?

In India, meditative "forest dwelling" in one's maturing years was an established tradition, accepted by Hinduism and Buddhism as an essential step on the path toward enlightenment. As those religions spread, particularly in the Far East, it took a form conditioned by local customs, and when, in sixth-century China, Buddhism joined with the indigenous Taoism to form Zen, the well-established practice of spiritual retreat was held to be of great importance.

The Zen sect established itself in Japan in the eleventh century, with the enthusiastic support of some of the reigning warlords, who were especially keen to exploit its disciplinary measures in the training of samurai. Little by little the more spiritual role of Zen came to the fore, and, as in China of the past, a period of retreat in the mountains was thought by the sect's masters not only meritorious but an essential preparation for enlightenment. Some masters who engaged in the practice, like Fugai (seventeenth century), were openly scornful of those unwilling to undergo hardships, as this anecdote, much admired in Zen communities, illustrates:

> One day the monk Bundo, fascinated by Fugai's famous austerities, called at the master's cave and asked if he could spend the night. The master seemed happy enough to put him up, and next morning prepared a breakfast of rich gruel for him. But not having an extra bowl he left the cave and a bit later returned with a skull found near a tomb. Filling it with gruel, he offered it to Bundo, who refused to touch it, staring at Fugai as if he thought him mad. At this the master became furious and drove the monk from the cave with blows. "Fool!" he shouted after him, "how can you, with your worldly notions of filth and purity, think yourself a Buddhist?"

Fugai was not only a Zen master, but also an illustrious painter and poet. Here is one of his best-known pieces:

> Only the Zen-man knows tranquility:
> The world-consuming flame can't reach this valley.
> Under a breezy limb, the windows of
> The flesh shut firm, I dream, wake, dream.

East or West, the achievement of serenity, arrived at by whatever means, has never been more important than in our time. As one who has lived in Japan, I am often asked whether the world I picture in books, so fragile, refined, is but a pretty anachronism in these days of roughhouse industry with its encroachments into everything. Such questions, faced honestly, are not easy to deal with. Sometimes the impulse to express one's fears is very strong:

> *Shrine of the Crane*
> *(Yamaguchi, Japan)*
>
> Once, far back in time, moving
> as slow shadows in a mime by
> the stone lanterns, chipped,
>
> discolored now, processions
> of shrine maidens, vestal sprigs
> crossed at their breasts, led
>
> by stiff-robed priests, black
> lacquered clogs tap-tapping on
> the path, filed by worshippers
>
> under red *toriis*, up the stone steps,
> passing three fox shrines aflush
> with offerings, coins, rice cakes,
>
> twigs embroidered with a paper-twist
> of prayer. Today those hungry
> ghosts with lofty dreams have fled
>
> the hum of useless prayer on prayer,
> to get ahead, outstrip, outdo,
> all dreams lost somewhere in the fold
>
> of time, deaf to the song of cranes.

DeKalb, Illinois, 1995

II   I sit at a window overlooking snow-heavy pines in DeKalb, Illinois. Juncos, sparrows, bluejays dart to and from the bird-feeder on this bitterly cold day, a new year begun. It seems only yesterday I sailed to Japan for the fourth time. Before boarding the freighter in Seattle, I visited the Art Museum's superb collection of Oriental art. Two Chinese works of the Yuan Dynasty (1279–1368) were particularly impressive: a supremely delicate scroll of flowering plum by Yang Hui, and an anonymous piece which seemed almost prophetic, a nearly life-size representation in polychromed wood called "Monk at Moment of Enlightenment." Overwhelmed, I thought of the Japanese master Daito's awakening poem, written in the same period:

> At last I've broken Unmon's barrier!
> There's exit everywhere—east, west; north, south.
> In at morning, out at evening; neither host nor guest.
> My every step stirs up a little breeze.

Often when translating Zen poems, I had touched such an experience; yet, though poems of enlightenment like Daito's gave its essence, this work shuddered with release. I stood before the figure for some time, then grasped the source of my fascination: the monk's face was familiar, that of a Zen priest in the mountains near Niigata, the first enlightened Zenist I had met, so many years before.

Now I was going back to question how life and art of such men are affected by the philosophy. Since having tried, as they, to shape my life and poetry according to Zen principles, having translated and commented on some of its great literature, I sometimes wondered whether insights gained might be substantiated through encounters with serious practitioners, whether Zen's truth still lived. To know seemed necessary. My plan to collaborate once again with Professor Takashi Ikemoto of Japan, who had taken part in earlier encounters, was not to be, for I found him too ill to contemplate such work. Hiroshi Takaoka, once my student in Niigata, helped arrange most of the meetings. I am always indebted to these good friends.

I would have liked to meet with more Zenists, had it been possible to convince them that they were worthy of being heard. Among those who would have proved to be fine subjects was Hachiro, a waste collector and very happy man, who once told me:

As a child I played in temple gardens—thought, why, here's the life! I watched disciples at their daily tasks, scrubbing, raking, steaming rice pots, chanting and, especially, just sitting! Here's the life for me, I thought. Only when it came to it, I found you have to learn all sorts of things, study hard. That's not for me, I thought, remembering how last time I saw the inside of a school-room, the teacher, foaming at the mouth, chased me out the door and down the path. They tried to make me go back in—I never did. Since then I've collected 'honey' in my wagon. The farmers pay well for it! Still, the life of those Zenists appeals to me. I learned some of the poems, like all children—they're so brief and clear and helpful. I make my own *zendo* in my head! Take it everywhere with me. For awhile I lived like a traveling monk, begging a bowl here and there. Some may consider my collecting of dung a common task—to me it's noble. What could be closer to the essence of things? Why, I forewarn of a sickness before the first symptoms hit them, and imagine—what the world reviles as waste, I put to work, to grow, marveling at the rebirth as I push my cart by all the fertile fields each day. It humbles me to know I have a hand in it! Zen? I'm a Zenist, yes, but that's all I can tell you.

My hope on setting out was to talk with others like Hachiro—fishermen, farmers, factory workers, Zen nuns—but it was impossible to get them to describe their feelings. Thus, I had to turn for the most part to Zen masters, artists, craftsmen, and poets, willing, or near will-ing, to articulate. If, therefore, my selection seems limited, the talk, I feel, is not. Once underway, my subjects spoke frankly, often with great warmth. Zenists value *mondo* (exchanges) and other forms of discussion highly; there are numerous Zen anecdotes, based on dialogue of great sophistication, some which read quite like poems. The following are sharp examples.

When Ninagawa-Shinzaemon, linked-verse poet and Zen devotee, heard that Ikkyu (1394–1481), abbot of the famous Daitokuji in Murasakino (violet field) of Kyoto, was a remarkable master, he desired to become his disciple. He called on Ikkyu, and the fol-lowing dialogue took place at the temple gate:
Ikkyu: Who are you?
Ninagawa: A Buddhist.
Ikkyu: You are from?
Ninagawa: Your region.

Ikkyu: Ah. What's happening there these days?
Ninagawa: Crows caw, sparrows twitter.
Ikkyu: And where do you think you are now?
Ninagawa: In a field dyed violet.
Ikkyu: Why?
Ninagawa: Miscanthus, morning glories, safflowers, chrysan-
themums, asters.
Ikkyu: After they're gone?
Ninagawa: It's Miyagino (field known for its autumn
flowering).
Ikkyu: What happens in the field?
Ninagawa: The stream flows through, the wind sweeps over.
Amazed at Ninagawa's Zen-like speech, Ikkyu led him to his room,
served him tea. Then he spoke the following impromptu verse:

I want to serve
You delicacies.
Alas, the Zen sect
Can offer nothing.

At which the visitor replied:

The mind which treats me
To nothing is the original void—
A delicacy of delicacies.

Deeply moved, the master said, "My son, you have learned much."

Son-O and his disciple Menzan (1683–1769) were eating melon
together. Suddenly the master asked, "Tell me, where does all this
sweetness come from?"

"Why," Menzan quickly swallowed and answered, "it's a product of cause and effect."

"Bah, that's cold logic!"

"Well," Menzan said, "from where then?"

"From that very 'where' itself, that's where."

Sometimes *mondo* is practically wordless, startling:

While drinking tea with his disciple Tetsumon, Zenkoku (1670–
1742) said, "A monk must be unfettered in life and death." Seeing
an opportunity to begin *mondo*, Tetsumon said, "What is life?"

Zenkoku held out his hands.

"What is death?"

Zenkoku joined his hands at his chest (a Chinese salutation).

"That may be your Zen," said Tetsumon, "but it isn't mine."
Now it was the master's turn: "What is life?" he said.
Tetsumon joined his hands at his chest.
"What is death?"
Tetsumon held out his hands.
"Ha!" Zenkoku said. "But you're not very firm, are you?"
Testumon smiled triumphantly, got to his feet, and strode out of the room. But it was long after, regretting his hauteur, that he realized perfect enlightenment.

At times when about to embark on a new meeting, I felt like a *tyro*. Fortunately my subjects, respecting the purpose of my questions, not only treated me with courtesy but seemed to realize how important their answers were to me. Thus, I found myself asking things which in other circumstances might have been held indiscreet.

One of the most interesting elements in the encounters was the occasional comparative judgment—Professor Ando's view of J. D. Salinger's "silence," for example—which he explains with great conviction in Zen terms. At such moments I felt treated to rare insights, whether or not I had reservations. Perhaps it helped that my subjects were aware of my interests, as when I spoke with Shinkichi Takahashi, whose translator I have been for many years and whose friendship I value. Sometimes, as in the encounter with Takahashi, there are references to my work. I ask the reader to bear with it, since I felt obliged to offer all that was said, even at risk of embarrassment.

I wanted more than anything to avoid disruption of a promising current of thought, often the result of natural feelings of discretion, sometimes pursuing doggedly a particular point. Yet, I was never made to feel that I had gone too far—it was only later that I felt shame. After all, I was there to discover and hope that I was never less than courteous in a country where manners are deeply refined. Having always believed not only in the possibility but necessity of serious communication, whether in statesmanship, philosophy, or poetry, I am conscious of the dangers of imprecision; the consequences, often appalling, of permitting discourse to fall apart. How many conflicts, both mental and physical, might be avoided were men to sit down not to talk but listen—how many misunderstandings swept away. As Albert Camus, whose life was sometimes poisoned by misunderstanding, said, "Naming an object inaccurately means adding to the unhappiness of the world."

I was hoping to find answers to questions which, though significant to Zenists, are infrequently asked, thus becoming sources of obfuscation. I wanted to know what sects think of each other, whether grudges sometimes sensed in the literature, early and recent, are common. If so, why? I hoped to discover the way an artist's work not only reflects Zen attitude but how the discipline guides the eye and hand. I hoped, above all, to learn whether *satori* (enlightenment), the point of meditation and Zen's greatest achievement, was realizable to most or a goal remote as Paradise. Was Zen meant for the superior, as the Sixth Patriarch Hui-neng maintained, or could all, as the Japanese master Bankei-Eitaku believed, benefit by sincere pursuit? How benefit, how was life affected?

On some matters I gained insight, on others offered but a glimpse, on some I still stand in the dark. So many things resist attempts at clarification; their darkness, as Lao Tzu proclaimed in the *Tao Teh Ching*, the greater part of their meaning. Like Taoism which, joining with Buddhism in the sixth century, gave it birth, Zen is a mystic way, and that which it insists cannot be revealed must be respected. Yet perhaps through attempting to understand, we show most respect; a paradox no more troubling than others associated with Zen.

If anything qualifies me for the task of such probing, it is more than likely my perpetual astonishment at the beauty and wisdom of Zen's humblest manifestations, from the daily conduct of Zenists I have known, to the words of masters and works of its artists, some represented in this book. Zen insists on the possibility of human integrality, offering guidance at every turn: a master for practitioners, works of imagination for those whose aim is the deepening and purification of vision. Surely it was Zen that Vincent Van Gogh had in mind when, in a letter to his brother Theo, he spoke of the Japanese genius for close observation, discovering more in less, infinity "in a grain of sand," or a blade of grass:

> If you study Japanese art, you see a man who is undoubtedly wise, philosophic, and intelligent who spends his time how? In studying the distance between the earth and the moon? No. In studying the policy of Bismarck? No. He studies a single blade of grass. But this blade of grass leads him to draw every plant and then the seasons, the wide aspects of the countryside, then animals, then the human figure. So he passes his life, and life is too short to do the whole.

It is an axiom in Zen that whatever his life, he who seeks finds, so long as the search is natural and the goal nothing more nor less than the awakened self. The encounters in this volume are meant to offer evidence that, in the face of all that would make it an absurdity in our time, Zen is being practiced seriously, sometimes with transfiguring results. No one I met, in or out of the temple, claimed superiority for himself or the work of his hands, yet each possessed a serenity, as unmistakable as it is rare.

DeKalb, Illinois, 1976

ESSAYS

Part I

BEGINNINGS, ENDS

I   My first encounter with an enlightened Zenist took place twenty-five years ago at his temple in the mountains south of Niigata in Japan. I knew little of Zen, but found myself responding with increasing warmth to its arts. I had gone to an exhibit of the priest's ceramics in Niigata, where I lectured on literature at the university, and was greatly taken by their purity and vigor. Asking about him, I was informed that his temple was in the mountains some fifteen miles from the city. Soon I was able to arrange a visit.

On a bright Saturday morning in autumn, accompanied by two of my students—Yoshki, whom I often think of, wondering where life has taken him, and Hiroshi, now a teacher and lifelong friend—I took a bus to the nearest stop, some miles from the temple. For two hours, we went on foot up a path deep into forests flaming with pine and maple, occasionally passing a farmer or woodsman, startled at the sight of a foreigner (I was told later that I was probably the first ever to walk that path). Finally we reached the temple, before which was a garden thick with vegetables piled up in the sun. The priest, bent over a spade, shouted a greeting, bowed, said he would join us before long.

To the right of the old tile-roofed temple was a small kiln, a dozen recently fired pots, and to its side, some farmers crouching besides baskets who, we later learned, bringing gifts of rice and mushrooms, had come to mull over plans with the priest and his wife for a coming festival. We joined them, amused at their good-natured laughter at the sight of such a stranger, exclaiming over the brightly packaged sweet beancakes we had brought. Finally the priest approached and, brushing earth from his hands, called to his wife to bring out tea for all. He chatted with his visitors—clearly a joyous occasion.

Soon he turned his attention to us, warmly insisting that we stay at the temple overnight. We gladly accepted, then followed to the kiln where he replaced new-fired pots. Every word and gesture flowed unhurried, as if he had known us always, genuinely pleased that we had come. We spent the day walking in all directions, gathering fallen nuts, and in the evening, after the chanted service and the sounding bell, we feasted on sweet pickles, rice, and vegetables served by his wife, so clearly proud that strangers had come from far Niigata to meet her husband. Then came our chance to really talk with him.

For one seeming so cut off from worldly matters, he was exceptionally informed in the arts, speaking easily, with much enthusiasm of ceramics, painting, and, when he became aware of my interest, poetry. He spoke of great Zen poets, of whom I knew next to nothing, and—to my surprise—of certain foreign writers in whom he had a strong interest, among them Whitman and Thoreau. He asked what was felt about them these days, whether I was teaching their works at the university. Impressed with the acuteness and boldness of his judgment, I began asking about Zen, his life as priest and artist. What he told me, his very manner, convinced me I would have to set about learning as much as possible about a philosophy which could inspire such a life, make a man content with his place, however obscure, and his work among people for whom he obviously cared deeply.

The visit left an extraordinary impression. Home again, sipping tea from the superb bowl he made for me (I still count it among my prized possessions), I began making plans. Soon I was inquiring seriously into Zen, reading everything available, and, for my own pleasure and enlightenment, making very tentative translations of some of its literature, particularly poetry. I visited temples and monasteries, meeting masters and priests throughout the country and, most important of all, began to meditate. I sensed most strongly that I had found something which could make a difference to my future. The intuition proved right, for that encounter in the mountains was among the most important of my life.

II   Japanese Zen poems, written by masters, priests, and laymen since the thirteenth century, are for the most part simple and highly suggestive. Rarely is a poem beyond understanding, though, to be sure, there is often symbolic
content requiring explanation. The poets rarely wrote about their
poems, for very good reason: to them poetry—for that matter, any
art—was not something to be cultivated but a means to self-judgment
and a gauge of spiritual growth. Often a poem was composed in response to a *koan* (problem for meditation) set by a master, such as,
"Describe the face you had before you were born." Some of the finest
poems have resulted from struggles with such problems: one of the
first *koans* given to disciples, "Joshu's Nothingness," is a source of
many. When Kuchu felt illuminated, he wrote:

> Joshu's word—Nothingness.
> In spring blossom everywhere.
> Now insight's mine,
> Another dust-speck in the eye!

Such poems gave graphic proof of the breakthrough to awakening,
and thus became for generations objects of meditation—important as
the *koans* which inspired them—on the harsh path to enlightenment.

Rarely in the history of religion has art played so fruitful a role,
however emphatic the disclaimers of many Zen practitioners. Shinkichi Takahashi, Japan's most celebrated contemporary Zen poet,
wrote: "As a follower of the tradition of Zen, which is above verbali-
zation, I must confess that I feel ashamed of writing poems or having
collections of them published in book form." This echo of Lao–Tsu
in the Taoist classic *Tao Teh Ching*—"He who knows does not
speak"—heard often in Zen communities, must not be taken lightly.
Zen came as the result of the fortunate merging in sixth century China
of Taoism and Buddhism and is still rooted in Taoism. There is the
exemplary, unbroken, wall-facing meditation of its first patriarch
Bodhidharma, for example, and the numerous anecdotes about the
power of the unspoken:

> Butei, Emperor of Ryo, sent for Fu-daishi to explain the Dia-
> mond Sutra. On the appointed day Fu-daishi came to the palace,
> mounted a platform, rapped the table before him, then descended
> and, still not speaking, left.
>
> Butei sat motionless for some minutes, whereupon Shiko, who

had seen all that happened, went up to him and said, "May I be so bold, sir, as to ask whether you understood?"

The Emperor sadly shook his head.

"What a pity!" Shiko exclaimed. "Fu-daishi has never been more eloquent."

Yet Zen is the least solemn of Buddhist schools and sometimes is caught spitting on itself—with glee. In the following anecdote, as well-known as the preceding, the self-mockery is compelling:

> A self-proclaimed Master of Silence had in attendance at all times two eloquent disciples. Never uttering a word himself, he was ever inscrutable. One day while his disciples were out, he was visited by a pilgrim, whose first question was, "What is the Buddha?" In his confusion Master of Silence looked around in all directions for the disciples. Satisfied by his "answer," the pilgrim went on to ask other questions, and each silent response, accompanied by strange looks and gestures, more than satisfied his curiosity. He left the Master to set out again on his journey, meeting the two disciples on the way. He was full of enthusiasm. "When I asked him," he said, "what Buddha is, he immediately turned his face in all directions, implying that humans are always looking for Buddha—but actually he is not to be sought in such a way. And his answers to my other questions were even more impressive—what a remarkable master!" When the disciples returned, the Master of Silence cried out, "Where have you been? Some crazy pilgrim has been driving me mad with impossible questions!"

Muga, the state of mind in which one identifies with an object without any sense of restraint, is achieved only by the enlightened, like Bunan:

> The moon's the same old moon,
> The flowers exactly as they were,
> Yet I've become the thingness
> Of all the things I see!

The moon, as here, is a common symbol. It should be borne in mind that Zen, however extraordinary it appears, is very much a school of Mahayana Buddhism, and like all Buddhists, the Zenist searches

within for the indivisible moon, reflected not only by the waves but
by each dew drop. Always Zen is to be found, if at all, in immediate
experience; the firefly rather than the star.

To discover the Buddha-nature (*Dharmakaya*) anywhere is for
the Zenist to find his own nature, and whether designated so or not
most Zen poems are *satori* poems. But there is another type of poem
which is unique in world literature, the death poem, traditionally
written or dictated just before death. The Zenist looks back on his life
and, steeled by necessity, expresses in a few terse lines his very being.
These are among the best known:

> Magnificent! Magnificent!
> No one knows the final word.
> The ocean bed's aflame,
> Out of the void leap wooden lambs.
> —Fumon

> Riding this wooden upside-down horse,
> I'm about to gallop through the void.
> Would you seek to trace me?
> Ha! Try catching the tempest in a net.
> —Kukoku

> The void has collapsed upon the earth,
> Stars, burning, shoot across Iron Mountain.
> Turning a somersault, I brush past.
> —Zekkai

The void, mentioned in all the poems, is Zen's great Penetralium: the mind is a void in which objects, stripped of their objectivity,
are reduced to essence. In this death poem there is another important
symbol, the ox, object of discipline.

> For seventy-two years
> I've kept the ox well under.
> Today, the plum in bloom again,
> I let him wander in the snow.
> —Bokuo

Bokuo, in his stoic acceptance, proves himself a true Zen-man.
Though *satori* and death are constants, many Zen poems deal with
nature and man's place in it. The Buddha-nature is not man's alone;
it is discoverable in all that exists, animate or inanimate. Perhaps in
this poem by Genko it is perfectly caught:

Unaware of illusion or enlightenment,
From this stone I watch the mountains, hear the stream.
A three-day rain has cleansed the earth,
A roar of thunder split the sky.
Ever serene are linked phenomena,
And though the mind's alert, it's but an ash heap.
Chilly, bleak as the dusk I move through,
I return, a basket brimmed with peaches on my arm.

III   Zen sermons are unlike those of any other religion, whatever the master's sect—Rinzai, which stresses sudden enlightenment, Soto, which maintains that gradually perfected meditation is equal to enlightenment, or Obaku,
which has more in common with Rinzai, practicing rigorous *zazen*
(formal meditation) and employing *koan*, though the chanting of the
Nembutsu (invocation of the Bodhisattva Amida) is also engaged in
by this sect. The purpose of the sermon is less to uphold what is
vaguely thought the ethical life than to point directly at awakening.
It is assumed by masters that those present at *teisho* (sermons) are
morally upright and that what they seek is a radical way of viewing
themselves in the world. Sometimes the sermons, invariably brief, are
more like demonstrations. The following report, by a disciple, of a
teisho by the modern master Joko Shaku on the Chinese poet Sotoba's
satori poem is illuminating.

> The master began by reciting the famous poem, which he said
> had been written by the layman Sotoba nearly òne thousand
> years ago:
>
>> The mountain—Buddha's body.
>> The torrent—his preaching.
>> Last night, eighty-four thousand poems.
>> How, how make them understand?
>
> After analyzing the poem, the master said that its most important
> words were "mountain" and "torrent." With growing interest,
> he continued, "Which of the two words is more important? Of
> course, 'torrent.' What's the sound of the torrent Sotoba heard at
> Rozan? Zaa-zaa-zaa—the sound fills the universe!" After paus-
> ing, he went on, "Good. Then is the torrent alone the Buddha's
> profound teaching?" He paused again. "Oh, I forgot about the

mountain. What's the mountain?" He looked around slowly, then said, "I'll have to let you see it." He then turned down his eyelid with a finger, saying, "Do you see any green in my eye?" With that he got up and left.

In spite of similarity in aims, whatever the sect, the sermons are as individual as the masters themselves. Bankei-Eitaku is a good example:

> The only thing I tell my people is to stay in the Buddha-mind. There are no regulations, no formal disciplines. Nevertheless, they have agreed among themselves to sit in Zen for a period of two incense sticks (an hour or so) daily. All right, let them. But they should understand that the birthless Buddha-mind has absolutely nothing to do with sitting with an incense stick burning in front of you. If one keeps in the Buddha-mind without straying, there's no further *satori* to seek.

Great masters are as vital in their sermons as in all else, and some like Shozan, a *samurai* (warrior) until he joined the priesthood in his forty-fifth year, are daringly iconoclastic:

> Unfortunately Buddhism has declined, going from bad to worse, with the result that most are milksops, critically lacking in vigor. Only the valorous can train properly; the ignorant being mild and sanctimonious, mistaken in the belief that such is the way of Buddhist practice. Then there are the madmen who go about trumpeting their attainment of *satori*—a bagatelle. Myself, I'm a stranger to sanctimoniousness and satorishness, my sole aim being to conquer all with a vivacious mind.

The historical continuity of the sermon, from earliest Chinese examples to the most recent Japanese, is possibly due to the fact that, when compared with other Buddhist schools, Zen has been able to absorb—at moments seemingly thrive on—shifts and upheavals in politics and culture normally bringing about changes in religion and philosophy. Not unexpected, perhaps, considering its avowed purpose to make it possible for man, whatever the challenge, to remain centered in his Buddha-nature—as true today as fifteen hundred years ago.   ·

Zen interviews are conducted in ways somewhat different from Western dialogues, the unspoken often held to be as important as what is said, meaning deduced from gesture, expression, the very atmosphere. In Zen communities, *mondo* (rapid exchanges) are thought reliable evidence of progress (or stagnation) and are frequently engaged in. Unlike dialogue in the Socratic tradition, in which the dominant party defends a viewpoint, Zen dialogue is at all times intensely exploratory, the participants tested at every turn—not viewpoint, but self. This gives an edge, a thrust, which can be bracing and revealing.

It is revelation which, at all times, is sought, and this accounts for the gravity of Zen dialogues, held for the most part between an enlightened master and either a disciple or one intrigued by the possibility of gaining rare insight. As one who has interviewed Zenists over the years—masters, craftsmen, artists, *Noh* actors—I can testify to astonishing depths of realization. The nature of the quest demands openness, largeness of vision, and, in the most fruitful encounters, there is palpable expansion. The master Tenzan Yasuda, for example, in a discussion of art, describes the effect on him of a painting by the great painter—and fellow Zenist—Sesshu, "Fisherman and Woodcutter": "To be sure, Western art has volume and richness when it is good. Yet, to me, it is too thickly encumbered by what is dispensable. It's as if the Western artist were trying to hide something, not reveal it." Whether or not one finds such judgment to be reasonable—perhaps few Westerners would—the comment, hardly meant to provoke, is deeply interesting.

Often Zen anecdotes concern confrontations between masters and disciples, and at times the disciple is shown "besting" his master:

> Pointing to the sea, Master Kangan said to his disciple Daichi: "You speak of mind over matter—well, let's see you stop those boats from sailing." Without a word the young disciple pulled the *shoji* (screen) across their view. "Hah," the master smiled and placed the *shoji* in position again. "But you had to use your hands!" Still without a word, Daichi then closed his eyes.

For the most part, however, the disciple is very much put in his place: Once a *tyro* asked his master, "What is the First Principle?" Without hesitation the master replied, "If I were to tell *you*, it would become the Second Principle!" Such anecdotes—and they are many—are chiefly responsible for Zen's appeal to those not normally aware of philosophy, yet capable of responding, if it is made palatable, to "wisdom literature." The best anecdotes share with good jokes of a certain order a degree of compactness and point found in only the finest writing. For many it is Zen's nonchalance which gives its greatest appeal. The popularity of the anecdote began with Taoism, particularly in the illustrious Chuang Tzu, who was born in central China around 300 B.C., and who became the toughest opponent of convention-ridden Confucianism. He maintained, in sayings like the following, that the best action is inaction:

—> The operations of Heaven and Earth proceed with the most admirable order, yet they never speak. The four seasons observe clear laws, but they do not discuss them. All of nature is regulated by exact principles, but it never explains them. The sage penetrates the mystery of the order of Heaven and Earth and comprehends the principles of nature. Thus the perfect man does nothing, and the great sage originates nothing. That is to say, they merely contemplate the universe.

Such sayings, uncompromising, unequivocal, greatly troubled Chuang Tzu's Confucian contemporaries, who were bitter in condemnation of what they understood to be Taoist indifference, if not hostility, to social order. It is equally a Western misconception that practitioners of disciplines like Zen are "quietists" turned from the world. So they are, to be sure, while in training, and are better for the experience when fully turned round again; self–discovered and ready as never before to respond to the world at its roughest. Surely Shinkichi Takahashi was not facing a wall when he wrote "Beach":

Gale: tiles, roofs whirling,
disappearing at once.

Rocks rumble, mountains
swallow villages,
yet insects, birds chirp by
the shattered bridge.

Men shoot through space,
race sound. On TV nations
maul each other, endlessly.

Why this confusion,
how restore the ravaged
body of the world?

The sense of Chuang Tzu's saying is not that one should avoid acting, rather it is that one should not act contrary to nature—one must not strain. In an anecdote like the following, the lesson is driven home:

> Kato-Dewanokami-Yasuoki, lord of Osu in the province of Iyo, was passionate about the military arts. One day the great master Bankei called on him and, as they sat face to face, the young lord grasped his spear and made as if to pierce Bankei. But the master silently flicked its head aside with his rosary and said, "No good. You're too worked up." Years later Yasuoki, who had become a great spearsman, spoke of Bankei as the one who had taught him most about the art.

The main purpose of the anecdote, often used in a master's *teisho*, is—very much like the *koan*—to jerk the unenlightened from a state of hebetude, induced by convention, and make it possible to experience awakening. Many of the anecdotes, as we have seen, are very old, drawn from works like the ancient collection of stories with commentaries, *Hekiganroku* (Blue Cliff Record), another Chinese book, the early thirteenth-century *Mu-mon-kan* (Barrier Without Gate), and the late thirteenth-century Japanese work, *Shaseki-shu* (Stone and Sand Collection). There are some anecdotes quite serious in tone, their purpose being to illustrate important Buddhist ideals:

> When wolves were discovered in the village near Master Shoju's temple, he entered the graveyard nightly for all of one week and sat in Zen. Strangely enough, that put a stop to the wolves' prowling. Overjoyed, the villagers asked him to describe the secret rites he had performed. "I didn't resort to such things," he said, "nor could I have done so. While I was in *zazen* a number of wolves gathered around me, licking the tip of my nose, sniffing my windpipe. They did all sorts of silly things. But because I remained in the right state of mind, I wasn't bitten. As I keep preaching to you, the proper state of mind will make it possible for you to be free in life and death, invulnerable to fire and water. Even wolves are powerless against it. I simply tried to practice what I preach."

For the most part, however, the anecdotes are farcical, illogical, and highly paradoxical. Whether its purpose is to amuse, shock or edify, or do all three together, like this one, greatly condensed, the story speaks for itself:

> Two monks were walking by the stream near their temple when

one spotted a leaf of lettuce floating downstream. "Master Gizan (abbot of a monastery a mile upstream) has become a wastrel, I'm afraid." The other nodded and sighed. Suddenly Master Gizan burst, panting, from a clump of bushes ahead and plunged into the stream for the lettuce-leaf. The monks bowed low, and walked on.

MAKING POEMS

I   "The thoughts expressed by music," wrote Mendelssohn in 1842, "are not too vague for words, but too precise." Replace "music" with "poetry" and, perhaps paradoxically, considering of what poems are made, you have a way of seeing into the difficulty of drawing conclusions about the nature of art. There are days when I feel that the main thing, all else equal, is what the poet has to say; other days, that it is his craftmanship, not what he's trying to express, that distinguishes him. What colors my view on any given day, tipping one way or the other, may be far more interesting than the whole issue of aesthetics, which is after all the sphere of aestheticians, not artists. All theories on art strike me as collections of truisms, though some ("The poet's theme dictates structure and is at the same time modified by it," might be one) seem pretty sound. Perhaps under the circumstances, and in spite of the great difficulty, the practicing artist should be willing, when called upon, to try to explain what it is he's after and how he goes about attempting to achieve it. That accepted, in what follows I shall try to give as clear an account as possible of the steps which led to where I now am as a maker of poems.

Some, aware of my work as a translator of Zen poetry, seem to feel that my poems are much affected by that interest, in content as well as structure. I believe they are right. Anyone serious about a discipline like Zen learns soon enough that much of his life, certainly any art he may practice, is being changed by it. When, as a visiting lecturer there, I began translating Zen texts in Japan, I asked the Zen master Taigan Takayama whether the philosophy might be useful to an artist. As an enlightened man (he is one of the most distinguished young masters in Japan), he did not show indignation, but he was most forceful in letting me know that Zen was not something to be "used" by anyone, including the artist, and that its arts were nothing more than expressions of the Zen spirit. That was the first "reprimand" I received. There was another, at the hands of the Zen master Tenzan Yasuda, of a more serious nature. I often went to his temple, the Joeiji, for the superb rock garden laid down by Sesshu, one of Japan's greatest painters who had been a priest at the Joeiji in the fifteenth century. In interviewing the master for the volume *Zen: Poems, Prayers, Sermons, Anecdotes, Interviews*, I said some very stupid things about the rock garden. Tenzan Yasuda was patient, but finally said (I quote from the interview), "In order to appreciate his garden fully, you must have almost as much insight as Sesshu himself. This, needless to say, very few possess. Ideally one should sit in Zen for a long period before looking at the garden; then one might be able to look at it, as the old saying goes, 'with the navel.'"

Even as those words were being spoken, I felt acute self-disgust, and resolved to try to overcome the vanity which had led me to utter empty phrases about something which I had not even "seen," let alone understood (the Sixth Patriarch of Zen, the Chinese master Hui-neng, insisted on "pure seeing"—one must not look *at* things, but *as* things). A few nights later, while working on a conventionally-structured poem set in Sesshu's rock garden, the sort of piece with which I'd already filled two "well-received" but unsatisfactory books, I remembered not only Taigan Takayama's reprimand but Tenzan Yasuda's specific comments on my "view" of the garden. Suddenly I became aware, *saw* with the greatest clarity: my failing in poetry was the result, in great part, of a grave misunderstanding concerning the very purpose of art. The Zen masters who had written the poems I was translating did not think of themselves as "poets" at all; rather, they were attempting to express in verse nothing less than the Zen spirit—and the results were astonishing. The poems, without any pretension to "art," were among the finest I had ever read, intense, compact, rich in spirit. Takayama and Yasuda were right.

Working for hours without a break, I transformed the poem I had been writing on the garden, ridding it of "filling," breaking down rigidly regular stanzas, a welter of words, to a few "image units" of around two and one-half lines, while keeping to a constant measure, the short line throughout being of the same syllabic length. In fact, though unintended, the stanzaic unit I came up with was in length and feeling very close to the *haiku*, and at its best as compact as the short Zen poems I was translating. Perhaps the fact that the "unit" was made up consistently of just so many lines, so controlled, was a matter of chance, the result simply of the way eye and ear, projecting my needs, meshed. I suppose anything leading to, or the result of, deep concentration might have worked as well, but, fortuitous or not, I was convinced that I had made for myself a profound discovery, and that henceforth I might work as an artist.

In the weeks following I wrote seven more pieces about Sesshu's garden; yet, given the challenge and because I wanted the sequence to be the very best I could make it, it took a few years to achieve what seemed to me altogether satisfactory versions of what eventually became:

Zen: The Rocks of Sesshu

I

What do they think of
    Where they lean
Like ponderous heads, the rocks?—

In prankish spring, ducks
    Joggling here
And there, brushing tails,

Like silly thoughts shared,
    Passed from head
To head? When, gong quavering

About a ripened sky, we
    Up and go,
Do they waken from a dream of flesh?

II

In the Three Whites of
    Hokusai—
Fuji, the snow, the crane—

What startles is the black: in
    The outline
Of the mountain, the branch-tips

Piercing the snow, the quills of
   The crane's wing:
Meaning impermanence.

Here, in stainless air, the
   Artist's name
Blazes like a crow.

III

Distance between the rocks,
   Half the day
In shadow, is the distance

Between man who thinks
   And the man
Who thinks he thinks: wait.

Like a brain, the garden,
   Thinking when
It is thought. Otherwise

A stony jumble, merely that,
   Laid down there
To stud our emptiness.

IV

Who calls her butterfly
   Would elsewhere
Pardon the snake its fangs:

In the stony garden
   Where she flits
Are sides so sharp, merely

To look gives pain. Only
   The tourist,
Kodak aimed and ready for

The blast, ship pointing for the
   Getaway,
Dare raise that parasol.

V

To rid the grass of weed, to get
   The whole root,
Thick, tangled, takes a strong mind

And desire—to make clean, make pure.
   The weed, tough
As the rock it leaps against,

Unless plucked to the last
  Live fiber
Will plunge up through dark again.

The weed also has the desire
  To make clean,
Make pure, there against the rock.

VI

It is joy that lifts those pigeons to
  Stitch the clouds
With circling, light flashing from underwings.

Scorning our crumbs, tossed carefully
  To corners
Of the garden, beyond the rocks,

They rose as if summoned from
  The futile
Groveling our love subjects them to.

Clear the mind! Empty it of all that
  Fixes you,
Makes every act a pecking at the crumb.

VII

Firmness is all: the mountain beyond the
  Garden path,
Watch how against its tawny slope

The candled boughs expire. Follow
  The slope where
Spearheads shake against the clouds

And dizzy the pigeons circling on the wind.
  Then observe
Where no bigger than a cragstone

The climber pulls himself aloft
  As by the
Very guts: firmness is all.

VIII

Pierced through by birdsong, stone by stone
  The garden
Gathered light. Darkness, hauled by ropes

Of sun, entered roof and bough. Raised from
  The temple
Floor where, stiff since cockcrow,

> Blown round like Buddha on the lotus,
>   He began
> To write. How against that shimmering,
>
> On paper frail as dawn, make poems?
>   Firm again,
> He waited for the rocks to split.

There were other poems to work on, and getting rid of much, overhauling what remained of a bulky manuscript, I finished what I have always considered to be my first real book, *Notes for a Guidebook* (though it was the third published and limited to a special type of poem: it does not include, for example, "Zen: the Rocks of Sesshu," which I saved for my next volume, *The Pit and Other Poems*). That was in 1965, the same year the first volume of Zen translations, done along with my Japanese friend Takashi Ikemoto, was brought out. No coincidence, for the translation of those profound and moving poems and the making of my own new pieces went on together for a long time. And it's been that way since: *The Pit and Other Poems* (1969) was written for the most part while I was at work on the books *World of the Buddha* (1968) and *After Images: Zen Poems of Shinkichi Takahashi* (1970); while I was at work on *Zen Poems of China and Japan: The Crane's Bill*, I was also composing the poems which appeared in *Awakening*, and the books were published only months apart in 1973.

That my poems owe much to the Zen aesthetic is undeniable, yet they owe as much surely to the many and various things which make up the life of a Midwestern American—husband, father, teacher—in our time, something perhaps most evident in *Awakening* and when I deal with the poems of others in the anthologies, *Heartland: Poets of the Midwest*, I and II, and which I have tried to explain in the interviews done with me.* It would be very disappointing to learn that, because of my interest in Asian philosophy, and the themes and settings of some of my poems, my work was read as that of someone who had gone "bamboo." I believe not only in the need to "hide traces," an invisible art, but as much in the wisdom of hiding sources. "South" is a typical poem:

> *South*
>
> Walking at night, I always return to
>   the spot beyond
> the cannery and cornfields where

---

* See, for example, *Chicago Review*, #88, 1973.

a farmhouse faces south among tall trees.
  I dream a life
there for myself, everything happening

in an upper room: reading in sunlight,
  talk, over wine,
with a friend, long midnight poems swept

with stars and a moon. And nothing
  being savaged,
anywhere. Having my fill of that life,

I imagine a path leading south
  through corn and wheat,
to the Gulf of Mexico! I walk

each night in practice for that walk.

II   T. S. Eliot, in an unpublished lecture on English letter writers, quoted by F. O. Matthiessen in *The Achievement of T. S. Eliot,* says something which, for me, virtually sums up the poet's ideal, one very close to the "less is more" aesthetic of Zen. Eliot refers to a passage in one of D. H. Lawrence's letters which runs: "The essence of poetry with us in this age of stark and unlovely actualities is a stark directness, without a shadow of a lie, or a shadow of deflection anywhere. Everything can go, but this stark, bare, rocky directness of statement, this alone makes poetry, to-day." Eliot's comment:

> This speaks to me of that at which I have long aimed, in writing poetry; to write poetry which should be essentially poetry, with nothing poetic about it, poetry standing naked in its bare bones, or poetry so transparent that we should not see the poetry, but that which we are meant to see through the poetry, poetry so transparent that in reading it we are intent on what the poem *points at,* and not on the poetry, this seems to me the thing to try for. To get *beyond poetry,* as Beethoven, in his later works, strove to get *beyond music.*

To get "beyond poetry," then, to avoid the hateful evidence of our will to impress (thereby perhaps losing that ambition), those handsprings and cartwheels, the heavy breathing down the line, so common to "early work" done at whatever age—the escape from such vulgarity—is the study of a lifetime. It can be furthered by a discipline

like Zen, but everything uniquely Western leading to a like realization will of course do as well. A man's poems should reveal the full
range of his life and hide nothing except the art behind them.

As much admiration as I have for a number of English-speaking
poets, I am very strongly affected by the work of—ranging both East
and West—Shinkichi Takahashi and Zbigniew Herbert, precisely because their poems appear to give the totality of their lives. We may not
know our neighbors, but such poets can become our intimates. The
fact that some of the poets I love write in other tongues is fundamentally of little importance, for they have been translated well
(though as his translator, I should not make such a claim for the
poems of Shinkichi Takahashi!). Never have so many poets turned
to translation, and all of us stand to gain by the collective energy and
dedication, but I admit readily that there are accompanying dangers
and that something very close to "translationese" is too often in evidence.

The range and swell of one of the poems of Theodore Roethke's
"North American Sequence," the superb concisions of his earlier
"greenhouse" poems, are unlikely to be matched in the translations
of even the greatest modern poets. And some of the greatest, Rilke
among them, have sometimes been very poorly served, with almost
criminal effect. A foreign poet is, after all, only as good as his best
translator. Still, to deny ourselves the profound satisfactions of the
best foreign poetry, for whatever reason, to hover timorously above
those deeps out of some theoretical fear, is to cut off a source of major
creative growth. Often foreign poetry offers something unique: all
sensitive people, for example, felt strongly about the reports of Buddhist monks burning themselves to death in Viet Nam—the ultimate
protest against that insane war, a protest not condoned by Buddhism,
but one powerful in its effect on the world as a whole. No response
to such acts by Western writers could have been as complex, as dev-
astatingly right as Shinkichi Takahashi's in his poem about a fellow
Buddhist, "Burning Oneself to Death":

Burning Oneself to Death

That was the best moment of the monk's life.
Firm on a pile of firewood
With nothing more to say, hear, see,
Smoke wrapped him, his folded hands blazed.

There was nothing more to do, the end
Of everything. He remembered, as a cool breeze

Streamed through him, that one is always
In the same place, and that there is no time.

Suddenly a whirling mushroom cloud rose
Before his singed eyes, and he was a mass
Of flame. Globes, one after another, rolled out,
The delighted sparrows flew round like fire balls.

In translating that poem, I was put to a grave test, for the responsibility was awesome, the sort felt, I imagine, by the translator of one of Zbigniew Herbert's poems about World War II resistance fighters in Poland. As I think back to its source, in my experience, I am certain that my work on poems like Takahashi's, my reading of Herbert and Char, among other foreign writers, lay behind the making of this poem:

> *Letter to Jean-Paul Baudot, at Christmas*
>
> Friend, on this sunny day, snow sparkling
> everywhere, I think of you once more,
> how many years ago, a child Resistance
>
> fighter trapped by Nazis in a cave
> with fifteen others, left to die, you became
> a cannibal. Saved by Americans,
>
> the taste of a dead comrade's flesh foul
> in your mouth, you fell onto the snow
> of the Haute Savoie and gorged to purge yourself,
>
> somehow to start again. Each winter since
> you were reminded, vomiting for days.
> Each winter since you told me at the Mabillon,
>
> I see you on the first snow of the year
> spreadeagled, face buried in that stench.
> I write once more, Jean-Paul, though you don't
>
> answer, because I must: today men do far worse.
> Yours in hope of peace, for all of us,
> before the coming of another snow.

I spoke of the responsibility felt when I was working on the Takahashi poem, but I felt it even greater when composing the piece about my friend, to the "experience" itself, one I wanted to share with (impose on?) as many as possible. I knew that in order to do so I would have to get "beyond poetry," put down, without faking, the truth of a young man's pain, which had nothing literary about it and was felt acutely over the years. A pain I was asked to share, and still do.

III   In an interview published by *Chicago Review* in 1973, I responded to the question "Does art do anything more than manifest moments of revelation?" I say something which relates not only to poems I am always hoping to write but also to those which most move me as a reader:

> It extends the imagination; more than anything else it does that. Perhaps the greatest poetry extends and directs it, but all fine poetry does extend, enlarge it. It makes us more than we have ever been. Really important poetry affects the imagination in something like a permanent way; it alters it. If we see the imaginative process (as perceivers or readers) as being constantly acted upon or acting itself, then those things which touch it have varying results. By some, the imagination is substantially affected; by others hardly at all, and, of course, the question is whether the latter are works of art.
>
> Once, in other words, you have read *Hamlet* as it should be read, you are no longer the same person. The possibilities of life have been altered, have been magnified. You read certain poems, they can be rather simple poems, in many ways. . . . I think a good example might be Blake's "London." It's a short poem that reveals, tremendously, a quality of life. When that happens, art takes on a kind of moral grandeur. And I choose as an example a short lyric poem because I think it would suggest what might be the hope of a poet like myself; I want, as a writer, to *reveal* in such a way, hardly with the expectation of achieving a poem like "London," but nevertheless, it offers an aesthetic ideal. . . . What I'm saying, I suppose, is that after reading "London" . . . I have a feeling that my view of that time and place is crystallized by the poem. Thus, it has historical importance. Whatever London was for Blake, and many others, is given, contained in, that poem.
>
> Now, I think this is what art should do. . . . When art can do this, it takes on a dimension that we sometimes forget it is capable of having. But one should not forget. A poet should never write without the vision that such things have been done,

that men have written *Hamlets* and poems like "London," because if he forgets that such things have been done, his work can become trivial. These things stand as warnings, as much as examples. Because by great works, the artist is warned: he cannot afford to use his art for unworthy purposes.

If it is true that, however full the imagination, what the poet experiences fixes the range of his art, then we should not expect him to be constantly touching the depths and the heights. He is often content to be somewhere between, unaware of the distinctions, boundaries set down about him, making some things more important than others. Poetry, not being producible, sometimes just comes, the result of miraculous convergences, the perfect meshing of eye, ear and heart. Some of my poems (the title poem of *The Pit and Other Poems* is a good example) have taken many years to complete; others—and for this I do not think less of them—have been written almost on the spot. I shall never forget wheeling around on my bike and speeding home to get "Étude" down, its music clear in my head:

Étude

I was cycling by the river, back and forth,
     Umbrella up against the
          Rain and blossoms.

It was very quiet, I thought of Woolworth
     Globes you shake up snowstorms in.
          Washed light slanted

Through the cherry trees, and in a flimsy house
     Some youngster practiced Chopin.
          I was moving

With the current, wheels squishing as the music
     Rose into the trees, then stopped,
          And from the house

Came someone wearing too much powder, raincape
     Orchid in the light. Middle-aged,
          The sort you pass

In hundreds everyday and scarcely notice,
     The Chopin she had sent
          Up to those boughs,

Petals spinning free, gave her grace no waters
     Would reflect, but I might
          Long remember.

As most poets, I have been much affected by the other arts, painting and sculpture especially, and along with my involvement in Zen has come a deepening appreciation of *sumie*, the monochromic black /white scroll painting associated with it. Perhaps nothing could illustrate better my turning Eastward and what it has meant to me than the differences—technically, in attitude—between two of my poems, written years apart and dealing with art and the life of the maker. Bartolomeo Ammanati (1511–92), when he was past seventy, wrote in "To the Academy of Design in Florence": "Beware, for God's sake, as you value your salvation, lest you incur and fall into error that I have incurred in my works when I made many of my figures entirely nude." Here is, from *Notes for a Guidebook*, a poem about his most important work:

The Fountain of Ammanati

Below the pigeon-spotted seagod
The mermen pinch the mermaids,
And you shopgirls eat your food.

No sneak-vialed aphrodisiac
Can do—for me, for you—what
Mermen pinching mermaids in a whack

Of sunlit water can. And do.
These water-eaten shoulders and these thighs
Shall glisten though your gills go blue,

These bones will never clatter in the breath.
My dears, before your dust swirls either up
Or down—confess: this world is richly wet.

And consider: there is a plashless world
Outside this stream-bright square
Where girls like you lie curled

And languishing for love like mine.
And you were such as they
Until ten sputtering jets began

To run their ticklish waters down your
Spine. Munch on, my loves, you are but
Sun-bleached maidens in a world too poor

To tap the heart-wells that would flow,
And flow. You are true signorine
Of that square where none can go

And then return. Where dusty mermen
Parch across a strand of sails and spars,
And dream of foamy thighs that churn.

By such works, I appear to be saying, man is made to feel his in-
significance: how pitiable those shop girls against the mermaids.
Whatever its worth as poetry, "The Fountain of Ammanati" is a piece
which examines one of life's profound discrepancies, measures a distance between its realities and ideals. Swirling and clashing, it makes
a harsh judgment. Perhaps the most, or least, that one can say about it
is that it is a young man's poem.

A growing awareness necessitates a changing language, a greater
seriousness, an altered structure. Just as at fifty a man has the face he
has earned, the lineaments of his poems reveal the range and depth of
his spiritual life. Simply by surviving I have become a middle-aged
poet, and as the result of many things which have made that survival
possible, this is where I am now:

Awakening
Homage to Hakuin, Zen Master, 1685–1768

I

Shoichi brushed the black
on thick.
His circle held a poem
like buds
above a flowering bowl.

Since the moment of my
pointing,
this bowl, an "earth device,"
holds
nothing but the dawn.

II

A freeze last night, the window's
laced ice flowers, a meadow drifting
from the glacier's side. I think of Hakuin:

"Freezing in an icefield, stretched
thousands of miles in all directions,
I was alone, transparent, and could not move."

Legs cramped, mind pointing
like a torch, I cannot see beyond
the frost, out nor in. And do not move.

III

I balance the round stone
    in my palm,
turn it full circle,

slowly, in the late sun,
    spring to now.
Severe compression,

like a troubled head,
    stings my hand.
It falls. A small dust rises.

IV

Beyond the sycamore
dark air moves
westward—

smoke, cloud, something
wanting a name.
Across the window,

my gathered breath,
I trace
a simple word.

V

My daughter gathers shells
where thirty years before
I'd turned them over, marveling.

I take them from her,
make, at her command,
the universe. Hands clasped,

marking the limits of
a world, we watch till sundown
planets whirling in the sand.

VI

Softness everywhere,
snow a smear,
air a gray sack.

Time. Place. Thing.
Felt between
skin and bone, flesh.

VII

I write in the dark again,
rather by dusk-light,
and what I love about

this hour is the way the trees
are taken, one by one,
into the great wash of darkness.

At this hour I am always happy,
ready to be taken myself,
fully aware.

WHAT?
WHY THIS.
THIS ONLY

Up in my eyrie-room atop the Chapel of the Madonna of Monserrato, perched on a cliff higher than the hawks above Lake Como, listening to the sweet bells of Bellagio's San Giacomo, I begin to cast into air and mind for an explication of "Awakening" (see pp. 39–41), a poem written years ago in homage to the great Japanese Rinzai Zen master Hakuin.* He expressed more fully than any before or since, through art, painting as well as poetry, the transforming power of Zen discipline. The poem attempts through the relationship of seven parts to suggest the nature of the Zen quest. I shall try to give an idea of each part, without apology but with sharp awareness that most such attempts are foredoomed. When the sequence came, however, I felt I was giving body, shape, to impulses born of my meeting with Zen.

---

* This essay was written while I was in residence, as a Rockefeller Foundation Fellow to complete my *Collected Poems 1953–1983*, at the Bellagio Center in Italy.

I   The artist Shoichi is brushing an *enso* (mystic circle, Zen's mandala), symbolizing Zen attainment. Often a poem is brushed above the *enso*, which in Japanese up/down script resembles "buds" rising from a bowl (image of the circle). In the second stanza, "pointing" suggests a mind sharply directed, the bowl—referred to as an "earth device"—the earth itself. Buddhist meditators often focus upon stone, water, stick, etc. The last part of the poem refers to an awakening. That this first part of the sequence moves to dawn, the last to dusk—however disjointed the in-between—has importance to me.

The assumption of the poem's first part, then, is that it is possible through meditation to transform one's world. The difference between the occasional epiphany, however startling, of Western experience—defined and justly considered by James Joyce in *Portrait of the Artist as a Young Man*—and Zen *satori* of the depth realized by Hakuin is, put simply, that the passing of the epiphanic moment (a return to reality rather like the street stepped back into after a luminous few hours in a theater) is invariably a comedown, whereas true *satori* is permanent in its effects: the world (that street) has been forever altered. I would not claim to have experienced *satori*. In Zen one cannot make such claims—only a master is qualified to judge—yet the experience was more than epiphany: something profound was grasped, had its effect upon my life. It has lasted, grows in strength each time in imagination I return to it.

That is very personal, only one way of putting it, possibly even misleading, for Zen insists the world, perfect just as is, needs no transformation. Rather it is we who must change our relationship to it—in effect, it is we who must undergo change, eyes seeing freshly. Thus responsibility is fully personal: no one to blame or praise, no condition to despair over, find fortunate, just the sudden (it is always that) awareness of where fault (answer) lies. It is never less than astonishing to regain the fullness of one's reality, to return to what we've ignored, possibly despised, and discover it marvelous. The last lines of the poem's first part attempt to express that recognition.

II *Zenkan* is meditation through close observation, leading sometimes to startling awareness. In the poem's second part such quality of perception is suggested by "ice flowers."

There is also associative process: a vision of the glacier leads rapidly (transitional leap) to thought of a moment in one of Hakuin's remarkable *satori* descriptions here modified in verse. In the last tercet there is profound identification with the master. Mind points like a torch because there is hope of escaping, by whatever means, the ice field, i.e., the frozen condition of one's life.

As process *zenkan* is obviously not unique to Zen, or for that matter to religious experience, yet it is practiced by all Zen artists, possibly accounting in large measure for the sharp particularity of their work, from ink painting to *haiku*. Deep, clean seeing, fully expressed, can say much, as in this *haiku* by Basho:

> Snowy morning—
> one crow
> after another.

The poet does not feel called upon to explain that one is more keenly aware of the crow in snow, to the point of "crow-viewing."

Emergence from the "glacier's side" of a meadow suggests perhaps hope (sign?) of awakening, which is of course the goal of meditation. At this moment of fire and ice, pure transparency, the meditator comes face-to-face with his true self, cannot see in or beyond, and cannot move. Facing his condition, his "original self," as Zen defines, he may be on the way to altering his life.

III By now the symbolic drift should be fairly clear, the gravity established. In this fragment the meditator closely observes another "device," this time a stone: slowly, as if a maker were examining a planet, with seasonal progression as the stone is turned, "spring to now." What follows might suggest rejection, by the stone, of such a role. It would seem that it is stone only, pure and simple, and like any other falling raises a "small dust."

I have written elsewhere, in the introduction to *The Penguin Book of Zen Poetry*, of the danger to the Zenist of such "mentalization," as in this passage:

> The Zen experience is centripetal, the artist's contemplation of subject sometimes referred to as "mind-pointing." The disciple in an early stage of discipline is asked to point the mind at (meditate upon) an object, say a bowl of water. At first he is quite naturally inclined to metaphorize, expand, rise imaginatively from water to lake, sea, clouds, rain. Natural, perhaps, but just the kind of "mentalization" Zen masters caution against. The disciple is instructed to continue until it is possible to remain strictly with the object, penetrating more deeply, no longer looking *at* it but, as the Sixth Patriarch Hui-neng maintained essential, *as* it. Only then will he attain the state of *muga*, so close an identification with object that the unstable mentalizing self disappears.

Why must we in order to value something imagine it larger, grander? Emptiness, in Zen, is what every thing *is*, alone, and what establishes *being* is context and relationship, as between the stone and the hand that holds it, the eye that examines it—not what the mind transforms it to. To make such an image of stone is to rob it of its essential being, and ourselves of the greatest possible source of integrality, identification with real things of this world.

IV   This part concerns occasional awareness, always startling, that we name things inadequately, reductively, relieving ourselves of burdens of the unknown. It asks: is certainty necessary, or is it possible to feel—like Keats's ideal poet, possessed of "negative capability"—at ease with uncertainty? Zen meditation inevitably pulls toward such challenging, just as its formal "problems," *koans*, if seriously faced, may lead to great doubt concerning the manners in which, hitherto, we explained reality to ourselves. The *koan* unties knots which have held the world together—rather it cuts them. We are set adrift by *koan*, forced to reexamine all, let the original man within us break free. The last lines of the piece suggest the meditator, uneasy at the prospect ("gathered breath"), ventures an answer, supplies a name. Just another name, as limiting as all the others have been, or one fully his own?

The Chinese master Ch'ing-yuan's famous saying may be appropriate:

> Before I had studied Zen I saw mountains as mountains, waters as waters. When I learned something of Zen, the mountains were no longer mountains, waters no longer waters. But now that I understand Zen, I am at peace with myself, seeing mountains once again as mountains, waters as waters.

And so may be this poem by the eighth-century Chinese poet Beirei:

> All Patriarchs are above our understanding,
> And they don't last forever.
> O my disciples, examine, examine.
> What? Why this. This only.

In a commentary on the poem in *Zen Poems of China and Japan: The Crane's Bill* (Grove, 1981), I write: "The objection to 'learning' is that it inevitably leads to presuppositions concerning the nature of the world, a philosophy the creation of others, whereas meditation and the pure perception which must accompany it may lead to insight into the very nature of things, the world not yet 'created, conceptualized, made philosophy.'"

It should be realized that the examination taking place in this part of "Awakening" is self-imposed, not a *koan* set by a master, that the meditator is so very far from Ch'ing-yuan's third stage, his doubts far from resolved.

V This segment might suggest that long before there is consciousness of meditation's power, as with a child, it is in a sense used. Here, too, "device" has place. What astonished the meditator, the girl's father, was that her command was urgent, suddenly she seemed possessed by will to understand: suddenly, on a Lake Michigan beach, she had to be given a picture of the universe. It was she who thought of clasping hands, so as to define that universe. In writing this, the poet was reminded of the profound structurings of his childhood, arrived at through a similar process of meditation, especially when exposed to nature—trees, flowers, birds, stones, shells.

Reminded of the self-created rituals, countings, touchings, all the secret ways which gave sense to his otherwise ruled world.

There is serious misunderstanding regarding Zen meditation. That it should be carried out, among fellow practitioners, in a *zendo*, that there should be, if only occasionally, the guidance of an authentic master, goes without saying. Yet unless the practice leads, slowly but surely, to new, permanent ways of dealing with reality, a constant state of meditation, it may be of little avail. Hakuin, most instructive of the great Rinzai masters, reveals to what degree he felt that meditation must be known by its fruits. Time and again he found it necessary, as the result of a strongly felt lapse, to return "to the mat" for prolonged sessions of *zazen*.

Hakuin was to insist, along with masters like Bankei-Eitaku, on the need to carry the meditative spirit out of the *zendo* into life. The meditative moment, we learn from such masters, is not special, something to be risen from, let alone descended into: it is every moment of full awareness, and can and should concern all. Children, at their best, well before learning to conduct their lives, do not discriminate between high, low, valuable, negligible. Simplest things, at the right moment, draw the deepest responses from them, become meditative devices. Surely it was in that sense Wordsworth understood the child to be father to the man.

VI   This snip of poem may appear to concern the process of de-creation, yet that was not the intention. The purpose was not to give dissolving body to Zen's first principle, that all passes, but to point at the relationship of all things, held together in the "gray sack" of air. It was also to image the essential formlessness of all, in a world of illusory forms—flesh "between" skin and bone. As in the case of all Zen expression, the poem is a meditation on the nature of Void, in which all forms and individuating characteristics are stripped away. All is empty. Nowhere is this fundamental fact of Zen given fuller expression than in the poetry of its masters.

It is also profoundly felt in the prose of great meditators, such as Pingalaka, best known as commentator on Nagarjuna, the late second-century Buddhist dialectician whose writings were all-important to the formation of Zen. Pingalaka writes:

> The cloth exists on account of the thread; the matting is possible on account of the rattan. If the thread had its own fixed, unchangeble self-essence, it could not be made out of the flax. If the cloth had its own fixed, unchangeable self-essence, it could not be made from the thread. But as in point of fact the cloth comes from the thread and the thread from the flax, it must be said that the thread as well as the cloth had no fixed, unchangeable self-essence. It is just like the relation that obtains between the burning and the burned. They are brought together under certain conditions, and thus there takes place a phenomenon called burning. The burning and the burned, each has no reality of its own. For when one is absent the other is put out of existence. It is so with all things in this world, they are all empty, without self, without absolute existence. They are like the will-o'-the-wisp.

It should not be necessary to comment on the moral implications of such a view, yet not to maintain the living dimension of Zen principles would be to do its practitioners an injustice. Suffice it to say that if one holds such a view, one cannot behave aggressively. Such feelings have had powerful expression in the West, as at the beginning of D. H. Lawrence's essay "We Need One Another":

> We lack peace because we are not whole. And we are not whole because we have known only a tithe of the vital relationships we might have had. We live in an age which believes in stripping away the relationships.

VII   The poem's conclusion offers something of a thematic summation: to one awakened, life in its fullness, beginning to end, is not only bearable but joyous. The preference for "dusk-light," the moment before day's (life's) end, suggests the profoundest segment of light's cycle, when meditation is most natural. Like the trees, man should release into the "wash of darkness," fully aware of what acceptance means.

It is one of the world's paradoxes that he who loves life most least fears its conclusion, yet there are few who attain such a state of acceptance. For the very religious especially there are needs of assurance of another chance, a further opportunity, miraculously in flesh. Karma, as real in Zen as in all Buddhism, does not offer comfort of bodily return. Perhaps the most helpful analogy is of a candle which, before expiring, passes its flame to another. The candle remains, only the flame endures. In man's most luminous relationships with the things of earth, including one's fellows, there can be a sense of profound exchanges, a passing on of the flame.

Perhaps the truest thing I can say about "Awakening" is that throughout its making I was struggling to find my way to clarity. Now, as I write these last few words, the bells peal again in the square below. Along the lake path to the church of San Giacomo comes a young bride clinging to her father's arm. They mount the steps, enter the door, and I can picture them moving past Perugino's great painting *The Deposition*, then down the aisle. Soon father will pass daughter, like a flame, on to another, and stand back as she goes on toward her new life.

LET THE SPRING BREEZE ENTER
The Quest of Zen

IN THE WAY OF DEFINITION

To begin, permit me to set you a *koan*, or Zen problem, for meditation: Chased by a tiger, you jump into an old well crawling with snakes. The vine you have miraculously snatched and which now sustains you a few feet from the brim of the well is being nibbled by a mouse.

As your *roshi*,* or master, I look you straight in the eye and demand that you tell me what you would do. Tricky, ingenious—like most Westerners—you may very well find a way out of the well, but none of your clever stratagems will satisfy me. Again and again you are sent back to the *zendo*,* or meditation hall, to ponder the *koan*; it may take you as long as a year to come up with a solution that does not disgust me. Meanwhile something is happening to you: slowly you realize that there is no "right" answer, that all you can do while grasping that vine for dear life (for you are living the *koan*) is accept the fact that dear or not it is no longer yours. This may make it possible for you to experience the bliss of a *satori* awakening and, by so doing, understand the essence of Zen said to be found in this four-line *gatha*:

---

* The terms *roshi* and *shike* are interchangeable, as are *zendo* and *sodo*.

Transmission outside doctrine,
No dependence on words,
Pointing directly at the mind,
Thus seeing oneself truly, attaining Buddhahood.

There are other, prosier ways of defining the spirit—life zest, awareness of the preciousness of each instant and every thing, a gay seriousness—but perhaps Zen is best expressed in that poetry, usually written in classical Chinese forms, which outstanding masters have traditionally composed. There is, for example, the poem by Daigu (1584–1669) from which I have drawn my title:

Who dares approach the lion's
Mountain cave? Cold, robust,
A Zen-man through and through,
I let the spring breeze enter at the gate.

It would *not* be in the spirit of Zen, which does not depend on words, to paraphrase; indeed any attempt to do so might resemble the tyro's abortive efforts with the *koan* above. There are some who have, through their well-meaning attempts to explain that spring breeze, well-nigh staled it for the man who would be refreshed by it. Like the famous wind of Archibald MacLeish, it "is trampled under the rain, shakes free, is again trampled." Which makes it (the spring breeze, the Spirit of Zen) something like freedom. Which is another way of saying that the *Tao*, the path, of Zen is the path of liberation.

JAPANESE BACKGROUNDS

The three major sources of Japanese thought are Shinto, the indigenous religion, the Way of the Gods; Confucianism, which was of course brought over from China and was concerned with the moral ordering of society and emphasized the present; and Buddhism, the religion of eternity, which originated in India and reached Japan by way of China and Korea.

Over two thousand years old, Shinto is a national cult, the spirit of "Nippon," and it has maintained its sacred sense of nature, which according to its mythology was not made but begotten. Hence the veneration of trees, mountains, waterfalls, and the pure lines of its central shrine at Ise. Evolved from Shinto, ancient state philosophy was based on the belief in the holy oneness of man and country. There has always been in Shinto a reverence for emperor and ancestors, and a faith in the communion of the living and the dead: there is, in other words, the sense of immortal presence.

Confucianism, on the other hand, has represented a rational, highly moral code of behavior and a system of firmly defined duties, with certain relationships—emperor-subject, father-son, etc.—particularly upheld. And there are the practical rules of etiquette and protocol, too numerous and intricate to go into here, but of great importance to the shaping of Japanese form. Also the family system is Confucian. The rather unfortunate overspecialization in certain areas and the for-the-most-part inflexible bureaucracy (those who have seen Kurosawa's great film *Ikiru* have had a glimpse of the latter), may be the result of Confucianism, and so, too, the exaggerated respect shown the *sensei*, or teacher, the title held by even an instructor in ping-pong. With the master in total control of his disciple or student, there has been little scope for the growth of originality as we think of it. Indeed the dismissive gesture, criticism, is in Japan the mark of a boor.

Mahayana Buddhism (the Great Wheel) has in spite of the demands of Shintoism and Confucianism dominated the Japanese mind for fifteen hundred years. All things, it claims, are predestined to become Buddhas, attain salvation. One must ignore the peculiarities of things and feel their absolute oneness. When, along with the human ego, the individuality of all is shed, then this oneness appears as emptiness. Through meditation of space can come the awakening to oneness, peace of mind, Nirvana—a concept which, as Dr. D. T. Suzuki explains in his *Zen and Japanese Culture*, is often misunderstood:

> . . . when we talk of nirvana we imagine that there is such a thing . . . as in the case of a table or a book. Nirvana, however, is no more than a state of mind or consciousness when we actually transcend relativity—the world of birth and death.

Zen Buddhism, which since the Kamakura Period (thirteenth century), has been truly important to Japanese life and arts, from the fine to the military, *ikebana* to *kamikaze*, does not use the word "God," nor (for the above reasons) does it speak of the individual soul. Various Buddhist sects, to be sure, differ in their methods of attaining salvation: in one, for instance, the mere invocation of the Buddha's name, if continuously and sincerely done, is sufficient. Other sects—Kegon, Tendai—seem more philosophical yet require, at the same time, rather elaborate devotional devices. But whatever the sect, because of Buddhism's "pantheism," it works harmoniously alongside Shintoism.

In contrast to Hinayana (the Small Wheel), Mahayana Buddhism is life-loving. Even the concept of *Mu* (nothingness) can be seen as positive, because of the principle of unity it implies. Perhaps the main difference between the two systems is to be found in their exemplars: the Hinayana Arhat seeks Nirvana and Buddhahood fervently, whereas the Mahayana Bodhisattva willingly postpones entering the blessed state until all others can be saved. It is for this reason that Mahayanists offer prayers to the Savior Bodhisattva Amida.

Zen is rooted squarely in Mahayana Buddhism, though it must not be seen as a theology. Rather it is a system of behavior based on the desire for salvation through revelation. What makes it virtually impenetrable to the uninitiated is the lack of dogma as such, and the fact that all Zen "statements" are in some manner paradoxical. Its chief practice, *zazen*, or formal sitting in meditation, goes back to Indian *dhyana*, and is said to be the search, always within the seeker, for the indivisible moon reflected not only on the sea but on each dewdrop and, perhaps most brightly of all, on the scummiest puddle. To discover this—the *Dharmakaya*—in all things, is for the Zenist to discover his own Buddha-nature.

The morality in all this is simple enough: like a tarnished mirror, the passion-twisted heart cannot reflect *Dharmakaya*. The injunction, then? Well, clean the mirror. By being perfect in conduct, by, as the master Fugai (seventeenth century) puts it in this poem, shutting the windows of the flesh:

> Only the Zen-man knows tranquility:
> The world-consuming flame can't reach this valley.
> Under a breezy limb, the windows of
> The flesh shut firm, I dream, wake, dream.

Zen tells that Gautama had his awakening under the *Bodhi*-tree and thus became the Buddha, but few scholars have dealt adequately, if at all, with the Buddha's early training in meditation under the tutelage of Alara Kalama and Uddaka Ramaputta. According to Sir Charles Eliot, in *Hinduism and Buddhism*, the first of these great teachers instructed the Buddha in the trances known as the formless states. The first taught the monk in meditation to rise above all ideas of form and multiplicity, and to pass by degrees into the sphere where nothing at all exists, while retaining consciousness of mental processes. Buddha's second teacher taught the attainment of a state in which neither idea nor its absence is present, a state which can be illustrated, to use Sir Charles Eliot's analogy, by a bowl whose inside has been coated with oil, a state in which consciousness is reduced to a minimum. As is well known, the Buddha was to reject those teachings which made hypnotic trances their chief aim.

Though perhaps too much has been made of it by the followers of Dr. Suzuki, there is no questioning Zen's similarity to mysticism. There is, for example, the Zen saying that the eye of divinity can be seen in a lotus blossom. In the same vein, that incredible German Meister Eckhart said, "The eye with which I see God is the eye with which God sees me." Instead of seeking God, Zen's adherents seek, and through *zazen* and its aim, *satori*, sometimes find, Nirvana. And they find the Way not by learning, but while in meditation, in the *tanden*, the body's exact center.

PHILOSOPHY AND ZEN

Those who should know maintain that Western philosophy received its greatest impetus at about the time of the Enlightenment in the eighteenth century, when having lost faith in religion's ready answers to the big questions, man tried on his own to fathom the only world he was ever likely to know. In a completely religious culture there would be little need for philosophy, because all answers would be supplied by dogma.

The most complete philosophers are those able to cope most thoroughly with the deepest problems: Kant, for example, with his Categorical Imperatives to guide conduct and his *Kosmos* to prefigure an essentially atomistic universe. Some thinkers have of course worked in a more fragmentary way—there are philosophical lyrics as well as epics—but, fragmentary or all-embracing, Western philosophy does not greatly interest the Zenist.

This lack of interest, it should be made clear at once, is not to be attributed to lack of curiosity, nor should it be seen as the result of religious thralldom. So far as Zen is concerned, it is just that most of the questions asked by Western thinkers are either frivolous or, worse, impertinent. If posed at all by a master, they are pondered in a very different manner, as in the case of the *koan*, for the mind, it is thought, severely limited and conditioned powerfully by egoistic needs, is simply not to be relied on in crucial issues. Intuition, mysterious as it may be, has always been considered by the Zenist a truer way of discovery, less a toying with the world.

Revelation of the kind sought by the Zenist is not to be confused with the Christian sort: for one thing, one need not be sporting a halo to experience it. Yet it often takes a superhuman effort:

Kando (1825–1904)

It's as if our heads were on fire, the way
We apply ourselves to perfection of That.
The future but a twinkle, beat yourself,
Persist: the greatest effort's not enough.

But when there is an awakening:

Tsugen (1322–1391)

Not a mote in the light above,
Soul itself cannot offer such a view.
Though dawn's not come, the cock is calling:
The phoenix, flower in beak, welcomes spring.

Always Zen is to be found, if at all, in immediate experience, the firefly rather than the star.

In Zen aesthetics there is a clear parallel to phenomenology. When, following Kierkegaard, Existentialists speak of the need to leap from one state of awareness—commitment—to another, higher, state they are saying what the Zen masters have always said. The *sumie* painter, perhaps without training in Zen but heir to its treasures, raises brush over blankness and at just the right moment takes such a leap into a free and floating world.

"The form of the object must first fuse with the spirit," wrote the great fifth-century Chinese painter Wang Wei "after which the mind transforms it in various ways. The spirit, to be sure, has no form; yet that which moves and transforms the form of an object is the spirit."*

That life is most vivid to one on the brink of death is a truism. The subjects of *sumie* painting—flower, rock, mountain, perhaps a human figure—are severely defined against the white background, thus taking on strong existential meaning. To most Japanese, certainly to those interested in Zen, the background clearly represents death,

---

* Mai-Mai Sze, *The Tao of Painting*, Pantheon Books, 1956.

the reality of man facing annihilation, fully aware of his *mujo*, or impermanence.

In the literature conditioned by Zen there is also a sense of this
nothingness against which the mortal drama unfolds, as in Yasunari
Kawabata's fine modern novel *Yukiguni*. Indeed the translator of the
English version (*Snow Country*, Knopf, 1956), Edward G. Seidensticker,
relates the technique of the book to the *haiku*, the seventeen-syllable
poems that have long been associated with Zen: "The *haiku* manner,"
he writes in a perceptive introduction to the book, "is notable for its
terseness and austerity, so that [the novelist's work] must rather be like
a series of brief flashes in a void." Then there are the early *Noh* plays,
perfect in their expression of Zen, and the dramas of Chikamatsu
Monzaemon, the eighteenth-century Japanese Shakespeare, so-called,
full, among other things, of the anguish of lovers about to commit
suicide.

Japanese suicide, or *hara-kiri*, has much Zen in it, it would seem,
for when a man finds himself faced, through an awakening sought or
unsought, with the absurdity of his lot, he may decide coldly to make
as honorable an end as possible by taking the existential leap—into the
grave. One thinks of the forty-seven Ronin, those fearless samurai who
committed *hara-kiri* at the command of the Tokugawa Shogun nearly
three hundred years ago; of the astonishing love suicides of the 1930s;
and most remarkable, of those ten members of the ultranationalist
Japan Productive Party, who on August 22, 1945, a week after the end
of World War II, sat in a circle in downtown Tokyo and, while chanting
apologies to the emperor for losing the war, pulled pins from hand
grenades and blew themselves to bits (less than a week later, three of
their widows went to the same spot and shot themselves to death). Not
as dramatic, perhaps, but of far greater importance to Zen, which, after
all, has never condoned suicide, is the stoic death:

Baiho (1633–1707)

Never giving thought to fame,
One troublesome span of life behind,
Cross-legged in the coffin,
I'm about to slough the flesh.

"If instead of the paradisiacal bliss promised by your faith," I was
once asked by a Japanese student trained in Zen, "you were threatened
with a chain of rebirths, each with its portion of misery, until by some

superhuman act you were able to snap that chain, would you not make every effort to order your life so as to be able to live it fully, now, while you have it?" In so bleak a scheme of things, the implication must be drawn: there is small reason for the rapturous faith many profess. Yet there is a way out: unswerving acceptance of the reality of self. Existence, of which for ages a single image has been held up to the Zenist, must be adjusted to: it cannot be altered. His training in the *zendo*, all rituals of his life, are meant to help him make that adjustment.

SHINKICHI TAKAHASHI

Contemporary Zen Poet

I   Like that of most important poets, East or West, Shinkichi
Takahashi's work can be read on a number of levels, each
rewarding, yet one must bear in mind that his poems are
those of a Zen Buddhist. The poet began as a dadaist at a
time in Japan when experimentation based on Western examples
flourished. The 20s and 30s were decades as restless in Japan as elsewhere, the best work of the leading modernists expressing that unrest.
Dadaism and surrealism especially, while foundering most, inspired
some interesting work and made a few reputations. Often translations, for the most part little more than passable, were made of such
poetry. There was inevitably more outright borrowing than serious
emulation, and the ambitious modernist was more likely to resemble
Tristan Tzara, say, than Basho, Buson, and other great masters of
Japan's past.

     Takahashi was born in 1901 in a fishing village on Shikoku,
smallest of Japan's four main islands. Largely self-educated, having
left a commercial high school just before graduation for Tokyo, he
hoped for a career in literature. He had no money and very little luck,
contracting typhus, winding up in a charity hospital, eventually
forced to return home. He did not give up. One day, reading a newspaper article on dadaism, he was galvanized. It was as if the movement

had been created those thousands of miles away with him in mind. He returned to Tokyo, worked a while as a waiter, then as errand boy in a newspaper office. In 1921 he produced a mimeographed collection of dadaist poems, the following year a dada manifesto and more such poems. In 1923 he published *Poems of Dadaist Shinkichi*, in 1926 *Gion Festival* and, in 1928 *Poems of Shinkichi Takahashi*. The books shocked and puzzled, but were warmly received by a few. A critic called him the Japanese Rimbaud.

Yet far from satisfied with life and work, he sought advice of the famed Rinzai Zen master Shizan Ashikaga, and was invited to come to his temple, the Shogenji. Takahashi participated in a special one-week retreat at the temple, applying himself strenuously to the very tough training. One day, walking in the corridor, he fell down unconscious. Coming to, his mind was shattered. At twenty-seven years old, it seemed his creative life was finished. Sent home, he was locked up in a tiny room for three years, during which, however, he continued to write poems. Before the disastrous incident at the Shogenji, and for years after, he was given to impulsive actions, often getting into trouble with the police. Indeed he was in a police cell when *Poems of Dadaist Shinkichi* appeared, and is said to have torn up the copy handed to him through the bars.

He slowly made a thorough recovery, and in 1939 visited Korea and China. He managed during the war to support himself as writer, and in 1944 began work for a Tokyo newspaper. The following year, the newspaper office bombed out, he turned to free-lance writing. He married in 1951, and lives with his wife and daughter in the Nakano Ward of Tokyo a serene yet active Zenist-writer's life.

Not long after his return to Tokyo in 1932 the poet heard Shizan Ashikaga's lectures on Zen, and in 1935 became the master's disciple at Shogenji. Through almost seventeen years of rigorous training, he, like all working under a disciplinarian, experienced many hardships, but unlike most gained genuine *satori* a number of times. He describes in an essay two such experiences. The first, at the age of forty during a retreat at a mountain temple. It came his turn to enter the master's room to present his view of a *koan* (problem for meditation, usually highly paradoxical). As is the practice, he struck the small hanging bell announcing his intention to enter. At the sound, he awakened to the keenest insight he had ever had. The sound, he describes, was completely different from what he had so often heard. His other experience came some years later while in a public bath:

stepping out, he stooped to grasp a wash-pail. In a flash he discovered that he had no shadow. He strained to see, but there were no other bathers, and washpails, voices, steam itself had all disappeared. He had entered the Void. He lay back again in the bath, at ease, limbs stretched out.

By 1952 Takahashi had learned all he could from the master, and the next year received in the master's calligraphy a traditional "The Moon-On-Water-Hall," formal testimonial of his completion of the full course of discipline. He was now recognized by the master as an enlightened Zenist, one of the handful of disciples so honored by Shizan. Now he was qualified to guide others, something Takahashi has done through his writings ever since. In addition to numerous books of verse, the poet has published books on Zen, among them *Essays on Zen Study* (1958), *Commentaries on Mumonkan* (1958), *Rinzairoku* (1959), *The Life of Master Dogen* (1963), *Poetry and Zen* (1969), and *Zen and Literature* (1970). Typically, in *Essays on Zen Study* he writes:

> Since, to my way of thinking, God transcends existence, to conclude there is no God is most relevant to him. As it is best not to think of such a God, praying to him is futile. Not only futile, but also immeasurably harmful; because man will make blunders, if, presupposing good and bad with his shallow wisdom, he clings to his hope of God's support.

II   Since the Kamakura period (13th century) many of Japan's finest writers have been, if not directly involved in its study and practice, strongly drawn to Zen Buddhism, which some would claim has been among the most seminal philosophies, in its effect on the arts, the world has known. A modern example, the late Yasunari Kawabata, Nobel Laureate and author of among other important works the novel *Yukiguni* (*Snow Country*), was as writer of fiction greatly indebted to the *haiku* aesthetic, in which Zen principles dominate. His Nobel Prize acceptance address was virtually a tribute to Zen. Another world-famous author, Yukio Mishima, wrote plays, a few of which have reached an international audience, based on the *Noh* drama, which like the art of the *haiku* is intimately associated with Zen. Many other writers have been affected by Zen, which, Arthur Waley has pointed out, has always been the philosophy of artists, its language that in which poetry and painting especially have always been discussed. Unlike Takahashi, however, few contemporary Japanese writers have trained under a Zen master. He is widely recognized as the foremost living Zen poet.

The poet's work is best read, then, in rather special context, its chief, perhaps most obvious, quality being what in Zen is called *zenki*, spontaneous activity free of forms, flowing from the formless self. This is best seen in the bold thrust of his images. No less important, and clearly Buddhist, is his awareness of pain, human and animal, though it should be evident that his frequent references to things "atomic" need not be seen as exclusively Buddhist or Japanese. That many of his poems are "irrational" cannot be denied, but if once irrationality was a suspect element in Western poetry (it has never been in Oriental), it is less so today—witness the acceptance of artists who, like Takahashi, employ the surrealistic method, if only in modified form. Zen and Taoist poets have always been unconventional in their methods and attitudes, and Takahashi's poems sin no more against the rational than Hakuin's, the greatest figure in Japanese Rinzai Zen. Here is a typical poem by the eighteenth-century master:

> You no sooner attain the great void
> Than body and mind are lost together.
> Heaven and Hell—a straw.
> The Buddha-realm, Pandemonium—shambles.
> Listen: a tortoise strains her voice, serenading the snow.
> Look: a tortoise wearing a sword climbs the lampstand.
> Should you desire the great tranquility,
> Prepare to sweat white beads.

In his preface to our *Zen: Poems, Prayers, Sermons, Anecdotes, Interviews,* Takashi Ikemoto wrote, "To a Zen poet, a thing of beauty or anything in nature *is* the Absolute. Hence his freedom from rationality and his recourse to uncommon symbols. Yet ultimately what he portrays is concrete, not a dreamy fancy or vision." Surely one of the strengths of Takahashi's poetry is its concreteness—a particular bird, beast or flower, a precisely rendered, however unusual, state of mind. And yet much of the poetry is admittedly very difficult, one reason being that as in the case of all Zen poets, many of Takahashi's poems read like *koans*, the purpose of which is to make clear to the seeker of answers that there is no distinction between subject and object, that the search and the thing sought are one and the same. One awakening

to such identification attains the state of *muga*, an important step
toward the goal of training, *satori*. One of the best known *koans* is
Hakuin's "What is the sound of one hand clapping?"

If read with some appreciation of the philosophy, Zen poetry
need not be obscure. A few more of its features may be cited. There are,
Takashi Ikemoto maintains, "conciseness, rigor, volitionality,
virility, and serenity." Yet, in spite of the importance, considering the
poet's intention, of analyzing the Zen elements in Takahashi's
poems, they should be fairly intelligible to those familiar with much
modern poetry, even in English translation (if not, the poet is less to
blame than his translators), for as has often been said that which is
most translatable in poetry is the image, and it is in his use of imagery
especially that Takahashi is perhaps most unique:

> My legs lose themselves
> Where the river mirrors daffodils
> Like faces in a dream.
>> —"A Wood in Sound"

> The peak of Mount Ishizuchi
> Has straightened the spine
> Of the Island of Futana.
>> —"Rat on Mount Ishizuchi"

> Sunbeams, spokes of a stopped wheel,
> Blaze through the leaves of a branch.
>> —"Sun Through the Leaves"

Yet Takahashi wishes to be judged—if as poet at all—as one
whose work expresses more than anything else the Zen spirit. A poem
like "Canna," which in addition to being effective poetry communi-
cates powerfully one of the Bodhisattva ideals of Mahayana Buddhism, sacrifice for others, is therefore of particular importance. In
Takahashi such ideals are everywhere given expression. Some of his
pieces concern Zen discipline, "Life Infinite" being typical.

> *Life Infinite*

> Beyond words, this no-thingness within,
> Which I've become. So to remain

> Only one thing's needed: Zen sitting.
> I think, breathe with my whole body—

> Marvellous. The joy's so pure,
> It's beyond love making, anything.

I can see, live anywhere, everywhere.
I need nothing, not even life.

In spite of its apparent simplicity, such a work is very difficult
to understand outside a Zen context—and extremely hard to render
properly in another tongue. Take the last line: if it had been given
somewhat less paradoxically, as, say, "I need nothing, fearing not
even death," the poet would have been misrepresented and the reader
misled, for there is no fear of death in Zen. While poems like "Life
Infinite" may not to some be quite as rewarding artistically as other
of Takahashi's pieces, they are understandably of great importance to
him and thus must not be passed over.

While an alert reader may find it possible to read a poem like
"Life Infinite" with not too much difficulty, there is another kind of
poem which, though dealing as directly with the Zen experience,
works somewhat more subtly and can prove most puzzling. "Destruction," which exhibits as well as any the quality of *zenki*, is such a
poem, for here there is not only "spontaneous activity free of forms,
flowing from the formless self," but the destruction of the most rigid
of all forms, a conceptual universe.

Destruction

The universe is forever falling apart—
No need to push the button,
It collapses at a finger's touch:
Why, it barely hangs on the tail of a sparrow's eye.

The universe is so much eye secretion,
Hordes leap from the tips
Of your nostril hairs. Lift your right hand:
It's in your palm. There's room enough
On the sparrow's eyelash for the whole.

A paltry thing, the universe:
Here is all strength, here the greatest strength.
You and the sparrow are one
And, should he wish, he can crush you.
The universe trembles before him.

What the poet says to us is man, unlike the sparrow, has created
forms which confine and frustrate, and until he sees that they have no
reality, are paltry, "so much eye secretion," will continue to tremble
before them, their prisoner. He must live freely as the sparrow who

can, should he wish, crush the universe and its creator. Indeed all forms, not the universe alone, "tremble before him."

Throughout Takahashi's work, as in all Zen writing, such attitudes are prominent, yet they need not be seen as peculiarly Zenist or, for that matter, Oriental. In his "Worpswede" the German poet Ranier Maria Rilke writes what could very well serve as paraphrase of a poem like "Destruction":

> We play with obscure forces, which we cannot lay hold of, by the names we give them, as children play with fire, and it seems for a moment as if all the energy had lain unused in things until we came to apply it to our transitory life and its needs. But repeatedly . . . these forces shake off their names and rise . . . against their little lords, no, not even *against*—they simply rise, and civilizations fall from the shoulders of the earth. . . .

III   Shinkichi Takahashi might have written, as Chekhov to a friend, "A conscious life without a definite philosophy is no life, rather a burden and a nightmare." That the poet has found such a definite philosophy in Zen Buddhism has perhaps been demonstrated, and it is doubtlessly true that his work is distinguished largely because of the philosophy underlying it. He has worked hard, as all Zenists must, to discover truths which can hardly be expressed in anything less than poetry. Indeed if the Western reader interested in Zen wants some indication of what the philosophy can mean to a practitioner, he might do well to seek it in the work of Takahashi. For centuries Zenists have through poetry expressed insights afforded by their discipline. With that in mind, it might prove useful at this point to give some idea of the manner in which the art has been employed, particularly by great masters.

Even in translation—such is the hope—Zen poetry is so suggestive in itself that, as in a piece like "Life Infinite," explication is rarely necessary. Older Japanese Zenists did not theorize about the poems they would write from time to time, for good reason: to them poetry was not an art to be cultivated for itself. Rather it was a means by which an attempt at the nearly inexpressible might be made. Though some poems are called "satori" poems, others "death" poems, and some are little more than interpretations, meant for presentation to a master, of *koans* (these may equally be *satori* poems), all the poems deal with spiritually momentous experiences. There are no "finger exercises," and though some Zen poems are comparatively light there are few less than fully inspired. Indeed when one considers the traditional goal, the all-or-nothing striving after illumination, this is hardly to be wondered at.

Poets of the Chinese Ch'an sect ("Zen" is the Japanese transliteration of "Ch'an"), on whose works early Zenists modeled, in every respect, their own, were less reluctant to theorize. They speak, for example, of the need to attain a state of calm, making it possible for the poet to get the spirit of nature into his poems. If Zen masters considered it out-of-role to write on the nature of poetry, many affected by Zen did not, and great *haiku* poets like Basho, an enlightened Zenist, had disciples who would transcribe their words. Here is Basho's disciple Doho:

> The Master said: "Learn about a pine tree from a pine tree, and about a bamboo plant from a bamboo plant." He meant that the poet should detach the mind from himself, and by "learn" that he should enter into the object, the whole of its delicate life, feeling as it feels. The poem follows of itself.

Another way of thinking about this most important principle of Zen aesthetics, and a suggestive one for Westerners, is to recall Keats's "Negative Capability," by which the poet implies that the true artist does not assert his own personality, even if imagining himself possessed of one. Rather he identifies as far as possible with the object of his contemplation, its "personality," without feeling that he must understand it. There are many Zen poems about this state of mind, one of the best being Nanei's:

> Splitting the void in half,
> Making smithereens of earth,
> I watch inching toward
> The river, the cloud-drawn moon.

Zen poetry has always been richly symbolic, and while hardly unique to Zen the moon is a common symbol. It should be remembered, in relation to the use of such symbols, that as religion Zen is a Mahayana Buddhist sect, and that the Zenist searches, always within, for the indivisible moon (essence) reflected not only by the sea but by each dewdrop. To discover this, the *Dharmakaya*, in all things, whether while in meditation or writing a poem, is to discover one's own Buddha-nature. Most Zen poems delineate graphically what the spiritual eye has been awakened to, a view of things seen as for the first time, in their eternal aspect. Here, a fourteenth-century piece by the master Hakugai.

> Last year in a lovely temple in Hirosawa,
> This year among the rocks of Nikko,
> All's the same to me:
> Clapping hands, the peaks roar at the blue!

One of the most important Zen principles, so appealing for obvious reasons to Westerners interested in the philosophy, is the need to "let go." It is a principle based on the idea, demonstrably true, that one never gets what is grasped for. Seek not, in other words, and ye shall find. Here is how the nineteenth-century master Kanemitsu-Kogun expresses it:

> My hands released at last, the cliff soars
> Ten thousand meters, the plowshare sparks,
> All's consumed with my body. Born again,
> The lanes run straight, the rice well in the ear.

Traditionally death poems are written or dictated by masters just before dying. The master looks back on his life and, in a few highly compressed lines, expresses for the benefit of disciples his state of mind at the inevitable hour. The Void, the great Penetralium of Zen, is often mentioned in the death poems. The mind, it is thought, is a void or empty space in which objects are stripped of their objectivity, reduced to their essence. The following death poem by the fourteenth-century master Yuzan is typical:

> What's life? What's death?
> I blast the Void.
> Winds spring up
> In every quarter.

It would be misleading to claim only Zenists exhibit such stoicism before death. In his brilliant essay, "Artists and Old Age," the

German poet Gottfried Benn tells of the diamond dealer Solomon Rossbach who, just before leaping from the top of the Empire State Building, scrawled what is by any standards a great death poem:

> No more above,
> No more below—
> So I leap off.

Because of the extremely private nature of *sanzen*, meeting of master and disciple during which the latter is expected to offer interpretations of *koans*, sometimes in the form of poetry, not too much can be said about those poems based on *koans*. Perhaps the following anecdote will give some idea of what takes place at such an interview, particularly the manner in which the disciple's poem is handled:

> Kanzan (1277–1360), the National Teacher, gave Fujiwara-Fujifusa the *koan* "Original Perfection." For many days Fujifusa sat in Zen. He finally had an intuition and composed the following:
>
>> Once possessed of the mind that has always been,
>> Forever I'll benefit men and *devas* both.
>> The benignity of the Buddha and Patriarchs can hardly be repaid.
>> Why should I be reborn as horse or donkey?

When he called on Kanzan with the poem, this dialogue took place:

> Kanzan: Where's the mind?
> Fujifusa: It fills the great void.
> Kanzan: With what will you benefit men and *devas*?
> Fujifusa: I shall saunter along the stream, or sit down to watch the gathering clouds.
> Kanzan: Just how do you intend repaying the Buddha and Patriarchs?
> Fujifusa: The sky's over my head, the earth under my feet.
> Kanzan: All right, but why shouldn't you be reborn as horse or donkey?

At this Fujifusa got to his feet and bowed. "Good!" Kanzan said with a loud laugh. "You've gained perfect *satori*."

Though *satori*, death and *koan* interpretation figure strongly in early Zen poetry, many of the poems deal with nature and man's place in it. The Buddha-nature is by no means man's alone, being discoverable in all that exists, animate or inanimate. As Arthur Waley puts it in *Zen Buddhism and Its Relation to Art*:

> Stone, river and tree are alike parts of the great hidden Unity. Thus man, through his Buddha-nature or universalized consciousness, possesses an intimate means of contact with nature. The song of birds, the noise of waterfalls, the rolling of thunder, the whispering of wind in the pinetrees—all these are utterances of the Absolute.

And as Shinkichi Takahashi expresses it in "Wind Among the Pines":

> The wind blows hard among the pines
> Toward the beginning
> Of an endless past.
> Listen: you've heard everything.

IV   It is clear that Shinkichi Takahashi is an important Zen poet, but what is it, apart from his philosophy, that makes him a remarkable contemporary poet, read with almost as much appreciation in the English-speaking world as in Japan? There are many reasons for the appeal of his work, but surely the chief is the breathtaking freedom of imagination, his capacity, as Robert Bly in his anthology *News of the Universe* claims, to handle seven or eight things at the same time and thus write "the poetry of the future." This is best seen perhaps in those poems dealing with the life of creatures, for in order to empathize in such ways the poet must imagine fully, enter the world of his subject spontaneously, no holding back. In poem after poem Takahashi reveals how totally he is able to identify with his subject.

In much of the poet's work, seemingly scornful of logical development, he achieves something close to pure poetry, which comes only of an unburdened imagination. Now pure poetry is as difficult to define as write, yet an attempt must be made. If we take into account those elements of poetry which, as far back as Aristotle, have been considered pre-eminent, chiefly vital metaphor and verbal energy, then we are forced to conclude pure poetry is very rare indeed, and much that goes by the name of poetry is really little more than metered prose. In modern criticism a great deal of space is devoted to the praise and refined analysis of experimentation, those ingenuities which so often cloak hollowness. Yet the serious reader is not so easily fooled, poets like Hart Crane and Dylan Thomas capture him readily enough, because their work is comparatively pure, charged with potent images.

A fine poet is something of an anomaly, and may be likened to a perfectly functioning sensorium, one sense related organically to all the others—eye to the ear, and so on. Whether he turns to poetry because it is natural for him to do so as the bird to sing, or because the making of poems may confer a distinction not attainable otherwise, I cannot say. Nor tell whether the themes associated with much serious poetry—social justice, for one—come naturally to a poet or are just used as suitable subjects to engage the imagination of the gifted human.

When we hear Takahashi claim his philosophy is more important to him than anything he writes, we are perhaps entitled to a degree of skepticism, yet bear in mind that traditionally Zen is not only the philosophy of artists, it is essentially, in its highest forms, unabashedly elitist. The Sixth Patriarch of Zen, the Chinese Hui-neng (683–713), who was handed "the robe and the law" of succession mainly because of the insight expressed in a short poem written for his master, claims in his *Platform Scripture*:

> . . . there is no distinction between sudden enlightenment and gradual enlightenment in the Law, except that some people are intelligent and others stupid. Those who are ignorant realize the truth gradually, while the enlightened ones attain it suddenly.

Just as the gifted man finds it possible to attain ends more quickly in a philosophy like Zen, he can, once setting mind to it, attain in the arts what others, however sincere and assiduous, cannot hope to reach. The fact is—were it acknowledged—that most critical writing deals with the phenomenology of failure, with why X, were he more like Z, might turn out to be slightly superior to Y. We wind up mistrusting much criticism, and aesthetic theorizing, because in spite of it, and all standards and criteria it propounds as essential to the judgment of art, a work either fully engages the imagination, or doesn't. Which is why Ezra Pound could claim audaciously that "It is better to

present one Image in a lifetime than to produce voluminous works."
The important artist stands alone.

Though as Zenist, Takahashi disclaims any ambition of the
kind, he must—as all poets, whether working within a particular discipline or not—be judged first as artist. In order for a poet anywhere
to become an artist, he must become maker of the new, and that which
chiefly distinguishes the poem of an artist from that of a writer of
verse is that it can live alone, palpably there, unsupported by anything outside itself, indifferent to the uses made of it. A work of art is
no vehicle of preachment or propaganda, and whatever the idea in the
name of which it was brought into being—Zen, Marxism, Art itself—
it lives or dies to the degree it possesses qualities which, though seemingly unique to its medium, are rightly seen as held in common by all
genuine works of art—appropriate form, freshness of detail, integrality of tone, and relevance to human experience.

I FEAR NOTHING:
A Note on the Zen Poetry of Death

A visit with my father is like coming from a *zendo*, thorny *koans* prodding at my half-cocked mind. My ninety-one-year-old inquisitor wheedles me to homilies on existence, non-existence. Impatient with my caginess, he whips me on to unmask secrets, write a masterpiece revealing Buddha-wisdom on life, on death. Driving home past autumn purples, bronzes, oranges, dark and soft golds, I'm suddenly aware of road-kill, mile on mile. Squirrels, opossums, skunks, and more, every few yards, it seems, poor things displaced by excavators turning meadows and cornfields into housing sites. Harsh contrast of ravaged dead and sensual drifts of nature into winter. There was a time when death came gentler to both man and beast, when words passed like seeds from those who went to those new-coming.

I wonder, in all literature can there be poetry so all-encompassing as the Zen poetry of death with its history of nearly fifteen hundred years. In T'ang China of the sixth century the first Ch'an (Zen) masters, accepting responsibilities that went with guiding a new generation, understood the exemplary nature of their role. Disciples were to be rescued from illusion, from dualistic traps set around them in a rigidly structured, Confucian-conditioned society. Only tough disciplines of Zen could possibly achieve that. The masters lived in every sense alongside their disciples, meditating and chanting with them, eating and sleeping with them, and, of course, making them talk out their fears, weaknesses, and hopes. They gave them *koans* to grapple with, again and again expressing dissatisfaction with their efforts, driving them ever harder to see, surpass themselves.

In the early days of Zen the vision of enlightenment and what it might achieve was very pure. All stages of progress in discipline were gauged most scrupulously, every hour offering its special challenge. How that challenge was met was most carefully judged, whether working in the vegetable garden, washing dishes, raking leaves, relating to fellows in the *zendo*, the daily begging round among laymen: all such things done by the master himself, done well in order for him to receive *inka* (testimonial to the disciple's enlightenment) from his own master. He would not only have had to perform such normal functions well, in the proper spirit, demonstrating growth in discipline, but—far more important—would have had to experience, in the judgment of his master, *satori*.

Zen's awareness of the spiritual potential of art, all arts, came early and was very keen. It was especially there that its connection with China's indigenous Taoism was apparent. Perhaps more than any spiritual discipline before or since, it would maintain that it was possible to realize oneself through the practice of a *do* (*Tao*, or Way): *Gado* (painting), *Shodo* (calligraphy), *Kado* (poetry), etc. Its masters, often expert in one or more of the arts, expected disciples to show strong interest in one or the other from the earliest period of training.

The art most accessible to Zen communities, one of its richest depositories of wisdom, was poetry, which even in early China had an ancient tradition, as in the Confucian *Book of Songs*. In order to do well in the annual state examinations, of crucial importance to all seeking advancement in the world, an appreciation of poetry was essential. Thus it was natural that disciples of a gifted master, who often employed poetry in his *teisho* (brief lectures to the assembled monks), might write *agyo* (poems of *koan* interpretation) such as the following by Seigensai of the twelfth century:

> This grasped, all's dust—
> The sermon for today.
> Lands, seas. Awakened,
> You walk the earth alone.

Seigensai had *satori* when he solved the *koan* "Maitreya preaches this," and his master approved the poem as evidence of the disciple's awakening. But very few *agyo* were approved, thus the disciple was forced to try again, again, sometimes choosing to interpret in normal speech. Chokei of the tenth century was to persist. After twenty years of serious application he was certain, on rolling up the blind in his room, that he had gained *satori*:

> Rolling the bamboo blind, I
> Look out at the world—what change!
> Should someone ask what I've discovered,
> I'll smash this whisk against his mouth.

When the poem was rejected as inadequate, he wrote the following, which more than satisfied his master:

> All's harmony, yet everything is separate.
> Once confirmed, mastery is yours.
> Long I hovered on the Middle Way,
> Today the very ice shoots flame.

There was one type of Zen poem, *jisei* (death poem), which was in a sense reserved for the master. Such a poem, sometimes composed well before death, was thought to be the expression of his very being. *Jisei* were thus considered of great importance, not only as personal testimonial, but as virtual *koans* themselves. They were pondered, lectured upon, and held to be revelatory of the deepest truths of discipline. Six hundred years after the first were composed in China, they were to take their honored place in Japanese Zen practice.

One of the most remarkable features of death poems, wherever written, is their stoicism, which when one considers the Buddhist attitude to death is not surprising. From the time of the Buddha himself it was considered essential to accept impermanence, without futile attempts to escape it. In the famous story of Kisagotami we find the Buddha dealing with an extreme case of delusion. After Kisagotami's son died, she simply refused to accept the fact, carrying his dead body everywhere. A wise man of her village told her to go to the Buddha, who assured her there was a medicine that could cure her son, but in order to prepare it he would have to have a handful of mustard seeds gathered at households that had never been visited by death. Kisagotami returned to the Buddha not only empty-handed but stripped of her delusion. Burying her son, she got on with her life. And here, one anecdote much admired in Zen communities of Japan:

> Dokuon was very sick, and Tekisui came to ask after him. Entering the sickroom, he announced himself, then straddled Dokuon. With his face almost touching Dokuon's, he said, "Well, how are you?" "Sick," answered Dokuon. "Think you'll pull through?" "No." Without another word, Tekisui got up and left.
>
> A few days before Tekisui's own death, Keichu came from afar to ask about him. "I hear," he said to the porter, "the master's very sick." "Yes, sir," said the porter. "Here's a box of cakes for him. When you hand it to him, give him this message: You're old enough to die without regret." With that Keichu left. When the porter brought the cakes to Tekisui and gave him Keichu's message, the master smiled sweetly, as if he had forgotten all pain.

Conditioned by training to accept life's inevitables and feeling they might inspire disciples by demonstrating strength and serenity, Zen masters wrote their death poems and made them public. Here is the great master Daito's poem:

> To slice through Buddhas, Patriarchs
> I grip my polished sword.
> One glance at my mastery,
> The void bites its tusks!

But before achieving the right to be heard at such a moment, Daito had to prove himself worthy of being followed by a generation of disciples exerting great effort to raise themselves before him. They listened to his subtle lectures, had confrontations with him during *dokusan* (meeting of master and disciple for discussion of *koans* and related matters). All knew, had examined carefully, his *satori* poem, which had convinced Daito's own master that he had won through:

> At last I've broken Unmon's barrier!
> There's exit everywhere—east, west; north, south.
> In at morning, out at evening; neither host nor guest.
> My every step stirs up a little breeze.

The relationship between master and disciple is often very lengthy, sometimes more intimate than that between the disciple and his parents. The master's death may overwhelm the disciple, but at the same time steel him for the traumas of his own life, especially at the end. One can easily imagine the effect of Fumon's death poem on disciples:

> Magnificent! Magnificent!
> No-one knows the final word.
> The ocean bed's aflame,
> Out of the void leap wooden lambs.

The astonishment of Kukoku's:

> Riding backwards this wooden horse,
> I'm about to gallop through the void.
> Would you seek to trace me?
> Ha! Try catching the tempest in a net.

And Zekkai's:

> The void has collapsed upon the earth,
> Stars, burning, shoot across Iron Mountain.
> Turning a somersault, I brush past.

How different from these wild challenges to the void is this, by Bokuo, with its reference to the ox, an animal closely connected with Zen, the taming of which is symbolic of enlightenment:

> For seventy-two years
> I've kept the ox well under.
> Today, the plum in bloom again,
> I let him wander in the snow.

The poem's serenity is palpable, as is that of the much more literal poem by Baiho, titled "On Entering His Coffin":

> Never giving thought to fame,
> One troublesome span of life behind,
> Cross-legged in the coffin,
> I'm about to slough the flesh.

The Chinese masters were on the whole somewhat more explicit in their *jisei*, even giving their ages, as in Fuyo-Dokai's:

> Seventy-six: done
> With this life—
> I've not sought heaven,

> Don't fear hell.
> I'll lay these bones
> Beyond the Triple World,
> Unenthralled, unperturbed.

The Triple World, in Zen, is that of desire, form, and spirit. Here is another such piece, by Unpo Bun-Etsu:

> Sixty-five years,
> Fifty-seven a monk.
> Disciples, why ask
> Where I'm going,
> Nostrils to earth?

Just as the master is constantly challenging his disciples, the boldest are as likely to challenge him. Thus the last three lines of the poem. A number of Zen anecdotes concern confrontations in which the disciple bests his master:

> Pointing to the sea, Master Kangan said to his disciple Daichi: "You speak of mind over matter—well, let's see you stop those boats from sailing." Without a word the young disciple pulled the *shoji* (screen) across their view. "Hah," the master smiled and placed the *shoji* in position again. "But you had to use your hands." Still without a word, Daichi then closed his eyes.

Small wonder Daichi was himself to become a great master, whose death poem inspired countless monks well beyond his own time and place:

> Thoughts arise endlessly,
> There's a span to every life.
> One hundred years, thirty-six thousand days:
> The spring through, the butterfly dreams.

From the moment the Zen master enters his *zendo* he is committed to a life of guidance, entering into a lasting and deeply caring bond with his disciples. In many of the death poems, as we have seen, he seems to be speaking well beyond the grave, addressing not only followers, but all men. The tenth-century Chinese master Hofuku Sei-katsu, waiting to die in the mountains, made this farewell poem standing on a bridge spanning the Dokei Gorge:

> Don't tell me how difficult the Way.
> The bird's path, winding far, is right
> Before you. Water of the Dokei Gorge,
> You return to the ocean, I to the mountain.

We can assume from this that disciples often complained to him of the obstacles placed before them, and the poem was meant to further encourage them to seek the Way in nature itself. An even more remarkable instance of truth revealed by nature is found in the eighth-century Chinese master Daibai's poem, which he recited while sitting in meditation with his followers, saying aloud for their instruction, "No suppressing arrival, no following departure":

> I'm at one with this, *this* only.
> You, my disciples,
> Uphold it firmly—
> Now I can breathe my last.

What is the "this" referred to? A weasel's shriek, simply that. It is said that on reciting the poem he died.

It is clear that without the anecdote about Daibai's last hour his death poem would be meaningless. When one knows that he was moved spontaneously by a weasel's shriek, as if summoned by death, then the poem is seen in all its profundity. Many other *jisei* are dependent for their effect on knowledge of the circumstances in which they were composed. Here is one from early China by the master Beirei:

> All Patriarchs are above our understanding,
> And they don't last forever.
> O my disciples, examine, examine.
> What? Why this. This only.

Beirei exhorts his followers to examine the only thing worthy of their awareness, oneself in the here and now, "this" of the last line. Attempting to understand the Patriarchs, Scripture, etc., distracts from real issues on the meditative path. The objection, generally, to such learning in the Zen community is that it inevitably leads to presuppositions concerning the nature of the world, those of others, whereas meditation may lead to insight into the very heart of things, a world not tampered by philosophy.

From its birth Zen Buddhism saw the necessity of creating conditions which might lead to personal salvation, as sought by generations

of Taoists long before Bodhidharma, Zen's First Patriarch, left India
for China in the sixth century. They had been inspired by Lao Tzu,
Taoism's founder, and his most illustrious follower Chuang Tzu, to
break free of the social and moral constraints of Confucianism, and
were considered anarchic. Yet when Taoism anchored itself in Buddhism, and thus became Zen, it acquired order and tremendous purpose, none other than spiritual transcendence. Here, a poem by
Ikuzanshu:

> I was born with a divine jewel,
> Long since filmed with dust.
> This morning, wiped clean, it mirrors
> Streams and mountains, without end.

Enlightenment, sudden, miraculous (it is said that the master gained
satori when, crossing a bridge, he was thrown by his donkey), is spiritual
cleansing, return to the purity of Original Self, of which the jewel is a
common symbol. Another way of seeing Ikuzanshu's poem is that, as
a natural Taoist, he was indeed born with a divine jewel but, lacking
the discipline of a path like Zen, allowed it to "film with dust." With
the achievement of Zen's greatest prize, *satori*, the world was transformed.

When, in the twelfth century, Zen reached Japan, it quickly attracted influential leaders, who saw its discipline as full of possibilities
for training followers, and thus became a great force. But its most
distinguished masters were wary of such associations and patterned
themselves and their temples on the most austere Chinese models. They
even wrote in Chinese, and there is a oneness in their poems with those
of their Chinese contemporaries. But soon masters like Dogen, of the
thirteenth century, began using their own language and the established
Japanese poetic forms. Here is one of the great master Dogen's early
poems:

> This slowly drifting cloud is pitiful:
> What dreamwalkers men become.
> Awakened, I hear the one true thing—
> Black rain on the roof of Fukakusa Temple.

And here, years later, is his death poem:

> Four and fifty years
> I've hung the sky with stars.

Now I leap through—
What shattering!

Another *jisei*, by Dogen's thirteenth-century contemporary, Doyu:

Fifty-six years, above Buddhas, Patriarchs,
I've stood mid-air.
Now I announce my final journey—
Daily sun breaks from the eastern ridge.

Thus like sun itself, which daily comes and goes, the poet came, must leave—after a life of standing mid-air in contemplative withdrawal. It is remarkable that men who did not make a practice of writing poetry, certainly did not think themselves poets, could at critical moments find it within themselves to compose masterly works.

A few more death poems of the Japanese masters:

These eighty-four years,
Still, astir, Zen's been mine.
My last word?
Spoken before time began.
                    —Kangan, 1217–1300

One thousand and one tumbles,
Ninety-one years through.
Snow covers reeds for miles,
Full in the midnight sky, the moon.
                    —Tettsu, 1219–1309

Drop by drop, seventy-seven winters,
Water's turned to ice.
Now this miraculous stroke—
I draw water from the flaming fount.
                    —Keso, 1352–1428

Coming and going, life and death:
A thousand hamlets, a million houses.
Don't you get the point?
Moon in the water, blossom in the sky.
                    —Gizan, 1802–1878

At all times conscious of examples they were setting, full of desire to guide disciples well beyond their earthly term, and continue in living memory, the Zen masters of China and Japan, and wherever else the discipline established itself, achieved the miracle of perfect art. Spurred on by my father's tireless curiosity and, most keenly, because of a recent close call of my own, these death poems have become ever more important to me. Perhaps it is because they reveal it is possible to face one's end without cowering, complaining, or perpetuating fairy tales. A final word should be left to Kokan (1770–1843), who not only accepted nearing death with calm and a touch of humor, but respected it for the mystery it will always be:

> For seventy-four years
> I've touched east, west.
> My parting word?
> Listen—I'll whisper.

POETRY
AND ZEN

I   One spring day in 1912, the German lyric poet Rainer
Maria Rilke had an extraordinary experience, which,
based on the poet's account to her, the Princess Marie von
Thurn und Taxis-Hohenlohe described in the following
manner:

> He wandered absent-minded, dreaming, through the under-
> growth and maze of briars, and suddenly found himself next to a
> huge old olive tree which he had never noticed before. . . . The
> next thing he knew he was leaning back into the tree, standing on
> its gnarled roots, his head propped against the branches. . . .
> An odd sensation came over him so that he was fixed to the spot,
> breathless, his heart pounding. It was as though he were ex-
> tended into another life, a long time before, and that everything
> that had ever been lived or loved or suffered here was coming to
> him, surrounding him, storming him, demanding to live again
> in him. . . . 'Time' ceased to exist; there was no distinction be-
> tween what once was and now had come back, and the dark,
> formless present. The entire atmosphere seemed animated,
> seemed unearthly to him, thrusting in on him incessantly. And
> yet this unknown life was close to him somehow; he had to take
> part in it. . . .

Of course, the princess was suitably impressed and saw the experience
as further proof of the poet's otherworldliness, romantic disposition.

Had Rilke spoken with a Zen master of the event, it would have been called perhaps by its right name, spiritual awakening. Zen Buddhism's main purpose is to make such experiences possible, for their result is liberation.

Because Zen exists as a discipline to make an awakening possible, and because its adherents are made aware, early in their training, that all their labors will be fruitless unless they are enlightened, many have at least simulacra of the event. If in the West the mystic realization is extremely rare, in the Zen communities of the Far East it is consciously worked for, induced in a thousand and one ways. Often the Zenist writes a poem expressing the essence of his awakening, the depth of which is suggested by the quality of the poem.

Zen is unique as a religion-philosophy of artistic manifestation, the attainments of its practitioners often gauged by the works of art they make. The disciple is expected to compose poetry of a very special kind (*toki-no-ge* in Japanese, or "verse of mutual understanding") on the occasion of the momentous event which the solving of his *koan*, or problem for meditation, always seems to be. *Koans* are set to disciples by the masters so as to make them realize that there are things beyond the reach of common sense and logic, that the sensible, normal way of handling things does not always work and that if they hope to win enlightenment they must break through the barriers created, in all of us, by "mind." *Satori* poems are always genuine because only those winning the approval of the poet's spiritual guide are designated as such: the poet does not himself refer to a poem as an enlightenment poem before the fact of his master's approval.

As a consequence of the anciently established practice, a rather natural process of criticism and selection takes place: what has passed down as *satori* poetry is, in other words, the cream—the rest, what in fact was not reproduced, was for some reason found wanting (this is true only of awakening poetry: "death" poems are written only by mature and established masters who have earned the right to be heard at such a time, and "general" poems written by those masters whose words are considered important enough to preserve). Enlightenment poems rejected by masters are sometimes, as the result of the poet's later eminence, reproduced, as in the case of the Chinese master Chokei, the first of whose following *satori* poems was rejected, the second approved:

> Rolling the bamboo blind, I
> Look out at the world—what change!

Should someone ask what I've discovered,
I'll smash this whisk against his mouth.

*

All's harmony, yet everything is separate.
Once confirmed, mastery is yours.
Long I hovered on the Middle Way,
Today the very ice shoots flame.

It would be presumptuous even to try to imagine why the first of
these poems was rejected as lacking sufficient insight by Chokei's
master (to assume that it was its "arrogance" would be risky, as many
true *satori* poems seem even more "arrogant"), but the second is
surely an extraordinary poem. Only the master, aware of his disciple's
barriers, can determine whether a breakthrough has been made: if it
has, the poem will show it. Such judgment, considering the spiritual
context, places the highest sort of value on art. The most famous example in Zen history of the manner in which a *satori* poem is written,
and the tremendous consequences it can have for the writer, is re-
counted in one of the most important Zen texts, the *Platform Scripture* of the Sixth Patriarch of Zen in China, Hui-neng:

> One day the Fifth Patriarch, Hung-jen, called all the disciples
> together and said: "Life and death are serious matters. You are
> engaged all day in making offerings to the Buddha, going after
> blessings and rewards only. You make no effort to achieve free-
> dom, your self-nature is obscured. How can blessings save you?
> Go and examine yourselves—he who is enlightened, let him
> write a poem, which, if it reveals deep understanding, will earn
> him the robe and the Law and make him the Sixth Patriarch.
> Hurry, hurry!" Shen-hsiu, the senior monk, wrote:

>> Our body is the tree of Perfect Wisdom,
>> And our mind is a bright mirror.
>> At all times diligently wipe them,
>> So that they will be free from dust.

> Then the humble Hui-neng, who as a mere "rice pounder"
> was practically unknown in the monastery, wrote in response to
> Shen-hsiu's poem:

>> The tree of Perfect Wisdom is originally no tree,
>> Nor has the bright mirror any frame.
>> Buddha-nature is forever clear and pure.
>> Where is there any dust?

> Which so impressed the Fifth Patriarch that Hui-neng was named his successor, saying: "You are now the Sixth Patriarch. The robe is the testimony of transmission from generation to generation. As to the Law, it is to be transmitted from mind to mind. Let men achieve understanding through their own effort."

Death poems are perhaps the most unusual of the Zen poems: rarely morbid, self-serving, or self-sorrowful, and never euphemistic, they serve a uniquely spiritual end, as inspiration for the master's immediate followers and for the Zen community at large. The tradition of the death poem is very old, and as with many traditions, it perpetuates itself. Expected to write such a poem, the master not only steels himself for the task but for death itself. He is, as a Zenist, expected to face the inevitable stoically, and he does not fail his disciples. There are many anecdotes about the valor, before death, of the masters, the following being well known:

> When a rebel army took over a Korean town, all fled the Zen temple except the Abbot. The rebel general burst into the temple, and was incensed to find that the master refused to greet him, let alone receive him as a conqueror.
> "Don't you know," shouted the general, "that you are looking at one who can run you through without batting an eye?"
> "And you," said the Abbot, "are looking at one who can be run through without batting an eye!"
> The general's scowl turned into a smile. He bowed low and left the temple.

In the Zen communities not only the masters were expected to write death poems. The greatest of the *haiku* writers Matsuo Basho (1644–94) was asked by his friends, when it was clear that he was about to die, for a death poem, but he refused them, claiming that in a sense every poem he had written in the last ten years—by far his most productive period and one of deep Zen involvement—had been done as if a death poem. Yet on the next morning his friends were called by the poet to his bedside and told that during the night he had dreamed, and that on waking a poem had come to him. Then he recited his famous poem:

> Sick on a journey—
> over parched fields
> dreams wander on.

There are perhaps as many ways of dying, or at least of facing death, as there are of living, and though all death poems are compact, deep, intense, they reflect, as might be expected, the many differences to be found among men, including Zen masters. There is, for example, the serenity of Hofuku Seikatsu:

> Don't tell me how difficult the Way.
> The bird's path, winding far, is right
> Before you. Water of the Dokei Gorge,
> You return to the ocean, I to the mountain.

The power of Dogen:

> Four and fifty years
> I've hung the sky with stars.
> Now I leap through—
> What shattering!

The self-honesty of Keisen:

> The first illusion
> Has lasted seventy-six years.
> The final barrier?
> Three thousand sins!

In the case of enlightenment and death poems, there are certain recognizable norms and standards, and it is possible to compare them for their concision and gravity, whatever the distinction of the poets. The general poems, as might be expected, are less easily judged and cover a multitude of subjects, for in spite of the exigencies of the Zen life, not to speak of the expectations from him of others—to be ignored at peril—the Zen man finds himself moved to poetry by things not ostensibly associated with his discipline (though many general poems are so associated). As some have remarked, Zen art, be it the monochromic inkwash painting (*sumie*) long connected with Zen, or poetry, is best characterized by its celebration of, its wonder at, the intimate relationship of all that exists in the world. Such feeling is, of course, not unknown in the West, and is beautifully expressed by Martin Buber:

> Believe in the simple magic of life, in service in the universe, and
> the meaning of that waiting, that alertness, that "craning of the
> neck" in creatures, will dawn upon you. Every word would fal-

sify; but look! round about you beings live their life, and to whatever point you turn you come upon being.

   In Zen poetry the phenomenal world is never treated as mere setting for human actions; the drama is there, in nature, of which the
human is an active part, in no way separated from his surroundings,
neither contending with them, fearing them nor—for that matter—
worshiping them. The Zenist is no pantheist: in order to feel at home
in nature he does not find it necessary to imagine it as a godly imma-
nence. Many of the general poems, then, express a simple awe at the
beauty of the world:

> *Hearing the Snow*
>
> This cold night bamboos stir,
> Their sound—now harsh, now soft—
> Sweeps through the lattice window.
> Though ear's no match for mind,
> What need, by lamplight,
> Of a single Scripture leaf?
>   —Kido
>
> Disciplined by wind and snow,
> The Way of Reinan opens.
> Look where—moon high, plums a-bloom—
> The temple's fixed in stillness.
>   —Eun

   Though most of the general poems are written in the spirit of
celebration, some are clearly meant to instruct or hearten the master's
disciples, or as in the case of the following *waka* by Dogen, inspire
those among the followers who might in moments of weakness question the purpose of what they are required to do:

> *Waka on Zen Sitting*
>
> Scarecrow in the hillock
> Paddy field—
> How unaware! How useful!

II   What have all Zen poems, of whatever type, in common
         and what distinguishes them from poems written by the

artistic equals of the masters who work in other traditions, or independently? Zen's aesthetics are well and very subtly defined.

The four traditionally recognized dominant moods of Zen-related art are: *Sabi, Wabi, Aware,* and *Yugen.* Often in large-scale works such as *Noh* plays, as the result of natural modulations, all the moods may be suggested, but in short literary works and in *sumie* painting the mood is clearly apparent. These moods are not consciously created, as in the case of Indian *rasas* (emotional "flavors" so precise that one *rasa*, say of a sitar melody, may "belong" to a particular time of the day and is always deliberately induced): they are experienced as we experience the light of the sky, hardly aware of the delicacy of its gradations.

Sabi may be defined as the feeling of isolation, or rather at a midpoint of the emotion when it is both welcome and unwelcome, source of both ease and unease. This mood, as all strong moods, comes as the result of many things, but clearly associated with *Sabi* is the sense of being detached, as in Honei's poem "Fisherman":

> On wide waters, alone, my boat
> Follows the current, deep/shallow, high/low.
> Moved, I raise my flute to the moon,
> Piercing the autumn sky.

Of importance to the mood of the poem is that in ancient China the fisherman, one of the so-called "four recluses" (the others being the farmer, the woodcutter, and the herdsman), was held in great esteem by Taoists and Zenists. Hakuin, greatest of the Rinzai Zen masters of Japan, significantly titled a remarkable account of his spiritual progress, *Yasenkanna,* which can be rendered as "talk in a boat at night."

Sabi is associated with the period of early monastic training when, if one is to succeed in Zen discipline, a strong detachment must be cultivated. While in training, the fifteenth-century Japanese master Saisho wrote as an interpretation of the *koan* on Joshu's Nothingness a poem the equal of Honei's in its spirit of *Sabi*:

> Earth, mountains, rivers—hidden in this nothingness.
> In this nothingness—earth, mountains, rivers revealed.
> Spring flowers, winter snows:
> There's no being nor non-being, nor denial itself.

Here the feeling of detachment is not only strong, it is identified as an essential precondition of enlightenment. Ch'ing-yuan's well-known words on the importance of *wu-hsin* (no-mind, detachment) will serve to paraphrase Saisho's poem:

> Before I had studied Zen I saw mountains as mountains, waters as waters. When I learned something of Zen, the mountains were no longer mountains, waters no longer waters. But now that I understand Zen, I am at peace with myself, seeing mountains once again as mountains, waters as waters.

Wabi is the spirit of poverty, the poignant appreciation of what most consider the commonplace, and is associated in Zen with one of the principal characteristics, if not ideals, of the sect, an anti-relativism: what's good? what's bad? what's valuable? valueless? The mood is perhaps most apparent in relation to that quintessential Zen art, the tea ceremony, which—from the utensils employed in the preparation of the tea to the very timber of the tea hut—is a celebration of the humble, the "handmade." The nineteenth-century *haiku* artist Masaoka Shiki writes:

> Thing long forgotten—
> pot where a flower blooms,
> this spring day.

Wabi is not to be found in objects alone. As in the following awakening poem by the sixteenth-century Japanese master Yuishun, it is the feeling of something hitherto ignored suddenly being seen for the precious thing it is (and always has been, though hidden from us by illusion):

> Why, it's but the motion of eyes and brows!
> And here I've been seeking it far and wide.
> Awakened at last, I find the moon
> Above the pines, the river surging high.

One day while practicing *zazen* (formal sitting in meditation) with his followers, the Chinese master Daibai was moved to say aloud for their benefit, "No suppressing arrival, no following departure." Immediately after the words were spoken, the shriek of a weasel pierced through the meditation hall, and Daibai recited this extemporaneous poem:

> I'm at one with this, *this* only.
> You, my disciples,
> Uphold it firmly—
> Now I can breathe my last.

To know what Daibai meant by asking his followers to "uphold" the simple fact of the weasel's shriek is to appreciate the importance of *Wabi* to Zen. How much more real, how much more relevant to the spiritual quest than even the wisest words is Nature's least manifestation, when accepted for the profound thing it is.

Aware is the sadness that comes with the sense of the impermanence of things, the realization that they are lost to us even as they are found. It is so constant a mood in the poetry touched by Buddhism, that as far back as the tenth century, when the Japanese poet Ki no Tsurayuki (died 946) compiled the anthology *Kokinshu*, the first done under Imperial order, he could write:

> When these poets saw the scattered spring blossoms, when they heard leaves falling in the autumn evening, when they saw reflected in their mirrors the snow and the waves of each passing year, when they were stunned into an awareness of the brevity of life by the dew on the grass or foam on the water . . . they were inspired to write poems.

A few centuries later, Kenko Yoshida, a famous poet and court official of his day who became a Buddhist monk in 1324, wrote in his *Essays in Idleness*:

> If we lived forever, if the dews of Adashino never vanished, the crematory smoke on Toribeyama never faded, men would hardly feel the pity of things. The beauty of life is in its impermanence. Man lives the longest of all living things—consider the ephemera, the cicada—, and even one year lived peacefully seems very long. Yet for such as love the world, a thousand years would fade like the dream of one night.

At times the sense of *Aware* is so powerful that the only way of coming to terms with it is to identify with it totally, perhaps retiring from the world and the constant reminders of its limited, conditioned nature. Many of the finest Zen poems, seemingly "escapist," have this spirit of acceptance, of oneness with what *is*, whatever it happens to be. Here is the fourteenth-century Japanese master Jakushitsu:

Refreshing, the wind against the waterfall
As the moon hangs, a lantern, on the peak
And the bamboo window glows. In old age mountains
Are more beautiful than ever. My resolve:
That these bones be purified by rocks.

And here the Chinese master Zotan is seen praising a fellow
monk, "Shooku" (Woodcutter's Hut), whose retirement very much
impressed him:

Is the live branch better than the dead?
Cut through each—what difference?
Back home, desires quelled, you sit by
The half-closed brushwood door the spring day through.

It is perhaps in *haiku* poetry that *Aware* is most keenly felt,
though, because it is so commonly suggested (*Sunt lacrimae rerum*—
There are tears for things), it is the spoiler of many otherwise acceptable verses. But by those who care for *haiku*, the sentimental is never
mistaken for the poignant, and a piece like the following by Yosa
Buson (1715–83), important Nanga-style painter as well as poet, is
greatly prized:

A sudden chill—
In our room my dead wife's
comb, underfoot.

Yugen, most difficult of the dominant moods to describe, is the
sense of a mysterious depth in all that makes up nature. Often the
term is used in almost a purely aesthetic way, as in the theoretical
writings on *Noh* theater by the most important figure in its development, Zeami (1363–1443). In his essay, "On Attaining the Stage of
Yugen," he speaks of the mood as that which "marks supreme attainment in all the arts and accomplishments" and describes its essence as
"true beauty and gentleness," a "realm of tranquility and elegance."
Though such may be the effect of *Yugen* on the *Noh* stage, perhaps a
better sense of what the mood can represent in Zen is suggested by
these words of the contemporary Japanese Soto master Rosen Taka-
shina:

The true basis of the universe is stillness, its real condition, for
out of it comes all activity. The ocean, when the wind ceases, is

calm again, as are the trees and grasses. These things return to
stillness, their natural way. And this is the principle of meditation. There is night, there is day, when the sun sets there is a
hush, and then the dead of night, when all is still. This is the
meditation of nature.

Yugen is the sense of the mystic calm in things (in T. S. Eliot's
phrase, in "Burnt Norton," "the still point of the turning world"),
which is always there, below the surface, but which reveals itself only
to the "ready."

Etsuzan, the Chinese master, aware that his time was nearly up,
looked into things as never before, and wrote:

> Light dies in the eyes, hearing
> Fades. Once back to the Source,
> There's no special meaning—
> Today, tomorrow.

For him the world had returned to a stillness, its natural condition,
and perhaps the realization gave him comfort in his final hour.
Yugen also suggests the sense of a strong communion with nature, a
descent into depths, as in this poem by the seventeenth-century Japanese master Manan:

> Unfettered at last, a traveling monk,
> I pass the old Zen barrier.
> Mine is a traceless stream-and-cloud life.
> Of those mountains, which shall be my home?

And in this poem, one of his most famous, by Dogen:

> This slowly drifting cloud is pitiful;
> What dreamwalkers men become.
> Awakened, I hear the one true thing—
> Black rain on the roof of Fukakusa Temple.

To hear that "black rain" with Dogen, to sense that it—or anything
like it, for though intensely particular it is symbolic—is the "one true
thing" is to enter the realm of *Yugen*, which as a mood is not of course
peculiar to Zen but which, nonetheless, is most commonly felt in its
art. Not to hear it, on the other hand, not to know if one hears that one
has identified with the Source is to remain a "dreamwalker," blind
not only to the beauty of the world but to its reality.

The four dominant moods, however closely associated with Zen art, are not exclusively related to the philosophy, whereas *zenki*, the sense of a spontaneous activity outside the established forms, as if flowing from the formless self, is the constant in its art. Without Zen there could not be *zenki*, just as without *muga* (so close an identification of subject and object that "self" disappears) the goal of Zen, *satori*, could not be realized. There have been occasional attempts to describe in detail the characteristics of Zen art, the most comprehensive being Dr. Hisamatsu's in *Zen and Fine Arts*, which gives as its chief qualities the following (all of which, according to Dr. Hisamatsu, are present harmoniously in every Zen work, whatever the medium): asymmetry, simplicity, freedom, naturalness, profundity, unworldliness, and stillness.

It is perhaps in poetry that these characteristics—subject and theme dictating to what degree, of course—are most apparent, the desired qualities of an aesthetic. The following poems have a common theme, and each in its way might be seen as representing the ideal Zen poem in Japan. This is by the thirteenth-century master Unoku:

> Moving/resting is meaningless.
> Traceless, leaving/coming.
> Across moonlit mountains,
> Howling wind!

And here is one by the fourteenth-century master Getsudo:

> The perfect way out:
> There's no past/present/future.
> Dawn after dawn, the sun!
> Night after night, the moon!

Against the facts of that wind, that sun, that moon, what are concepts such as time? these poems seem to be asking. And as in all genuine Zen art, calm replaces restlessness.

In Zen painting there are only the essential strokes, the space surrounding them being filled in by the mind, which poises itself on (imagines) what it knows best, that which is always tranquil, agreeable. The brush strokes, however few, serve to make the mind aware of the space, suggested not so much by the absence of objects but by the manner in which the objects are absorbed. And in poetry, perhaps the most important things are to be found in the silence following the words, for it is then that the reader or listener becomes conscious of the calm within. It is something felt, not known, and precious in the way that only the spiritual can be.

III   There are distinct types of Zen poetry, and distinguishing qualities, but what makes it unique in world literature is that it is recognized as a mystic Way—to a most difficult truth. Zen has other Ways (dō) but Kadō, the Way of poetry, is one that has always held a place of honor in its culture, which has always valued directness, concision, and forcefulness of expression. As Dr. D. T. Suzuki writes in one of his essays, "The Meditation Hall":

> The Zen masters, whenever they could, avoided the technical nomenclature of Buddhist philosophy; not only did they discuss such subjects as appealed to a plain man, but they made use of his everyday language. . . . Thus Zen literature became a unique repository of ancient wisdom . . . [refusing] to express itself in the worn-out, lifeless language of scholars. . . .

The masters also discouraged the dependence on scriptural writings, and a master like Tokusan could proclaim (in one of the stories of the *Mumonkan* [Barrier Without Gate], an early thirteenth-century classic of Chinese Zen): "However deep your knowledge of the scriptures, it is no more than a strand of hair in the vastness of space; however important seeming your worldly experience, it is but a drop of water in a deep ravine." And as the fourteenth-century Japanese master Shutaku wrote:

> Mind set free in the Dharma-realm,
> I sit at the moon-filled window
> Watching the mountains with my ears,
> Hearing the stream with open eyes.
> Each molecule preaches perfect law,
> Each moment chants true sutra:
> The most fleeting thought is timeless,
> A single hair's enough to stir the sea.

While discouraging dependence on scripture (sutra learning), the masters strongly encouraged the cultivation of non-attachment, upheld by all the sects of Buddhism, the ultimate aim of whose discipline was, quoting from Dr. Suzuki again, "to release the spirit from its possible bondage so that it could act freely in accordance with its own principles—that is what is meant by non-attachment."

To give some idea of the manner in which such an important ideal, one with scriptural authority, is dealt with by Zenists, here is the Japanese master Takuan (1573–1645) in a "Letter to the Shogun's Fencing Master":

> If your mind is fixed on a certain spot, it will be seized by that spot and no activities can be performed efficiently. Not to fix your mind anywhere is essential. Not fixed anywhere, the mind is everywhere. . . . The Original Mind is like water which flows freely . . . whereas the deluded mind is like ice. . . . There is a passage [in the *Diamond Sutra*] that says: "The mind should operate without abiding anywhere."

Presumably dissatisfied with his explanation, Takuan goes on:

> It is like tying a cat with a rope to prevent it from catching a baby sparrow which is tied up nearby. If your mind is tied down by a rope as is the cat, your mind cannot function properly. It is better to train the cat not to harm the sparrow when they are together, so that it can be free to move anywhere. . . . That is the meaning of the passage [in the *Diamond Sutra*]. . . .

How bumbling and obvious when compared with the poem Takuan was to write on the theme some time later:

> Though night after night
> The moon is stream-reflected,
> Try to find where it has touched,
> Point even to a shadow.

Which is perhaps the equal of Dogen's poem on the same passage in the *Diamond Sutra*:

> Coming, going, the waterfowl
> Leaves not a trace,
> Nor does it need a guide.

And resembles the eighteenth-century master Sogyo's:

Careful! Even moonlit dewdrops,
If you're lured to watch,
Are a wall before the truth.

And the contemporary Japanese Zen poet Shinkichi Takahashi's
"Fish":

I hold a newspaper, reading.
Suddenly my hands become cow ears,
Then turn into Pusan, the South Korean port.

Lying on a mat
Spread on the bankside stones,
I fell asleep.
But a willow leaf, breeze-stirred,
Brushed my ear.
I remained just as I was,
Near the murmurous water.

When young there was a girl
Who became a fish for me.
Whenever I wanted fish
Broiled in salt, I'd summon her.
She'd get down on her stomach
To be sun-cooked on the stones.
And she was always ready!

Alas, she no longer comes to me.
An old benighted drake,
I hobble homeward.
But look, my drake feet become horse hoofs!
Now they drop off
And, stretching marvelously,
Become the tracks of the Tokaido Railway Line.

Thus an important Buddhist principle, first advanced by scripture, often quoted and allegorized by masters (as in Takuan's "Letter
. . . " or Hyakujo Ekai's famous injunction, *Fujaku fugu*—No
clinging, no seeking), is transmuted into superb poetry by men who
not only know truth but feel.

We have examined the nature of the three main types of Zen
poetry, its characteristics, and have shown the manner in which it
expresses insights afforded by the philosophy. Perhaps from our discussion something like a viewpoint has emerged; namely that if one
wishes to "understand" Zen Buddhism, one could do worse than go to
its arts, especially the poetry, compared with which the many dis-
quisitions on its meaning are as dust to living earth.

BUDDHISM AND MODERN MAN

What think you, disciples, whether is more, the water which is in the four great oceans, or the tears which have flowed from you while you strayed and wandered on this long pilgrimage, because that was your portion which you abhorred and that which you loved was not your portion?

Samyutta-nikaya

Buddhism, better than most religions, seems to have adapted to modern life, many considering it to be, among other things, not only a method of self-discovery but a source of ideas for social orientation without equal in the West. By some, it is not thought to be a religion at all: it lacks the ritualism of most world religions, including the hebetude-inducing regularity of church going, and the one thing all the others most certainly have—a God. As a religion-philosophy it has had for centuries a strong appeal to rationalists, who have felt the need for spiritual guidance but wanted, at the same time, some assurance that it was toward a realizable end.

There has been in recent years much discussion of Buddhism, most of which has been the kind hardly conducive to appreciation, let alone understanding, of the twenty-five-hundred-year-old doctrine. One suspects for example that those who have been quick to

draw parallels between its metaphysics and those of the most prominent schools of Western philosophy have been in part motivated by
the desire to establish a base of respectability, however exotic, for
generally unpopular views. There is nothing reprehensible in that,
surely, and, if anything, the perception of such similarities can lead
to the sort of mutual respect many have assumed could never be
brought about, yet the result is often confusion.

Schopenhauer was among the first of the major Western philosophers to find in Buddhism true parallels to his own thought, and it
is in his *The World as Will and Idea* (1818) that these are best seen:

> If that veil of Mâyâ, the principle of individuation, is lifted from
> the eyes of a man to such an extent that he no longer makes the
> egotistical distinction between his person and that of others, but
> takes as much interest in the suffering of other individuals as in
> his own, and therefore is not only benevolent in the highest de-
> gree, but even ready to sacrifice his own individuality whenever
> such a sacrifice will save a number of other persons, then it clear-
> ly follows that such a man, who recognizes in all beings his own
> inmost and true self, must also regard the infinite suffering of all
> suffering beings as his own, and take on himself the pain of the
> whole world.

But Schopenhauer was an exception, perhaps a natural Buddhist; he
wrote:

> If I am to take the results of my philosophy as the standard of
> truth, I should be obliged to concede to Buddhism the pre-
> eminence over the rest. In any case it must be a satisfaction to me
> to find my teaching in such close agreement with a religion pro-
> fessed by the majority of men. This agreement must be all the
> more satisfactory because in my philosophizing I have certainly
> not been under its influence.

Remarkable as such similarities in thought may be, and in spite
of the value of having them pointed out, Buddhism should not be
considered, as it apparently is in some quarters, an ancient form of
phenomenology. That it is phenomenological in its approach to
matter and experience, that certain of its sects developed techniques of
psychic control suggestive of the aims of current psychotherapy, can
hardly be questioned, yet the doctrine is far more than the pragmatic-
minded would make it out to be, offering most when there are no
preconceptions concerning it.

One reason for the contemporary interest in Buddhist psychology is that most of its literature is that of dramatic confrontation between master and disciple, the one dedicated to helping the other rid himself of illusion and egoism. In the West, such relationships are understood chiefly in psycho-therapeutic terms, yet those who have observed their results in the East respect more than anything else their naturalness. By and large, the differences between Western and Eastern, particularly Buddhist, dialogues are due to the former being based on the effort of the stronger party to formulate and defend ideas, as in the Socratic tradition, whereas the latter concern problems of a more ontological order: the question most frequently heard in Western dialogue is "Who am I?" in Buddhist, "What am I?" In other words, the Occident's view of the natural scheme is essentially idealistic, with everything in its place and man somewhere in the center—doubting and perplexed at times, to be sure, but never questioning his right to be, perpetually. This view of the world may be the source —and the result—of the West's reliance on empiricism, which can be made to offer proofs and invest the shakiest theories with invincibility. It is also behind the West's distrust of intuition and the Eastern penchant for will-lessness, which it has somewhat scornfully named "quietism."

I recall being asked by a well-meaning, though skeptical student, what a Buddhist, particularly a Zenist, would do in a calamity of some sort, say a flood. My answer was that Buddhists, as all men, act when they are forced to, whether in response to natural disaster or social disorder, but—and this is crucial—they act with their hands, not permitting their minds to wobble, lose center. Such objectivity results often in more effective action and is fully in accord with the Buddhist principle of non-attachment, a principle extremely difficult for Occidentals to understand, suggesting as it admittedly does unconcern and coldness. In Zen terms, attachment is a spiritual malady, *chin*, which is a state, attained through meditation, in which one feels gay and immaculate. As a Zen master explained, *"Satori* (sudden awakening) will make it possible for you to live constantly in a state of joy. But remember that one needs further discipline to rid oneself of this joy, for there must not be even the shadow of attachment, any kind of attachment, in Zen. In this way you can attain a genuine awakening."

Part of the difficulty experienced by Westerners with such ideas is the result, simply, of imperfect translation of terms, especially those of Far Eastern origin. It is practically impossible to suggest with one English word the full meaning of a *kanji* (ideogram), which is why the Japanese are puzzled by foreign attempts to render with only seventeen syllables their *haiku* poems (a more realistic ratio, they maintain, would be two syllables in a Western language to one in the Chinese or Japanese). English being far less specific, the word "attachment" vaguely suggests feelings such as love and duty. In any case, as men everywhere, the Buddhist is involved emotionally in the life of his time and place. Yet if able to resist attaching himself to the impermanent, he may find it possible to avoid the suffering which the Buddha claimed was caused by craving and illusion.

THE REALISM OF BUDDHIST AIMS

No philosophy is more realistic in its methods and aims than Buddhism. Much has been said in recent years about the realism of Existentialism, and many presumably consider it to be a total philosophy with adequate answers to man's major questions, yet its chief theorist and spokesman Jean-Paul Sartre, among the most brilliant of contemporary thinkers, speaks of death as the one absurdity, an abyss before which man must tremble. In so far as such an attitude betrays a slavish attachment to life, something man possesses temporarily and cannot own, Existentialism is, in comparison with Buddhism, an incomplete, thus unsatisfactory philosophy. It would be impossible for a Buddhist to comprehend how men can hope to find comfort, not to speak of guidance, in a system leaving perhaps their main question unanswered.

The Zen master Shozan was typical in not shirking the issue. He lived in a period of Japanese history, the seventeenth century, when likely death by the sword was an everyday reality, and because many coming to his temple were involved in that reality, he chose to try to make it possible for them to overcome their fear. To turn his back on them would have been unthinkable to the master, and accepting the world for what it was, while doubtless wishing it were otherwise, he performed his duties with such success that he had a following among the samurai, the warrior class. To consider any part of life, even its natural end, an absurdity, to quake before it, is to make of it something which does not exist, a cosmic agent the purpose of which is to act on man.

A MEASURE OF THE BUDDHA'S ACHIEVEMENT

In order to appreciate the magnitude of the Buddha's achievement, it is necessary to try to imagine what life was like in early India, particularly in towns of the Ganges Valley like Kapilavastu, eighty miles north of Benares, where he was born about 560 B.C. Every year the river flooded the valley, overnight destroying crops wrung from a harsh earth, spawning famine and spreading its leavings—dysentery, cholera, and countless other ills; weakening men for the predatory beasts, particularly tigers and snakes. Meanwhile the Brahmanas, Hindu priests, chanted the Vedic hymns and offered fire sacrifices to Brahma, in one of his many forms, yet nothing they did could improve the conditions of the common man.

From earliest times Hindu society was stratified to such a degree, caste so firmly established in the economy that to rise against it, as the Buddha in his own way certainly did, questioning even the wayward nature of asceticism, was to arouse anger. The Brahmanas, creators and perpetuators of a social order highly favorable to themselves, must have thought him a dangerous lunatic. Of caste the Buddha said, "A man does not become a Brahmana by his family or by birth. In whom there is truth and righteousness, he is blessed, he is a Brahmana." Nor did the Buddha accept the existing belief that because of their caste some were naturally unworthy of salvation: "My doctrine makes no distinction between high and low, rich and poor; it is like the sky, it has room for all; like water it washes all alike." And, worst of heresies, the Buddha went so far as to deny the existence of Brahma himself: "Is there a single one of the Brahmanas . . . who has ever seen Brahma face to face? Does it not follow, then, that it is foolish talk to point the way to a state of union, with that which we have not seen?" The gods, to the Buddha, were creatures with very human attributes, as much in need of salvation as men.

Perhaps the Buddha's greatest spiritual accomplishment was the doctrine of the Middle Way, which he discovered only after renouncing the harsh practices of the forest dwellers, among whom he lived as an ascetic for some time. And yet, despite his doubts about existing religious practices, and his strong sense of mission, he did not think of himself as the creator of a new religion. Rather—and in this he was like Jesus Christ—he felt the need to purify the religion of his day. He took for granted the truth of Hindu conceptions such as *Karma* (causality), while insisting that they be examined in relation to their psychological sources. It must have been evident to him that the Brahmanas, whether consciously or not, used a number of means to preserve the status quo, especially caste, which seemed almost designed to prove their superiority over the three other *varnas—Kshatriyas* (warriors), *Vaisyas* (traders and farmers), *Sudras* (serfs)—whom they considered to be little more than attendants upon themselves. It was not difficult for the Brahmanas to keep the lower groups in line, and they were actually able to convince the *Sudras*—so powerful was their hold—that their lot was miserable, because in past lives they had accumulated a store of bad *Karma*. These lowest of the low were good enough to sweep roads and cart dung, but not worthy of entering a temple in the hope of purification. The Buddha described the caste arguments of the Brahmanas as casuistical as well as cruel, and he declared that all men lived within reach of Nirvana.

The sixth century B.C. has been called the most remarkable in the spiritual history of mankind, producing in addition to the Buddha, Mahavira, Lao-Tsu, Confucius, Zarathustra, and Parmenides. The main events of the Buddha's life are well known: the miraculous birth and precocious childhood, the princely upbringing, his marriage and the birth of his son, the fatal encounters with the old man, the sick man, the corpse, and the religious ascetic, which made him aware of suffering and convinced him that his mission was to seek liberation for himself and others; his renunciation and the six years spent in studying doctrines and undergoing yogic austerities, the giving up of ascetic practices for normal life, the seven weeks spent in the shade of the Bodhi tree until, finally, one night toward dawn, enlightenment came; then his sermons and missionary travels, which lasted forty-five years, during which he affected the lives of thousands, high and low; and, at the age of eighty his *parinirvana*, extinction itself.

Such is the simple, dramatic outline of his life and mission, yet, as in the case of all great religious leaders, the literature inspired by the Buddha's story is as various as those who have told it in the last twenty-five hundred years. To the first of his followers and the tradition associated with Theravada Buddhism, and figures like the great Emperor Ashoka, the Buddha was a man, not a God; a teacher, not a savior. To those who, a few hundred years later, formed the Mahayana school, he was a savior and often a God, one concerned with man's sorrows above all else. To this day, the former tradition prevails in parts of India, Ceylon, Burma, Cambodia, and Thailand; the latter in Tibet, Mongolia, Vietnam, Korea, China, and Japan.

THE THERAVADA AND MAHAYANA SCHOOLS

Exactly how and when the Mahayana school came into being is one of the mysteries of world religion, yet most Buddhist historians seem fairly certain that of great importance to its inception was the Fourth Council of monks convened by King Kanishka, a convert to Buddhism, around 100 A.D. Whatever the purpose of the council, which has never been recognized by the Theravada, it represents an epoch-making event in the story of Buddhism in that it established Sanskrit as the language of the scriptures. Certainly the proceedings of the council resulted in a new atmosphere which, not long after, made it possible for figures like the metaphysician Nāgārjuna, thought to be the founder of Mahayana, to work in a spirit of free inquiry.

The simplest description of the differences between the schools is that of the Chinese traveler I-Tsing (635–713), who saw both, impartially, as living realities in India: "Those who worship Bodhisattvas (enlightened beings) and read Mahayana Sutras are called Mahayanists, while those who do not do this are called Hinayanists (Theravadins)." Sir Charles Eliot, in his *Hinduism and Buddhism* (Volume II), enlarges on I-Tsing's definition by conveniently listing seven lines of thought or practice found in Mahayana:

1.   A belief in Bodhisattvas and in the power of human beings to become Bodhisattvas.

2.   A code of altruistic ethics which teaches that everyone must do good in the interest of the whole world and make over to others any merit he may acquire by his virtues. The aim of the religious life is to become a Bodhisattva, not to become an Arhat.

3.   A doctrine that Buddhas are supernatural beings, distributed through infinite space and time, and innumerable. In the language of later theology a Buddha has three bodies and still later there is a group of five Buddhas.

4.   Various systems of idealist metaphysics, which tend to regard the Buddha essence or Nirvana much as Brahman is regarded in the Vedanta.

5.   A canon composed in Sanskrit and apparently later than the Pāli Canon.

6.   Habitual worship of images and elaboration of ritual. There is a dangerous tendency to rely on formulae and charms.

7. A special doctrine of salvation by faith in a Buddha, usually Amitâbha, and invocation of his name. Mahayanism can exist without this doctrine, but it is tolerated by most sects and considered essential by some.

Though it was during the reign of the third century B.C. Theravadin, King Ashoka, that Buddhism began to spread from India to other parts of Asia, there is little question that its greatest expansion, particularly in East Asia, was inspired by the altruistic Bodhisattva ideals of Mahayana, which was as a school less monastic, more outgoing, warmer in charity, and more disposed to evolution and development than Theravada. As a result of this new spirit, Buddhism began to be felt as a force in the secular history and art of China around the second century A.D. A few centuries later, largely due to China's great influence, it reached, with like impact, Korea and Japan.

THE NOBLE TRUTHS

To bring about a change in the way man views himself in the world is the highest purpose of religion and philosophy, and if today many are turning to Buddhism as the doctrine best able to help them achieve such transformations, it is not because other systems of belief have failed in their purpose but because, simply, they have been unable to co-exist with those views of reality offered by science and humanistic disciplines, such as psychology, conditioned if not created by the empirical approach. That is claiming much, but many of the most penetrating thinkers of our time, from Jung to Toynbee, have for one reason or another been strongly attracted by Buddhism. In any case, it is apparently with the greatest sense of relief that some Occidentals have discovered a doctrine which, while dispensing with ritualistic trappings and other hindrances to intelligent appraisal, offers answers both profoundly spiritual and fully rational. The Buddha stated his views in the clearest possible manner, according to the capacity for understanding of his listeners, sometimes through the use of analogies and parables, sometimes straightforwardly, as when he claimed that man's subjection to *Samsara* (time, life-and-death consciousness) is due to *avidyā* (ignorance) leading to *āsava* (illusion, depraved craving), from which state he must rise to *vidyā* (enlightenment). From the moment of his own awakening to his death, he attempted to show men how to transform themselves, proclaiming the Four Noble Truths, the Noble Eightfold Path, and the Middle Way.

The Middle Way was meant to help men find peace with themselves and the world, whose Four Noble Truths were that there is *Dukkha* (suffering), that its origin is *Samudaya* (thirst, desire), that men can bring about its cessation, *Nirodha*, through the attainment of Nirvana, and that the only way to achieve Nirvana is to follow the *Magga* (the Noble Eightfold Path): Right Views, or acceptance of the Buddha's teaching; Right Thought, or aspirations leading to purity and charity; Right Speech; Right Conduct; Right Livelihood; Right Effort, or avoidance of lapses into frailty; Right Mindfulness, or constant awareness of the truth of the doctrine; and Right Concentration, or spiritual exercises leading to an awakening.

KARMA AND SAMSARA

The Buddha's doctrines were centered in two basic Hindu conceptions, *Karma* and *Samsara*. The Hindus believed that the universe is inhabited by numberless souls in various degrees of elevation, each passing through many births and deaths in a variety of bodily forms. Each instant of existence experienced by the soul, in each incarnation, is directly the result of action performed in a former birth, and in its turn affecting future experience. In short, each soul is made up of an endless chain of sorrow, and the only escape possible is spiritual insight and union with the supreme being, Brahma. As is well known, the Buddha formulated the doctrine of *anatta* (no-soul), rejecting not only the idea of self but of God as well. He felt that by denying them he could rid humanity of its moral and intellectual weakness, caused in part by an insistence on individuation and its accompanying dualisms. One of the most strongly held views in the Buddha's time was that, "Whatsoever happiness or pain or neutral feeling the person experiences, all that is due to the creation of a Supreme Deity." In the *Anguttara-nikāya*, a book of the Pāli Canon, his comment on this fatalistic view is quoted:

> So, then, owing to the creation of a Supreme Deity men will become murderers, thieves, unchaste, liars, slanderers, abusive, babblers, covetous, malicious, and perverse in views. Thus for those who fall back on the creation of a God as the essential reason, there is neither the desire to do, nor the effort to do, nor necessity to do this deed or abstain from that deed.

Though much has been written about *Karma* (Pāli: *Kamma*) and the principle of no-soul, they are still poorly understood, the chief

reason being that few have gone for clarification to Buddhist literature itself—the *Questions of Milinda*, for example—preferring, as is
unfortunately the custom in the West, to consult expositions of the
subjects which, for the most part, are ponderously tricked out with
psychological jargon. Avoiding such an approach, and using one of
the best known analogies and inventing an extremely effective one of
his own, Ananda Coomaraswamy, in his *Buddha and the Gospel of
Buddhism*, discusses *Karma* and no-soul:

> Many are the similes employed by Gautama to show that no
> *thing* transmigrates from one life to another. The ending of one
> life and the beginning of another, indeed, hardly differ in kind
> from the change that takes place when a boy becomes a man—
> that also is a transmigration, a wandering, a new becoming.
> Among the similes most often used, we find that of the flame
> especially convenient. Life is a flame, and transmigration . . .
> is the transmitting of the flame from one combustible aggregate
> to another; just that, and nothing more. If we light one candle
> from another, the communicated flame is one and the same, in
> the sense of an observed continuity, but the candle is not the
> same. Or, again, we could not offer a better illustration, if a mod-
> ern instance be permitted, than that of a series of billiard balls in
> close contact: if another ball is rolled against the last stationary
> ball, the moving ball will stop dead, and the foremost stationary
> ball will move on. Here precisely is Buddhist transmigration: the
> first moving ball does not pass over, it remains behind, it dies;
> but it is undeniably the *movement of that ball*, its momentum,
> its *kamma*, and not any newly created movement, which is re-
> born in the foremost ball. Buddhist reincarnation is the endless
> transmission of such an impulse through an endless series of
> forms; Buddhist salvation is the coming to understand that the
> forms . . . are compound structures subject to decay, and that
> nothing is transmitted but an impulse . . . dependent on the
> heaping up of the past. It is a man's character, and not himself,
> that goes on.

In order to explain the nature of being in the light of his doctrine, the Buddha hit upon the important formula of "Origination in
a Sequential Series" (Pāli: *Patichchasamuppāda*), which is made up
of the following: Ignorance caused by *Karma*, the false belief in self;
Conformations issuing from ignorance, the potentialities of love,
hatred, and similar attachments which are the results of actions in a

former existence and inspire to future actions; Consciousness of finite beings, resulting in "Name and Form" (Pāli and Sanskrit: *nāma-rupā*), the conception of a world of particulars; Six sense organs, from such a conception, which make contact with these particulars, leading to sensations of feeling and desire which, in turn, lead to the attraction of individual life and its attachments; Being (Pāli and Sanskrit: *Bhava*), or finite existence and the passing of consciousness through its stages of birth, sorrow, death. Then, as the result of the old *Karma* and reinforced by that newly acquired, the process begins again.

In other words, the Buddha reasoned that the individual is merely a combination of name and form, the former including all the subjective phenomena of thought, feeling, and the above-mentioned conformations, all of which are called "aggregations" (Pāli: *khand-has*); the latter standing for the four elements of physical nature (earth, water, fire, air) and their products, a fifth *khandha*. It is *Karma* which unites the five *khandhas* into an apparent individual, and represents the link preserving the identity of a being through the countless changes undergone in its progress through *Samsara*. Buddhism's purpose is to destroy *Karma*, which can be accomplished only by voyaging the Eightfold Path to salvation, either in the present or, as the result of perfections, in the future.

NEITHER PESSIMIST NOR OPTIMIST

Because of such doctrines, it is quite naturally assumed by Westerners that Buddhism is pessimistic, but to consider it as such is to grossly simplify and infer, at the same time, that even in the face of incontrovertible evidence that they live in a fool's paradise, men prefer their illusions. Buddhism is neither pessimistic nor optimistic; it is realistic, dealing objectively with the human experience. What the Buddha meant by *Dukkha* was not suffering alone but impermanence and imperfection, and he was very far from denying the possibility of happiness, spiritual and material. He simply maintained that it could not last and that to believe otherwise was to court disappointment. Yet there was a form of happiness that could endure, and it came with the knowledge and acceptance of the universal essence, manifesting itself as the *Tri-kāya* (Three Divine Bodies): *Dharma-kaya*, or Essential Body, which is primordial, formless, and eternal; *Sambhogakaya*, or Reflected Body, wherein dwell the Buddhas and the Bodhisattvas while embodied in superhuman form; and *Nirma-nakaya,* or Incarnated Body, in which exist the earth-bound Buddhas.

It is the first of these, *Dharmakaya,* which is considered to be the Buddha-nature and noumenal source of the cosmic whole, the One Mind which, when grasped, leads to the perception of the undifferentiated nature of *Samsara* and *Nirvana.* Though *Samsara* and *Nirvana* form an inseparable entity, the Buddha himself declared that *Nirvana* is a state of transcendence over "that which is become, born, made and formed." Thus it is realized as the result of the stripping down of appearances, the penetration of their reality. As has been seen, the concept of *Samsara,* in which the law of *Karma* operates, is based on the belief that nothing is permanent, not even death, which must turn to new life. The Buddha was no fatalist. He maintained that man can work out his future, conquer time, but only at the cost of great sacrifice and the rooting out of self.

In his "Psychological Commentary" on *The Tibetan Book of the Great Liberation* (ed. by W. Y. Evans-Wentz, Oxford University Press, 1954), Dr. Jung writes:

> The fact that the East can dispose so easily of the ego seems to point to a mind that is not to be identified with our 'mind.' Certainly the ego does not play the same role in Eastern thought as it does with us. It seems as if the Eastern mind were less egocentric, as if its contents were more loosely connected with the subject, and as if greater stress were laid on mental states which include a depotentiated ego. It also seems as if Hathayoga were chiefly useful as a means for extinguishing the ego by fettering its unruly impulses. There is no doubt that the higher forms of *yoga,* in so far as they strive to reach *samādhi,* seek a mental condition in which the ego is practically dissolved. Consciousness in our sense of the word is rated a definitely inferior condition, the state of *avidyā* (ignorance), whereas what we call the 'dark background of consciousness' is understood to be a 'higher' consciousness. Thus our concept of the 'collective unconscious' would be the European equivalent of *buddhi,* the enlightened mind.

There have been many attempts in the West to describe philosophically and morally the "collective unconscious," yet it is one thing to claim that all men share in something, another to behave as if one really believed that they do. As the Buddhist scholar and translator

Edward Conze, discussing the Western interest in the philosophy, has said, "Although one may originally be attracted by its remoteness, one can appreciate the real value of Buddhism only when one judges it by the result it produces in one's own life from day to day."

The failure in such terms of much Western philosophy, even the most progressive, is due largely to its being too easily acquired, calling for very little discipline and sacrifice on the part of its adherents. If one reads Plato and approves of his view of the world, one is automatically a Platonist; if one "understands" the phenomenologists and appreciates the imaginative writings of Jean-Paul Sartre one can call oneself an Existentialist, and so on. Of course there are Occidentals who accept, as if converts, a rather spurious neo-Buddhism which, as one commentator claimed, "Plays amongst living religions the part of Esperanto amidst the natural languages." Yet when one takes into account the varying capacities of men, one finds it possible to tolerate almost anything, even the apparent need for escapism satisfied by a strange doctrine. By and large Western response to Buddhism is based on the most human of needs, that of self-understanding, and the philosophy's value is judged by the result it produces.

THE QUEST FOR PEACE

Regarding Western religious practice, it would appear that in order to "belong" to a church very little effort is required and less questioning countenanced. To become a Buddhist, the Emperor Ashoka knew that he must renounce all that he had hitherto believed and lived by, including warfare. His Thirteenth Rock Edict, which refers to his decimation of the Kalingas, suggests how complete was the transformation brought about in him through his conversion:

> When the king, Beloved of the Gods and of Gracious Mien, had been consecrated eight years, Kalinga was conquered, 150,000 people were deported, 100,000 killed, and many times that number died. But after the conquest of Kalinga, the Beloved of the Gods began to follow Righteousness (Dharma). . . . Now [he] regrets the conquest of Kalinga, for when an independent country is conquered people are killed, they die, or are deported, and that [he] finds very painful and grievous. . . . For all beings the Beloved of the Gods desires security, self-control, calm of mind, and gentleness. [He] considers that the greatest victory is the victory of Righteousness.

Echoing Ashoka, the contemporary Japanese Zen master Tenzan Yasuda, in an interview dealing in part with warfare, had this to say: "In a sense, Buddhism is the only religion capable of helping the world achieve peace. Its fundamental teaching is that all things are Buddhas—not men alone but all things, sentient and non-sentient. And not merely the earth, but the other planets as well. Universal peace will be realized when men all over the world bow to the preciousness and sacredness of everything." According to Buddhism, then, there is no justification whatsoever, least of all political expediency, to think of another human being as an enemy.

In the essay from which I have already quoted, Dr. Jung describes the Western religious attitude:

> In its religious attitude, too, the West is extraverted. Nowadays it is gratuitously offensive to say that Christianity implies hostility, or even indifference, to the world and the flesh. On the contrary, the good Christian is a jovial citizen, an enterprising business man, an excellent soldier, the very best in every profession there is. Worldly goods are often interpreted as special rewards for Christian behavior, and in the Lord's Prayer the adjective . . . *supersubstantialis*, referring to bread, has long since been omitted, for the real bread obviously makes so very much more sense! It is only logical that extraversion, when carried to such lengths, cannot credit man with a psyche which contains anything not imported into it from the outside, either by human teaching or divine grace. From this point of view it is downright blasphemy to assert that man has it in him to accomplish his own redemption. Nothing in our religion encourages the idea of the self-liberating power of the mind.

Yet, today, it is precisely that which is being attempted by many in the West, if not through the study of Eastern philosophy, particularly Zen Buddhism and Yoga, then with the aid of the so-called consciousness-expanding drugs such as LSD, which as one chiefly responsible for the interest in them has explained, make of the body a virtual laboratory if not temple, the last refuge of the freedom-seeking man. Now no one seriously involved in the study of Buddhism can witness such short-cuts to nowhere as less than pathetic, but equally appalling are the conditions forcing men to grope in such directions.

To many, modern life is simply unbearable, and there are things happening, or threatening to, which make of our time a perilous absurdity. Man's choices have been so severely curtailed, his involvement in decisions of life-or-death magnitude so limited, that he often finds himself lacking totally in purpose. Paradoxically, Western man's strong response to Buddhism may very well be the result of his being forced by circumstances to accept one of its major premises, that human experience is not individualistic. Those things which have made of life, for some, a veritable hell, have at the same time thrown its richest possibilities into relief, the chief being the sense of man's oneness with others.

If the writings of authors like Hesse and Salinger are popular with the young, it is because they too seem to offer alternatives to what is clearly no longer acceptable. When they think back to their own school years, it must seem incredible to the parents of today's students that they have chosen as models, even heroes, figures like Siddhartha of Hesse's story of the same name, or the suddenly enlightened coed, Franny, of Salinger's. Siddhartha, another of the Buddha's titles, meaning "he whose aim is accomplished," is made to say things by Hesse which in this age are well-nigh blasphemous: "Wisdom is not communicable. The wisdom which a wise man tries to communicate always sounds foolish," and "The world is not imperfect or slowly evolving along a long path to perfection. No, it is perfect at every moment."

If formerly it was customary to cite philosophers like Bergson when questioning some of the findings of science, today one is as likely to hear quoted an authority like the thirteenth-century Japanese Zen master Dogen, who in his great work *Shobogenzo* (The Correct-Law Eye Treasury), a collection of ninety-five essays dealing with Zen dialectics, said of time that it is man's experience of it which gives it form and duration—it is otherwise nonexistent. Everywhere one turns one observes doubt concerning thought structures of the past, a questioning of the very nature of our response to the physical world, our measuring, codifying, categorizing, the neat formulae and pat answers. If once it was natural to look out and name the day and the hour, experiencing Wednesday as something different from Sunday, we now realize that these equivalent periods of "time" have no consciousness of the roles we have given them. The solipsistic fairyland and pathetic fallacy men have made of the world is being shattered, partly as a result of the interest in Oriental philosophy.

BUDDHISM AND MODERN SCIENCE

Indeed, as has already been suggested, and as Maurice Percheron points out (*Buddha and Buddhism*, Harper and Brothers, New York,

1957), modern science fully supports the earliest findings of Buddhism:

> And so we see physics joining Buddhism in its theory of universal flux, of the lack of substance inherent in matter, of impermanence, of fundamental error attaching to the testimony of the senses and consequently of doubt over the validity of the mind's speculations. We also see modern psychology concerned only with an essentially labile psyche: a fluid personality governed by temporary conjunctions escaping all control, and depending more or less on circumstances, acts, and thoughts either barely acknowledged or not acknowledged at all. What else did the Buddha understand two thousand five hundred years ago but this?— that man has a certain vision of the universe through the medium of his senses; that he has another if he disengages himself from his sensory impressions; and yet another if he goes beyond perception of the laws that rule the balances of the universe and outside the causal sphere, to reach the domain of the unconditioned, which is an unthinkable for the intellect as is the identity of matter with magnetic fields and energic forces of attraction or repulsion. If we accept atomic physics as true . . . it is perfectly legitimate to accept the idea of vacuity, a state of unconditionedness outside phenomenal perceptions of time and space.

If Occidentals have been able to find in Buddhism parallels to their own thought and ideas sufficiently novel to make of it a source of insight and discovery, they have by and large proved themselves insensitive to its spiritual content. Many books of a generally pragmatic nature have been produced in recent years, showing the usefulness of Buddhism, especially Zen, to the development of new approaches to psychotherapy, literature, architecture, sports, even organized religion, yet for the most part their authors view the philosophy as technique and discipline, or one which perhaps more than any other offers concrete evidence, particularly in the arts, of its vitality. There is no gainsaying that aspect of Buddhism, and its gifts to the West have been substantial, yet Buddhists are often made uncomfortably aware of what they sense to be an exclusively utilitarian involvement in their doctrine. They would prefer, without proselytizing, to make Westerners conscious of Buddhism as religion, or at least as keenly melioristic philosophy.

The Occident's difficulty in accepting Buddhism's spiritual role is due in part to certain historical misconceptions. Even those familiar with its literature do not distinguish properly between the Theravada and Mahayana, assuming their differences, some of which have already been discussed, to be similar to those between, say, the Catholic and Protestant churches. The fact is that in comparison, and in the things that most matter, the differences between the schools are, if not considerable, certainly of great importance. As has been seen, Mahayana not only elevated the Buddha from noble teacher to virtual God, but even created something very close to a pantheon, in which the Bodhisattvas (enlightened beings) had their just place.

. The Bodhisattva, unlike his Theravada counterpart the Arhat, who is concerned mainly with self-salvation, voluntarily renounces the bliss of *Nirvana*, though fully qualified for it, so as to remain among the still unenlightened and work for their salvation. He is reverenced, even worshiped, for his ardor and compassion. Small wonder, then, that Mahayanists consider "Hinayanists" to be selfish. Their views on such matters led the Mahayanists to an acceptance—often reluctant—of myth and superstition associated with popular worship, resulting in the formation of, among others, the Japanese Pure Land Sect, which promises its followers a heaven as delectable in every way as the Christian or Muslim, and the Nembutsu cults, which consider the invocation of the Buddha Amida's name, and his praise, in this formula, *Namu Amida Butsu* (Honor to the Buddha Amida), as sufficient, if sincerely repeated, to assure salvation. Yet, balancing this tendency and of much more importance to Mahayana is the metaphysical speculation the most gifted of its followers have always engaged in, on subjects which in Theravada literature the Buddha refused to take seriously, and the like of which has rarely been witnessed elsewhere. The differences between the schools are dealt with openly throughout Buddhist literature, and in the *Lotus Sutra* the Buddha is quoted as claiming that he had first taught the Theravada doctrine because men were not yet ready for the more advanced ideas of the Mahayana.

THE TEN STAGES OF ENLIGHTENMENT

So far as the West is concerned, it is perhaps in Mahayana literature that Buddhism's spiritual message is most clearly heard, and it is as exalting as that of any comparable doctrine. As much as anything else in the literature, the *Dacabhûmî* (Ten Stages of Bodhisattva-hood), as given in the Avatamsaka Sutra, suggests the purity and zeal of Mahayana faith. As they fully represent salvational Buddhism and define the ideal Buddhist, in what follows, a paraphrasing of Dr. Suzuki's account of them in his *Outlines of Mahayana Buddhism*, an attempt is made to relate the Ten Stages, briefly, to the philosophy as a whole.

Pramuditâ (Joy), the first stage of Bodhisattvahood, is the result of turning from what Mahayanists see as the nihilistic contemplation of *Nirvana* practiced by Hinayanists, and is inspired by the realization that self-salvation is not enough, that there are others walking about in ignorance who must be made to recognize the error of their ways. It is only when men are made aware of suffering that the greatest joy possible to them, sacrifice for others, can be achieved. Once this stage is reached, it is natural for the enlightened man to teach and exhort, to go among the people, without discrimination, bearing his gifts.

Vimulâ (Purity) is attained through the spiritual insight gained at the first stage. Now that he is selfless, the enlightened one is without anger or malice. No longer can he conceive of taking the life of a living creature, no longer does he covet what belongs to others. His speech is direct and considerate, though never flattering. Now he is not only possessed of a sense of mission, he is morally qualified to carry it out.

Prabhâkari (Brightness) characterizes the intellectual condition of the awakened man, and is the result of newly acquired insight into the nature of things. He now understands that all is impure, impermanent, subject to sorrow and without soul, and recognizes at the same time that the real nature of things is neither created nor subject to death. All share in the selfsame essence, which is above time and space. It is only the unenlightened man, consumed with worry over the passing of grasped things, who adds to his store of *Karma* and is certain to suffer for it in future states. Yet it is precisely such a man that the Bodhisattva is sworn to save, his plight which fills him with spiritual energy. The following prayer by the Japanese Zen master Daichi expresses the feeling of this stage:

> My one desire is to dedicate this body born of my parents to the vow-ocean of Buddha, Law and Order. May I in all bodily actions be fully in accord with the holy rules, cherishing Buddha's Law throughout the rounds of birth and death until my reincarnation as a Buddha. May I never grow tired of saving all that is sentient wherever I happen to be. May I ever be masterful, whether in the forest of spears, the mountain of swords, the boil-

ing caldron, or the heap of burning coals, always bearing the Treasure of the Correct-Law Eye. May Buddha, Law and Order testify to my faith! May Buddhas and patriarchs safeguard me!

And here is a similar prayer by the Zen master Bassui:

May I, with clear *Marga* (truth)-eye, inherit the wisdom of Buddhas and patriarchs and, training superior beings, pitying those in error, conduct men and *devas* along the road to enlightenment. If any be so unlucky as to fall into the three hells—fire, blood, swords—I will suffer for him. Should the torment last a hundred million *kalpas* (aeons), I will not retreat.

Arcismatî (Burning) refers to the manner in which the enlightened man consumes all elements of evil and illusion in the purifying crucible of his new insight. It is at this stage that he practices strenuously the thirty-seven *Bodhipâksikas* (Virtues Conducive to Enlightenment), among the seven categories of which are the "Four Contemplations": on the impurity of the body, the evils of sensuality, the passing away of worldly interests, and the soul-less quality of things.

Sudurjayâ (Invincibility) is reached by the awakened man when, armed with the Virtues, he breaks the hold of all evil passions. Feeling intense love for humanity, inheriting the wisdom of past Buddhas, he is fearless in his quest for even greater truth, which in its highest form is perceived by him as an essence manifesting itself in a world of particulars. He also sees that absolute and relative knowledge are one and the same, and that the quality of particularity appears only when subjectivity is disturbed.

Abhimukhî (Revealing Oneself) is entered upon when the enlightened man reflects on the essence of all *Dharmas* (doctrines), which are of a piece. Perceiving their truth, he feels compassion for those still straying in *Samsara* and meditates on *Karma*, which brings about and is, at the same time, brought about by the hunger for individuation. His insight makes it possible for him to see beyond what is created and destroyed.

Dûrangamâ (Going Far Away) is the stage in which the awakened one attains *Upâyajñâ*, the knowledge which enables him to find whatever expediency is necessary to the work of salvation. Though he realizes that the Buddhas are no different from himself, he does not cease to do them homage, though he thinks constantly on the nature of the absolute, he does not abandon merit-accumulation, though no longer troubled by worldly thoughts, he does not disdain secular affairs. He knows that life is illusion, yet he toils on in the world of particulars and submits to the workings of *Karma*. He knows that the language of the Buddhas is beyond normal comprehension, yet he uses many devices to make it intelligible to the people. All of which suggests that while he lives on the highest plane of spirituality, he does not withdraw, preferring to engage himself in *Samsara* for the benefit of mankind.

Acalâ (Immovability) is the state attained by the Bodhisattva when he acquires the very highest knowledge, which is that everything in the world partakes of Suchness (Sanskrit: *Tathatā*). This knowledge, unconscious, intuitive, is the opposite to that derived by logic. Suchness is the term used by Mahayanists for the absolute and unconditioned quality of life, and in a sense is the positive expression of Voidness (Sanskrit: *Sūnyatā*), for it is to be found in all separate things and is neither different from nor divided by them. As it is not distinct from anything, it cannot be named the One as distinct from the Many, and nothing concerning it can be affirmed or denied, for these are modes of expression which by excluding suggest opposition. Nāgārjuna, the greatest Mahayana metaphysician and founder of the Madhyamika school, was the first to teach the doctrines of Suchness and Voidness. Possessing such knowledge, the awakened man enters a stage where all is immediately brilliant and his actions are spontaneous, innocent, even playful. He wills and it is done, he is nature itself.

Sâdhumatî (Good Intelligence) is the stage reached by the enlightened man when already sentient beings benefit by his works, and he is led to the *Dharma* of the deepest mystery, the penetration of which requires the four aspects of comprehensive knowledge: the self-essence of all beings, their individual attributes, their indestructibility, and their eternal order.

Dharmameghâ (Clouds of Dharma), the last stage of Bodhisattvahood, is attained when the enlightened man has practiced all the virtues of purity, has accumulated all that constitutes transcendent power, is fortified with intelligence men see as genius, practices universally the principle of compassion, and has followed with vigor the path of the Buddhas. His every thought now reaches the realm of eternal tranquility, for he has the knowledge of all things and has arrived at the summit of all activities. He is the personification of love, sympathy, and the Good Law, and the least of his actions results in benefit to mankind.

In the *Dacabhûmî*, we see detailed not only those qualities gained, step by step, by the Bodhisattva but the specific ideals of Mahayana throughout the Buddhist world it dominates. The first step in the pilgrimage to the Mahayana was the idealization of the Buddha, the second the positive view of *Nirvana,* and the last, and perhaps most important, the salvational mission of the Bodhisattvas, founded on the conviction that at the heart of the Eternal there is a love which surpasses all human understanding. The Mahayana brought about great changes in Buddhism, but the philosophy's major goals remained the same, and so did its chief assumptions regarding the world and man's journey through it. Without *Kshanti* (patience), *Karuna* (compassion), and *Prajna* (wisdom) it would be a chaos, and man could never liberate himself from *Samsara.*

"The West will never be 'Buddhist,'" Christmas Humphreys, who is in a position to speculate, has said (*Buddhism*, Penguin Books, 1957), "and only the most unthinking zealot would strive to make it so." He goes on:

> The Western mind will never be content with second-hand clothing, and all that Western Buddhists have the right to do is to proclaim the Dhamma to all who have "ears to hear," and to suggest why, and in principle how, it should be applied. It may be that from the mingling streams of the Pali Canon, the compassionate splendour of the Mahayana, and the astringent force of Zen will come a Navayama, a new "vehicle" of salvation.

But is there need for a Navayama? In his syncretistic approach to Buddhism, however noble its aim, does the Occidental betray the very characteristic which places its greatest truth beyond his reach? If the most cherished of Buddhism's gifts to the West is the pointing out of the path to self-discovery, its most valuable lesson is that as the consequence of that discovery the self is lost. With that in mind, why should not the West be Buddhist? Why should Westerners resist, merely because it is "second-hand clothing," a doctrine which can lead to the vision of a realm which knows neither East nor West? The Buddha, who spoke the first and must have the last word concerning the doctrine, never stated it more simply or movingly than while staying at Kosambī in the Sisu Grove:

The Buddha gathered up a handful of sisu leaves and addressed the monks: "Which do you think are the more numerous, monks, this small handful of leaves or those in the whole grove?"

"Very few in number are the leaves you have taken up. Much more in number are those in the whole grove."

"Even so, monks, much more in number are those things I have discovered but not revealed. And why, monks, have I not revealed them? Because they are not concerned with profit, they do not conduce to the holy life, nor to aversion, to detachment, to cessation, to tranquility, to comprehension, to wisdom, to Nirvana. That is why I have not revealed them.

"And what is it, monks, that I have revealed?

"Why, that this is suffering, this the arising of suffering, this the ceasing of suffering, this the practice leading to the cessation of suffering.

"And why did I reveal this alone?

"Because, monks, this is concerned with profit and is the beginning of the holy life; this conduces to aversion, detachment, cessation, tranquility, comprehension, wisdom, Nirvana. Therefore have I revealed it."

ZEN POETRY

I   The Golden Age of China, T'ang through Sung dynasties (AD 618–1279), began not long after the Western Roman Empire came to an end and lasted well beyond the First Crusade. One of the most cultivated eras in the history of man, its religious, philosophical, and social ground had been prepared centuries before Christianity, and men perfected their lives and arts certain that they gave meaning to something higher than themselves. To artists of the time, numerous and skilled, poetry and painting were Ways—two among many, to be sure, but glorious Ways—to realization of Truth, whose unfolding made possible not only fulfilled life but calm acceptance of its limitations. They saw in the world a process of becoming, yet each of its particulars, at any moment of existence, partook of the absolute. This meant that no distinction was drawn between the details of a landscape—cliffs, slopes, estuaries, waterfalls—shaped by the artist's emotions. Foreground, background, each was part of the process, in poetry as in painting, the spirit discovering itself among the things of this world.

> On the rocky slope, blossoming
> Plums—from where?
> Once he saw them, Reiun
> Danced all the way to Sandai.
>   —Hoin

The artist's visions were held to be revelatory; painting, poem meant to put men in touch with the absolute. Judgment of art works was made principally with that in mind. Some might delight the senses, a few exalt the spirit, whose role was taken for granted to be paramount, the greatest artists respecting its capacity to discover itself anew in their works. Over centuries the West has deduced the guiding aesthetic principle of such art to be "less is more," and a number of stories bear this out.

One concerns a painting competition in the late T'ang dynasty, a time of many such events and gifted competitors, all of whom, brought up in an intellectual and artistic meritocracy, were aware of what success might mean. Judged by master painters, most carefully arranged, each had its theme, that of our story being "Famous Monastery in the Mountains." Ample time was provided for the participants to meditate before taking up brushes. More than a thousand entries of monasteries in sunlight, in shadow, under trees, at mountain-foot, on slopes, at the very peak, by water, among rocks— all seasons. Mountains of many sizes, shapes, richly various as the topography itself. Since the monastery was noted "famous," monks abounded, working, praying, all ages and conditions. The competition produced works destined to be admired for centuries to come. The winning painting had no monastery at all: a monk paused, reflecting, on a misty mountain bridge. Nothing—everything—more. Evoking atmosphere, the monk knew his monastery hovered in the mist, more beautiful than hand could realize. To define, the artist must have learnt from the Taoism of Lao-Tsu or the Zen of Hui-neng, is to limit.

II   Zen began its rapid growth in early T'ang China, a product of the merging of the recently introduced Buddhism of the Indian monk Bodhidharma, who reached China in 520, and Taoism, the reigning philosophy of poets and painters for some thousand years. Providing a rigorously inspiring discipline, insisting on the primacy of meditation, its temples and monasteries were havens for seekers after truth throughout the T'ang, Sung, and Mongol-shadowed Yuan dynasties. Zen masters, religious guides, often themselves poets and painters, made judgments concerning the spiritual attainments of artist-disciples on the basis of works produced. Neither before nor since has art had so important a role in community life, and there are countless instances of poems or paintings affecting the development of the philosophy itself.

Writers of enlightenment poems did not think themselves poets. Rather they were gifted men—masters, monks, some laymen—who after momentous experiences found themselves with something to say which only a poem could express. Enlightenment, point of their meditation, brought about transformation of the spirit; a poem was expected to convey the essential experience and its effect. Such an awakening might take years of unremitting effort, to most it would never come at all:

> One day Baso, disciple of Ejo, the Chinese master, was asked by the master why he spent so much time meditating.
> Baso: "To become a Buddha."
> The master lifted a brick and began rubbing it very hard. It was now Baso's turn to ask a question: "Why," he asked, "do you rub that brick?"
> "To make a mirror."
> "But surely," protested Baso, "no amount of polishing will change a brick into a mirror."
> "Just so," the master said: "no amount of cross-legged sitting will make *you* into a Buddha."

Yet masters did their best to guide disciples: one device was the *koan*, which they were asked to solve. As no logical solution was possible, the meditator was always at wits' end—the intention. One of the *koans*, usually first given, was Joshu's "Oak in the courtyard," based on the master's answer to the standard Zen question "What's the meaning of Bodhidharma's coming to China?" These awakening poems, responses to this question of the masters, suggest the range of possibilities:

> Joshu's "Oak in the courtyard"—
> Nobody's grasped its roots.
> Turned from sweet plum trees,
> They pick sour pears on the hill.
> —Eian

> Joshu's "Oak in the courtyard"
> Handed down, yet lost in leafy branch
> They miss the root. Disciple Kaku shouts—
> "Joshu never said a thing!"
> —Monju-Shindo

Given their importance, it is not surprising to find in early Chinese enlightenment poems frequent references to *koans*. Most poems, though, deal with major aims of the philosophy, escape from space-time bondage, for example, a hard-won precondition of awakening:

> Twenty years a pilgrim,
> Footing east, west.
> Back in Seiken,
> I've not moved an inch.
> —Seiken-Chiju

> Earth, river, mountain:
> Snowflakes melt in air.
> How could I have doubted?
> Where's north? south? east? west?
> —Dangai

Many express swift release from conventional attachments:

> Searching Him took
> My strength.
> One night I bent
> My pointing finger—
> Never such a moon!
> —Keppo

Need for such release, transcending of doctrine (finger pointing at the moon, never taken for the moon itself), was the theme of Bodhidharma's historical interview with Emperor Wu of Liang, shortly after his arrival in China (by then some schools of Buddhism had been established there a few hundred years):

> Emperor Wu: From the beginning of my reign, I have built many temples, had numerous sacred books copied, and supported all the monks and nuns. What merit have I?
> Bodhidharma: None.
> Emperor Wu: Why?
> Bodhidharma: All these are inferior deeds, showing traces of worldliness, but shadows. A truly meritorious deed is full of wisdom, but mysterious, its real nature beyond grasp of human intelligence—something not found in worldly achievement.
> Emperor Wu: What is the first principle of your doctrine?
> Bodhidharma: Vast emptiness, nothing holy.
> Emperor Wu: Who, then, stands before me?
> Bodhidharma: I don't know.

Not long after this, Bodhidharma wrote his famous poem:

> Transmission outside doctrine,
> No dependencies on words.
> Pointing directly at the mind,
> Thus seeing oneself truly,
> Attaining Buddhahood.

As might be expected, awakening poems were held precious in Zen communities, serving for generations as *koans* themselves or as subjects for *teisho* (sermons). Interpretation was often made in the light of the master's life, what led to his experience. Nan-o-Myo, awakened when asked by his master to interpret "Not falling into the law of causation, yet not ignoring it," wrote:

> Not falling, not ignoring—
> A pair of mandarin ducks
> Alighting, bobbing, anywhere.

Every utterance of a worthy master was thought significant. The late Sung master Tendo-Nyojo, an example, guided Japan's great Dogen (1200–1253) to enlightenment, which alone made his death poem, simple as it is, glorious to the Japanese:

> Sixty-six years
> Piling sins,
> I leap into hell—
> Above life and death.

Zen death poems, remarkable in world literature, have a very ancient tradition. On their origin one can only speculate, but probably in early communities masters felt responsibility to disciples beyond the grave, and made such poems in the hope that they would help point the way to attainment, not only for disciples but for posterity. To some the final poem was not felt to be itself of much importance:

> Life's as we
> Find it—death too.
> A parting poem?
> Why insist?
>   —Daie-Soko

Many, however, considered it to be a symbolic summation, quite possibly preparing well before the inevitable moment. It would stand, every syllable pondered, and lives might well be affected by truth, absolute, whatever its message and worth as "poetry." Differences between death poems give a sense of the variety of temperament among Chinese masters. Fuyo-Dokai's vital self-assurance:

> Seventy-six: done
> With this life—
> I've not sought heaven,
> Don't fear hell.
> I'll lay these bones
> Beyond the Triple World,
> Unenthralled, unperturbed.

Koko's sense of release from a harsh existence:

> The word at last,
> No more dependencies:
> Cold moon in pond,
> Smoke over the ferry.

Shozan's astringent mockery:

> "No mind, no Buddha"
> Disciples prattle.
> "Got skin, got marrow"
> Well, goodbye to that.
> Beyond, peak glows on peak!

There is no way of telling, records being scant and unreliable (there are wild variants of birth and death dates), whether all wrote death poems, but given their solemn purpose they probably did. By 1279, when China was overrun by Mongols, Zen had flourished for almost one hundred years in Japan. There from the start death poems of masters were thought to have great religious meaning. Dogen left, exulting:

> Four and fifty years
> I've hung the sky with stars.
> Now I leap through—
> What shattering!

III   Centuries before the introduction of Zen in the Kamakura Period (1192–1333), Japan had been virtually transformed by Chinese Buddhism. Every aspect of life, from the Nara Period (710–84) on, reflected in one way or another the Chinese world vision. Painters and poets looked to China constantly, as did the greatest painter in the Chinese style, Sesshu, who crossed there for instruction and inspiration. Not all became Zenists like Sesshu, who was to join the priesthood, but most were guided by the philosophy, their works revealing the extent. In the earliest Zen communities enlightenment and death poems were written strictly in *kanji* (Chinese characters), in classical verse forms preferred by the Chinese masters—there is little to distinguish poems of the first Japanese Zenists from those written in China centuries before.

Here is the 12th century master Kakua's enlightenment poem:

> How can I tell what I've seen?
> Fall, stand—it's clear at once.
> Wearing my cowl backwards, I
> Trample the old path. And the new.

And here is the 13th century master Doyu's death poem:

> Fifty-six years, above Buddhas, Patriarchs,
> I've stood mid-air.
> Now I announce my final journey—
> Daily sun breaks from the eastern ridge.

The Japanese masters composed not only enlightenment and death poems in Chinese verse forms, they often wrote of important events in the history of Zen, like Bodhidharma's interview with the Emperor Wu. Here is Shunoku's poem on the subject. ("Shorin" is the temple where Bodhidharma, on discovering that the emperor lacked insight, sat in Zen for nine years. To reach the temple he had to cross the Yangtze River.)

> After the spring song, "Vast emptiness, no holiness",
> Comes the song of snow-wind along the Yangtze River.
> Late at night I too play the noteless flute of Shorin,
> Piercing the mountains with its sound, the river.

Even in writing on general themes associated with Zen life, the masters employed the purest literary Chinese. Since few Japanese knew the language, this practice made the Zen poems élitist, leading to the feeling on the part of masters like Dogen that an indigenous verse form, *tanka* (or *waka*), should be utilized. Such works would be understood in and out of the Zen communities, and surely it was possible to be as inspiring in Japanese which, though using *kanji*, had a syllabary and was very different from Chinese. The most important collection of early Japanese poetry, the *Manyoshu* (eighth century), contains three kinds of verse forms: *choka, tanka*, and *sedoka*, all based on arrangements of 5-7-5 syllable lines, the most popular, *tanka*, structured as 5-7-5-7-7 syllables—strictly, without any possible variation.

In the Heian Period (794–1185), which immediately preceded the first age of Zen, *tanka* was the favorite verse form at the courts. Towards the end of Heian, *renga* (linked verse), became popular: a chain of alternating fourteen and twenty-one syllables independently composed but associated with the verses coming before and after. By the fifteenth century, *renga* expiring of artificiality, something more vital was found, the *haikai renga*, linked verses of seventeen syllables. Later came individual poems of seventeen syllables, *haiku*, the earliest authentic examples by writers like Sogi (1421–1502), Sokan (1458–1546), and Moritake (1472–1549).

Basho, thought by many Japanese to be their finest *haiku* writer and greatest poet, lived from 1644 to 1694. Like almost all noted *haiku* writers he was a Zenist, practising discipline under the master Butcho, with whom, according to Dr. D. T. Suzuki, he had the following exchange:

> Butcho: How are you getting along these days?
> Basho: Since the recent rain moss is greener than ever.
> Butcho: What Buddhism was there before the moss became green?

Resulting in enlightenment and one of Basho's best-known *haiku*:

> Old pond,
> leap-splash—
> a frog.

Whether or not they undertook discipline, *haiku* writers thought themselves living in the spirit of Zen, their truest poems expressing its ideals. To art lovers, the appeal of *haiku* is not unlike that of a *sumie* (ink-wash) scroll by Sesshu, and many *haiku* poets, like Buson, were also outstanding painters.

Zenists have always associated the two arts: "When a feeling reaches its highest pitch," says Dr. Suzuki, Zen's most distinguished historian, "we remain silent, even seventeen syllables may be too many. Japanese artists . . . influenced by the way of Zen tend to use the fewest words or strokes of brush to express their feelings. When they are too fully expressed, no room for suggestion is possible, and suggestibility is the secret of the Japanese arts." Like a painting or rock garden, *haiku* is an object of meditation, drawing back the curtain on essential truth. It shares with other arts qualities belonging to the Zen aesthetic—simplicity, naturalness, directness, profundity—and each poem has its dominant mood: *sabi* (isolation), *wabi* (poverty), *aware* (impermanence), or *yugen* (mystery).

If it is true that the art of poetry consists in saying important things with the fewest possible words, then *haiku* has a just place in world literature. The limitation of syllables assures terseness and concision, and the range of association in the finest examples is at times astonishing. It has the added advantage of being accessible: a seasonal reference, direct or indirect, simplest words, chiefly names of things in dynamic relationships, familiar themes, make it understandable to most, on one level at least. The *haiku* lives most fully in nature, of great meaning to a people who never feel it to be outside themselves. Man is fulfilled only when unseparated from his surroundings, however hostile they may appear:

> To the willow—
> all hatred, and desire
> of your heart.
> > —Basho

> White lotus—
> the monk
> draws back his blade.
> > —Buson

> Under cherry trees
> there are
> no strangers.
> > —Issa

In the West, perhaps as a result of fascination with the *haiku* (its association with the development of modern poetry at one extreme, its universal appeal in schools at the other), it arouses as much suspicion as admiration. It looks so easy, something anyone can do. A most unfortunate view, for *haiku* is a quintessential form, much like the sonnet in Elizabethan England, being precisely suited to (as it is the product of) Japanese sensibility, conditioned by Zen. For Basho, Buson, Issa, *haiku* permitted the widest possible field of discovery and experimentation.

The Zen experience is centripetal, the artist's contemplation of subject sometimes referred to as "mind-pointing." The disciple, in an early stage of discipline, is asked to point the mind at (meditate upon) an object, say, a bowl of water. At first he is quite naturally inclined to metaphorize, expand, rise imaginatively from water to lake, sea, clouds, rain. Natural perhaps, but just the kind of "mentalization" Zen masters caution against. The disciple is instructed to continue until it is possible to remain strictly with the object, penetrating more deeply, no longer looking *at* it but, as the Sixth Patriarch Hui-neng maintained essential, *as* it. Only then will he attain the state of *muga*, so close an identification with object that the unstable mentalizing self disappears. The profoundest *haiku* give a very strong sense of the process:

> Dew of the bramble,
> thorns
> sharp white.
> > —Buson

> Arid fields,
> the only life—
> necks of cranes.
> > —Shiko

To give an idea of the way *haiku* work, without making an odious cultural comparison, here is Ezra Pound's "In a Station of the Metro," perhaps the most admired (and for good reason) *haiku*-like poem in English:

> The apparition of these faces in the crowd;
> Petals on a wet, black bough.

A simile, the poem startles as *haiku* often do, but much of what is said would, to a *haiku* poet, be implied. Incorporating the title (*haiku* are never titled), he might make the poem read:

> Faces in the metro—
> petals
> on a wet black bough.

If asked why, he might answer: the first few words, "The apparition of these," though sonorous enough, add nothing. Nor does the reference to "crowd," metro "stations" usually being crowded—besides, the "petals" of the simile would make that clear. His revision, he might claim, transforms the piece into an acceptable *haiku*, one rather like, perhaps less effective than, Onitsura's:

> Autumn wind—
> across the fields,
> faces.

Without using simile, Onitsura stuns with an immediacy of vision—those faces whipped by a cold wind.

For centuries *haiku* has been extremely popular, and there are established schools with widely differing views. Typical is the Tenro, truly traditional, working with the 5-7-5 syllabic pattern, clear seasonal reference, and possessing a creed—*Shasei*, on-the-spot composition with the subject "traced to its origin." There are around two thousand members all over Japan, and it is usual for groups to meet at a designated spot, often a Zen temple, and write as many as one hundred *haiku* in a night, perhaps only one of which, after months of selection and revision, will be adequate. It will then be sent to one of the school's masters and considered for the annual anthology, representing poems of some thirty members.

Untypical by comparison is the Soun (free-verse) school, which feels no obligation to stick to the seventeen-syllable pattern. Short and compact, however, its poems are written in the "spirit of Basho." Their creed is more general—Significance—and is very close to Zen, many of the members involved in discipline. They follow an ancient dictum, *Zenshi ichimi* (Poetry and Zen are one), and *Kadō*, the Way of poetry. As they strive for the revelatory, fewer poems are written than in the Tenro. Both schools, while opposed in principle, relate *haiku* to Zen, as do all other schools. Yet very few contemporary *haiku* could have pleased Basho, for, however lofty the ideals, they are generally derivative.

Kadō, the Way of poetry to self-discovery, is similar in aim to other *dō* (Ways) of Zen: *Gadō* (painting), *Shodō* (calligraphy), *Jindō* (philosophy), *Judō* (force). *Haiku* teachers and Zen masters expect no miracles of disciples, yet maintain that with serious practice of an art, given aspirations, men perfect themselves: farmers, professors make their *haiku*, most egalitarian of arts. To those who find art a mystery engaged in by the chosen, the sight of a *haiku*-school group circling an autumn bush, lined notebooks, pens in hand, can be sharply touching. Only a cynic would think otherwise.

The few, of course, achieve true distinction in the skill, and are known to all who care for poetry. Usually they echo early masters, but some find that language cramping and consciously introduce the modern—factories, tractors, automobiles. They will admit, without derogating, to taking little pleasure from old *haiku*. They are, however, generous readers of each other's work and that of certain contemporary poets. One in whom many are interested, despite his not being a writer of *haiku*, is Shinkichi Takahashi, regarded throughout Japan as the greatest living Zen poet.

IV   Overlooking the sea in a fishing village on Shikoku Island, a poem is carved on a stone:

Absence

Just say, 'He's out'—
back in
five billion years!

It is Shinkichi Takahashi's voice we hear. He was born in 1901, and the commemorative stone, placed by his townsmen, is one of many honors accorded him in recent years: another is the Ministry of Education's prestigious Prize for Art, awarded for *Collected Poems* (1973). In Japan poets are often honoured in this way, but rarely one as anarchical as Takahashi. He began as a dadaist, publishing a novel, *Dada*, in 1924, and defied convention thereafter. Locked up in his early life a few times for "impulsive actions," when his newly printed *Dadaist Shinkichi's Poetry* was handed to him through the bars of a police cell, he tore it into shreds.

In 1928 Takahashi began serious Zen study under the master Shizan Ashikaga at the Shogenji Rinzai Temple, known for severity of discipline. He trained for seventeen long years, doing *zazen* (formal sitting in meditation) and studying *koans*—on which he wrote numerous poems. He attained enlightenment (*satori*) the first time on reaching the age of forty. In 1953, when fifty-two, he was given *inka* (his awakening testified to) by Shizan, one of six or seven disciples so honored. In addition to some fiction and much poetry, he has written books on Zen highly regarded by Zenists, among them *Stray Notes on Zen Study* (1958), *Mumonkan* (1958), *Rinzairoku* (1959), and *A Life of Master Dogen* (1963).

Takahashi has interested fellow-poets and critics, East and West. A Japanese poet writes:

> Takahashi's poetry is piquancy itself, just as Zen, the quintessence of Buddhism, bawls out by means of its concise vocabulary a sort of piquant ontology. . . . Where does this enlivened feature come from? It comes from his strange disposition which enables him to sense the homogeneity of all things, including human beings. It is further due to his own method of versification: he clashes his idea of timelessness against the temporality of all phenomena to cause a fissure, through which he lets us see personally and convincingly the reality of limitless space.

The American poet Jim Harrison comments in the *American Poetry Review* on his "omniscience about the realities that seems to typify genius of the first order," and goes on:

> Nothing is denied entrance into these poems. . . . All things are in their minutely suggestive proportions, and given an energy we aren't familiar with. . . . Part of the power must come from the fact that the poet has ten thousand centers as a Zenist, thus is virtually centerless.

Philosophical insight is uncommon enough, but its authentic expression in poetry is extremely rare, whether found in T. S. Eliot's "Four Quartets" or in Shinkichi Takahashi's "Shell":

> Nothing, nothing at all
>   is born,
> dies, the shell says again
>   and again
> from the depth of hollowness.
>   Its body
> swept off by tide—so what?
>   It sleeps
> in sand, drying in sunlight,
>   bathing
> in moonlight. Nothing to do
>   with sea
> or anything else. Over
>   and over
> it vanishes with the wave.

On one level a "survivor" poem, inspiring in its moral grandeur, on another, surely important to the poet, expressing dramatically Zen's unfathomable emptiness. Here is the Chinese master Tao-hsin, Zen's Fourth Patriarch, in a sermon on "Abandoning the Body":

> The method of abandoning the body consists first in meditating on Emptiness . . . . Let the mind together with its world be quietened down to a perfect state of tranquillity; let thought be cast in the mystery of quietude, so that the mind is kept from wandering from one thing to another. When the mind is tranquillized in its deepest abode, its entanglements are cut asunder . . . the mind in its absolute purity is the void itself. How almost unconcerned it appears . . . . Emptiness, non-striving, desirelessness, formlessness—this is true emancipation.

According to the great Taoist philosopher Chuang-tzu, his admirer, Tao-hsin said, "Heaven and earth are one finger." In the poem "Hand," Takahashi writes, "Snap my fingers—/ time's no more." He concludes, "My hand's the universe, / it can do anything." While such a poem may show indebtedness to masters like Tao-hsin, in a piece like the following, deceptively light, the poet's grasp is equally apparent:

Afternoon

My hair's falling fast—
this afternoon
I'm off to Asia Minor.

Always in Takahashi there is evidence of profound Zen, in itself distinguishing. His appeal, though, is by no means limited to Zenists, for his imagination has dizzying power: cosmic, surging through space and time ("Atom of thought, ten billion years— / one breath, past, present, future"), it pulls one beyond reality. At times, among his sparrows, he resembles the T'ang master Niao-k'e (Bird's Nest), so called because he meditated high in a tree, wise among the creatures.

Yet Takahashi is never out of this world, which for Zenists is a network of particulars, each reflecting the universal and taking reality from its relationship to all others: it has otherwise no existence. This doctrine of Interpenetration, as known in Zen and all other schools of Mahayana Buddhism, cannot be understood without being felt: to those incapable of feeling, such ideals have been thought mere "mysticism." Poets and philosophers have attempted for centuries to explain interdependence. Here is the late second-century Indian philosopher Pingalaka:

> If the cloth had its own fixed, unchangeable self-essence, it could not be made from the thread . . . the cloth comes from the thread and the thread from the flax . . . It is just like the . . . burning and the burned. They are brought together under certain conditions, and thus there takes place a phenomenon called burning . . . each has no reality of its own. For when one is absent the other is put out of existence. It is so with all things in this world, they are all empty, without self, without absolute existence. They are like the will-o'-the-wisp.

For one who believes in the interpenetration of all living things, the world is a body, and if he is a poet like Takahashi, troubled by what the unenlightened inflict upon one another, he will write:

> Why this confusion,
> how restore the ravaged
> body of the world?

And against this confusion he will invoke the saving force of Buddhism, the layman Vimalakirti who "at a word draws galaxies to the foot of his bed," and Buddha himself, in a poem like "Spinning Dharma Wheel," which ends:

> Three thousand years since Buddha
> found the morning star—now
> sun itself is blinded by his light.

The poet once wrote, "We must model ourselves on Bodhidharma, who kept sitting till his buttocks grew rotten. We must have done with all words and letters, and attain truth itself." This echo of Lao Tsu in the Taoist classic *Tao Teh Ching* ("He who knows does not speak") is, as truth, relative: to communicate his wisdom, Lao Tsu had to speak, and Takahashi's voice is inexhaustible. No one would question his seriousness, the near doctrinal tone of some of his work, yet his best poems pulse with *zenki* (Zen dynamism), flowing spontaneously from the formless self and partaking of the world's fullness:

> *Camel*
>
> The camel's humps
> shifted with clouds.

Such solitude beheads!
My arms stretch

beyond mountain peaks,
flame in the desert.

V   Such are the three major phases of Zen poetry, spanning
        nearly fifteen hundred years from the earliest examples to
        the present, and displaying distinctive characteristics: the
        Chinese master Reito would very likely have appreciated
Shinkichi Takahashi, much as Takahashi values Reito. This consistency, while very special, is by no means inexplicable. The philosophy underlying the poetry is today, in every respect, precisely what
it was in T'ang China: it worked then, it works now, in the face of all
that would seem bent on undermining it. In Japan, where industry is
king, the need for Zen intensifies, and particular care is taken to preserve its temples and art treasures, numbered among the nation's
glories.

Perhaps today Zen's spirit shines most purely in its poetry, some
of which is familiar to all, wherever they happen to live and however
limited their knowledge of the philosophy. Yet consciously or not,
those who care for Fuyo-Dokai, Issa, Shinkichi Takahashi, *know*
Zen—as much as those who revere Mu-ch'i and Sesshu. For to respond
strongly to poetry and painting is to understand the source of their
inspiration, just as to relate fully to others is to understand Zen's interpenetration—more completely than do those who, though familiar with its terminology, are incapable of attaining its spiritual
riches. Walt Whitman, a poet much admired by Zenists, wrote in
"Song for Occupations":

> We consider bibles and religions divine—I do not say they are
>   not divine,
> I say they have all grown out of you, and may grow out of you
>   still,
> It is not they who give the life, it is you who give the life,
> Leaves are not more shed from the trees, or trees from the earth,
>   than they are shed out of you.

Zen always travelled well in time and space, through denying them. Its poetry will continue to move some to heroic efforts towards light, constantly delight others—which is as it should be. "Zen is offering something," the master Taigan Takayama said, "and offering it directly. People just can't seem to grasp it." Zen not only offers itself directly, but everywhere, and nowhere more authentically than in poems written in its name and honor, as the Chinese layman Sotoba realized a thousand years ago when he wrote in his enlightenment:

> The mountain—Buddha's body.
> The torrent—his preaching.
> Last night, eighty-four thousand poems.
> How, how make them understand?

WHY ZEN?

I   The question "Why Zen?" is one often asked of Zenists, even mere novices like me. When thus confronted, I find myself rushing ass-backwards into the thunder zone of World War II. I was fresh out of high school, where in 1942 the rallying cry, sloganed on walls, was "Slap a Jap." Mentors like the chorus director we nicknamed Bilious exhorted boys, soon to be uniformed and buzzed off to battle, to shape up, stop caterwauling, else we'd end up sounding like the enemy. They rigged us to pick off a brutal foe, fanatically inspired by divine winds to make kamikaze dives onto our ships.

We went off in different directions, but I wound up in the South Pacific and, unbelieving, gaped as hulls smithereened around us and our comrades fell, broken bodies facedown on the waves. The smoldering ammo, those festering dead on the beaches of Saipan and Okinawa, dog me yet. When news reached us of the fireballs razing Hiroshima and Nagasaki, we rose like ghosts, shooting carbines into the air. A maniacal celebration. Primed for the invasion of Japan, counting our chances zero, we had reflected obsessively on home, times that might never be. Now we might live?

Soon in Japan, face-to-face with the defeated, we saw with shock that our enemies were simply human. These "savages" were gentle, courteous to each other, welcoming to us. We discovered these folk had a remarkable culture and a powerful kinship with nature—mountains, rivers, plains, all colors of the earth. Amid such delicate, refined beauty, I felt an intense spirituality that would never leave me. Shuttled back home, I knew I'd return some day to learn more of this world.

In his fine book *Basho's Ghost* (Broken Moon Press, 1989), Sam Hamill tells of a return to that world, of experiencing revelations close to mine. While a young Marine, stationed in Okinawa in 1961, he began the practice of *zazen*. There is a disarmingly frank picture of his troubled youth (a judge suggested he join the Marines to keep out of further trouble with the law), and a glowing account of the deep impression Japanese Buddhist culture made on him, transforming him from roughneck to sensitive lover of beauty, from rootlessness to a keen sense of belonging. One of the most compelling things in the book is the growing awareness, chapter by chapter, that his feelings about the culture have, if anything, intensified. There are moving passages in which we find him reflecting on the good fortune that made his return possible. There are rare insights, such as the following, into the nature of the Japanese psyche:

> Nothing in this world is as beautifully containing as a thoughtful Japanese room. Paper diffuses like nothing else. Tatami mats are firm, but soft enough for comfortable kneeling. The painted portions of the wall are a soft sandy green. The simple unpolished grain of the main beam reflects not only the growth of the natural world, but the growth of the human soul as well. A dark table in the center of the room reflects everything that passes by like a pond or a lake reflecting winter and summer skies, like ricefields reflecting a thousand moons at night. Such a room carries a great sense of warmth during the long winters of the north, a cool austerity during the swelter of deep summer. Such a room fills one with the elegance of silence, with interior vision composed of shadow, with the awe not of religion, but of the elementally holy.

The title essay of *Basho's Ghost*, first in the book, is a masterful rendering of Basho's life, poetry, and importance to Japanese culture. Everywhere there is a strong sense of Hamill's oneness with his subject. His enthusiasm is engaging, one is convinced that it is based on deeply considered confrontation with the whole of Basho's life and art. Compared with that of others, this author's approach is a personal, very specific response to the poems. Here we find him writing about one of the best known of these:

> For Basho, the grass blowing in the breeze seems especially poignant, so much so that his eyes well into tears. . . . The grasses bend. Basho moistens his brush months later and writes remembering,

> | *Natsugusa ya* | Summer grasses— |
> |---|---|
> | *tsuwamono doma ga* | after great soldiers' |
> | *yume no ato* | imperial dreams. |

After an interpretation of the poem, he continues:

> The haiku itself is spare, clean, swift as a boning knife. The melopoeia combines *a, o* and *u* sounds: *tsu, gu* in line 1; *tsu* and *yu* in lines 2 and 3; the *tsu* sound is very quick, almost to the point of silence. The *a* sound punctuates the whole poem: *na, sa, ya* among the five syllables of line 1; *wa* and *ga* among the seven syllables of line 2, the four remaining being *mono* and *domo*; and a semiconcluding *a* before *to*. Among the seventeen syllables are six *a* syllables, six *o* syllables, and four *u* syllables. . . . Onomatopoeia, rhyme and slant rhyme are Basho's favorite tools, and he uses them like no one else in Japanese literature. He wrote from within the body; his poems are full of breath and sound as well as images and allusions.

Admirable analysis, so different from the ordinary treatment of *haiku* aesthetics, which often ignores the music, indeed even at times denies that it has any importance to the form. Throughout the essay the author demonstrates the seriousness of Basho's art, the nature of his extraordinary achievement: total resuscitation of a withered form. I recall being struck while translating Basho by something in the master's *haibun* (mix of *haiku* with prose) *The Records of a Travel-Worn Satchel:*

> In this poor body, composed of one hundred bones and nine openings, is something called spirit, a flimsy curtain swept this way and that by the slightest breeze. It is spirit, such as it is, which led me to poetry, at first little more than a pastime, then the full business of my life. There have been times when my spirit, so dejected, almost gave up the quest, other times when it was proud, triumphant. So it has been from the very start, never finding peace with itself, always doubting the worth of what it makes. . . . All who

achieve greatness in art—Saigyo in traditional poetry, Sogi in
linked verse, Sesshu in painting, Rikyu in tea ceremony—possess
one thing in common: they are one with nature.

Though Basho remains at the very center of this book, throughout,
the author finds Ryokan, the eighteenth-century monk-poet of Japan's
north country, a worthy follower and fellow spirit. His account of Ryokan's world is thorough, very moving. As one who spent two years in
that region, while teaching in Niigata in the fifties, I can vouch for the
accuracy of his vision. Ryokan is among the most loved of Japanese
poets, in the way the *haiku* master Issa is loved. His poetry is simplicity
itself, the innocence palpable (I translate the following two pieces
freely):

> Without a jot of ambition left
> I let my nature flow where it will.
> There are ten days of rice in my bag
> And, by the hearth, a bundle of firewood.
> Who prattles of illusion or nirvana?
> Forgetting the equal dusts of name and fortune,
> Listening to the night rain on the roof of my hut,
> I sit at ease, both legs stretched out.

> Spring come again, after moody
> Wintering indoors, I left the hermitage
> With begging bowl. The village children
> Played in long-awaited sun. I bounced
> Ball with them, chanting—
> One-two-three-four-five-six-seven.
> They bounced while I sang, they sang
> While I bounced. So I've wasted,
> Joyfully, a whole spring day.

Throughout the book, Sam Hamill's poems, and there are quite
a few, conform to the spirit of *haibun*. One of the best comes after a
visit to Ryokan's grave behind Ryusen Temple. An observation, then
the poem:

> The rain has almost stopped. We take a few more photographs
> and make our bows. The beautiful old temple is absolutely silent.
> Its shoji screens are patched, the wood worn to smooth ripples.
> We are soaked to the skin and unspeakably happy and filled with
> an inner lightness. We stop at the hondo to make a last bow and
> a small donation before turning back to the road. Just above the

fence, a single cherry branch is blooming, and children shout and laugh somewhere far in the distance.

> Ryusen-ji—two graves
> for Ryokan and his brother.
> A heavy mist shrouds the world,
> wrapping things in dream.
> Birth-death cycle?—All the same:
> cherry blossoms float downstream.

The author's joy, devotion is wonderful. I do not doubt for a moment that, in spite of being soaked to the skin, he was unspeakably happy and "filled with an inner lightness." Of such emotion—and only of such emotion—fine books are made. Yet, unlike many who dabble in Asian thought, Hamill is conscious of limitations, the fact that he lives in a conditioned world:

> I have never been to Nirvana and I don't know anyone there. In *this* world, Samsara, the cycle-of-birth-and-death, I am witness to the innumerable births and deaths of each inevitable day. Nirvana is not my problem . . . because I know I will die, because I live my own death as surely as I live my own life, I inhabit the world of Samsara.

Sam Hamill has the Zenist's suspicion of words, remembering that "even Basho tried desperately to give up poetry in order to embrace the grand silence of *mushin* (nothingness), but try as he might, the poetry spoke again." He remembers also a poem by the great modern Zen poet Shinkichi Takahashi (again, I translate freely):

> *Wind Among the Pines*
>
> The wind blows hard among the pines
> Toward the beginning
> Of an endless past.
> Listen: you've heard everything.

Finally, he remembers:

> Samuel Beckett, awarded the Nobel Prize in literature, had no comment. After days or weeks holed up in his room, he was finally persuaded to appear for a photograph. Still he had no comment. Eventually, an old friend persuaded him, "Please Mr. Beckett, just a comment on receiving the Nobel Prize." "Every word," Sam Beck-

ett replied, "is an unnecessary stain on silence and nothingness."
Mushin, Sam Beckett, crown prince of the comedy of Zen.

> Even daybreak,
> such a momentary thing.
> What is it in the heart?
> With no word to explain it,
> something sings.

II   So much for that strange Western idea of Zenist wall-gazing, back turned to the world's problems. Nothing could be further from the truth, as Thich Nhat Hanh, Vietnamese Zen master and internationally known peace activist shows us. In 1964 he was nominated by Martin Luther King for the Nobel Peace Prize, has published over sixty books, among them the best-selling *Miracle of Mindfulness* (Beacon, 1992). A leading proponent of politically engaged Buddhism, co-founder of the School for Youth for Social Service (a "third world" movement based on Buddhist compassionate action), his role is stirring and exemplary, his influence broad and most important. Reading of his life, and heroic acts, I think of the Zen master Taigan Takayama in Japan, leading an intensely spiritual life as the chief priest of the Toshunji Temple in Yamaguchi while serving as director of the Yamaguchi Council of Social Welfare, the prefectural Association for the Protection of Cultural Properties, and the Yamaguchi Orphanage, subsidized by the prefecture and located on the grounds of Toshunji.

The poems in *Call Me by My True Names*, accompanied by the author's comments and with drawings and photographs by Vietnamese and Western artists, reflect throughout the poet's powerful spirit, reaching out, comforting, embracing, encouraging those who seek his advice on the best way to conduct their lives. Again and again one sees his capacity to feel the pain of others, shoulder their burdens, and, yes, wipe their tears. True, some serious allowances must be given to what I can't help feeling must have been lost in translation, which he has acknowledged was done with the help of a number of friends. I find myself wondering, as I move through the collection, how the language must ring in Vietnamese. For one thing, Thich Nhat Hanh, on the evidence of this book—and it must be borne in mind that he is one of his nation's major writers—is attuned to nature, and finds its person-ification irresistible. Here, a few lines from a typical poem, "Illusion Transformed":

> Horizon's heavy eyelids,
> mountains leaning,
> seeking rest from Earth's pillow—

In so many of the poems there are references, direct or indirect, to Buddhist principles, which may very well be due to his role as spir-itual guide in the West. Rarely in the Far East does one find Zen masters, let alone Zen poets, so involved in the interpretation of pre-cepts, presumably because they take for granted that they are under-stood, have been absorbed into the lives of those they guide. Indeed as far back as ninth-century China, where Zen was born, the masters would express disdain for such pursuits. Here, from *Zen Poems of China and Japan: The Crane's Bill*, the Zen master Mokuchin Juro's "death poem":

> I've remained in Mokuchin thirty years.
> In all that time not one disciplinary merit.
> If asked why Bodhidharma came for the West
> I'll say, unknitting my brow—"What's that?"

And here is my comment on the poem:

> In thirty years Juro would have gained many "disciplinary merits," else he could not have remained at one temple for so long a time. The self-effacing tone of the first two lines is countered by the confidence of the last two. The question "Why did Bodhidharma come from the West?" is often asked, as a koan. Mokuchin's non-chalance has precedence in the founder of one of the three major sects of Zen, the Master Rinzai:
>
> > Those who are true seekers of the truth must take nothing as Buddhas . . . nothing as admirable in the world. They are to be completely independent, un-concerned. They should smash the Buddhas, Bodhi-sattvas and Arhats, attaining freedom only when they have attained freedom from them.

So, if at times the poems in this collection seem somewhat doctrinaire, at other times they are wonderfully fresh and imaginative, as in this piece on the importance of remaining centered, "Froglessness":

> The first fruition of the practice
> is the attainment of froglessness.
>
> When a frog is put
> on the center of a plate,
> she will jump out of the plate
> after just a few seconds.
>
> If you put the frog back again
> on the center of the plate,
> she will again jump out.
>
> You have so many plans.
> There is something you want to become.
> Therefore you always want to make a leap,
> a leap forward.

The poem continues, in the same vein, for another two stanzas, displaying well the writer's imagination and his strongly felt need to guide.

It was the Vietnam War which brought Thich Nhat Hanh to a prominence well deserved and lasting, for his response to that tragedy was total. In poem after poem on war, in the detailing of harrowing event after event, in the compassionate sharing of suffering, he lives the Bodhisattva ideal, expressed movingly in this prayer, from *World of the Buddha: An Introduction to Buddhist Literature* (Grove, 1982), by the Japanese Zen master Daichi (1290–1366):

> My one desire is to dedicate this body born of my parents to the vow-ocean of Buddha, Law and Order. May I in all bodily actions be fully in accord. . . . May I never grow tired of saving all that is sentient wherever I happen to be. May I ever be masterful, whether in the forest of spears, the mountain of swords, the boiling caldron, or heap of burning coals. . . .

To illustrate his deep commitment and involvement in the suffering of his land, I quote stanzas from Thich Nhat Hanh's Vietnam War poem "Flesh and Skin, Bricks and Tiles" in which he describes the bombing of a Buddhist temple where children, all killed, were taking lessons in reading and writing:

The bombers are gone.
Beneath a still sun,
in the dying light of noon,
our ancient land stirs again.

The curved temple roof
is burnt out, crumpled.
But Lord Buddha sits,
his gilt all smeared,
smiling ineffably at bricks and stones.

O sisters and brothers,
what will you do
with these bullets and steel,
broken and burst in you?
O flesh and skin,
bricks and tiles.

Need one say more?

ENCOUNTERS

Part II

RINZAI
ZEN MASTER
—SATORI

Yamaguchi, the "Kyoto of the West," is one of the best preserved castle towns of Japan and is well known for its superb Zen temples, among them Toshun, one of the most beautiful in spite of its age (or because of it), which the billowy green of the young bamboo trees planted on the slope of the mountain against which it was built tends to belie. As has so often been the case in this crowded land, the mountain has served to protect the temple from the encroachment of those seeking breathing space on the outskirts of town. In this respect it most clearly resembles Kyoto: to its ring of mountains might be attributed the fine state of its shrines and temples, if not their very survival.

If the reader has seen Kurosawa's *Rashomon*, he will remember the opening scene: the rain, the old gate, the wasted grandeur of the temple. Well, it was raining when Takashi Ikemoto and I bicycled up from the national university where we were teaching, and I was strongly reminded of that scene. We parked our bicycles and entered the temple. A few minutes later we were met by Taigan Takayama, master of the Toshun, and led to his reception hall, which overlooks a lovely garden. Takayama is young (thirty-four), intellectual (a graduate in Chinese Philosophy of Kyoto University) and, Ikemoto has informed me, he journeys to Kyoto a few times a year to undergo more discipline.

Though we had about a week to mentally prepare for the exchange, we did not think it in the spirit of Zen to prepare a list of questions. Perhaps this would turn out to be a mistake. It was agreed that we take turns asking questions and that Ikemoto would record what was said and translate the difficult parts.

Before we begin, a few words from Takayama: "I know very well that Zen is above explanation, and that the Westerner may find expository remarks in a Zen interview inadequate. Nonetheless, an exchange between a Westerner and a Japanese master might very well serve as a stimulant toward the reader's further efforts for a better appreciation of Zen. Indeed, the remark that Zen is above explanation applies only to those destined to remain ignorant of it. As for those, on the other hand, possessed of insight keen enough, they will be able to intuit a Zen meaning in a master's words, spoken or written. It is my hope that the reader will read the following exchange in the proper way and, thus, see into the spirit of Zen."

STRYK: Takayama-san, as a Zen priest, you have been trained in the ways of proper meditation. Now, if I were to undertake Zen discipline it would be with the view of achieving something like inner peace. Is it that which the priest seeks when meditating, or does his meditation lead him to other, more "religious" things? And if the latter is true in the case of the priest, what is it the serious lay Zen Buddhist seeks when he attempts to gain a *satori* awakening?

TAKAYAMA: In a sense Zen is a religion of peace of mind; therefore Zen and "inner peace" seem to be connected. But all depends on what is meant by this "inner peace," inasmuch as, complications being incidental to life, we must invariably confront them. The way of coping with them determines the nature of the "inner peace" experienced.

STRYK: You surprise me. Rightly or wrongly, I have always considered inner peace to be a rather absolute thing. If I understand correctly, you feel that the peace achieved through *zazen* and through *satori* itself is dependent on the circumstances of one's life at the time of meditation, on the things, perhaps, which made one turn to meditation in the first place. Is that right?

TAKAYAMA: Yes.

STRYK: But if a person seeks shelter in a storm, it doesn't much matter, does it, whether it is a rain or snow storm, so long as he finds on entering the shelter the protection he sought?

TAKAYAMA: This type of inner peace is different from that offered by Zen. A Zen-man, you see, must be able to keep his mental serenity in the midst of life's greatest difficulties. Here is a well-known Zen poem by Manura, the Twenty-second Patriarch of India:

> The mind moveth with the ten thousand things:
> Even when moving, it is serene.
> Perceive its essence as it moveth on,
> And neither joy nor sorrow there is.
> (translated by D. T. Suzuki)

This "being serene" is the inner peace of Zen. As to your second question, of course both priest and layman seek the self-same serenity.

IKEMOTO: When recently questioned about the secret of manipulating his puppets, a prominent American artist replied: "The most important thing is to love the puppets. When I manipulate Judy, my fingers become Judy. When I move the monkey, they become the monkey. I forget myself and become the thing I handle. That's the secret." Now, it seems to me that his words resemble those of a Zen master. Am I right in thinking that the puppeteer has realized a Zen state, at least as far as his art is concerned?

TAKAYAMA: Perfectly right.

STRYK: I dislike leaving that puppeteer, but there is something that interests me very much. Ikemoto-san has pointed out to me that, unlike Christian mystics who seek vision, the Zen-man seeks release from vision. It is sometimes described, is it not, as a vision of emptiness? Now, is this image of nothingness complete and instantaneous or, to use the metaphor of the room, does one cushion at a time, say, then the walls themselves, have to be removed?

TAKAYAMA: I'm very much afraid that Zen has nothing to do with your vision of nothingness. How can one have such a vision?

STRYK: Well, we've all tried to vision the reaches of space, haven't we? Surely the open eye sees, even emptiness.

TAKAYAMA: Nevertheless Zen, which disowns all that has form, rejects any and all kinds of vision. According to it, a mountain is not high, nor is a pillar vertical. Emptiness in Zen is that in which being and non-being originate. It is realized, if you continue to insist on the term, when the dualism of being and non-being is done away with. The emptiness is not there as something to be seen or not seen, it is what you have become. And its realization is instantaneous, meaning timeless, without beginning or end. It is perhaps to be conceded that one can experience emptiness at a given moment, but the experience itself transcends time.

IKEMOTO: While we're on the subject of that experience, Dr. Daisetsu Suzuki, who as you know is a follower of the Rinzai sect, has always been of the opinion that there is no Zen without *satori*. It appears that Western readers of Dr. Suzuki have been intrigued above all by his dramatic descriptions of *satori* awakening. Yet the Soto sect, which has many more adherents, insists on the primacy of sitting in meditation without seeking *satori*. With Westerners in mind, what is your opinion of the Soto standpoint?

TAKAYAMA: Simply, though perhaps inadequately put, it seems that Rinzai Zen is more accessible to Westerners.

STRYK: To continue our discussion of *satori*, exactly what does one feel as distinct from what one sees, or no longer sees, at the moment of the awakening, and how long does the feeling last?

TAKAYAMA: The feeling will differ with individuals, of course, but perhaps I can say this much. Until the coming of *satori*, one's being is filled with doubt. At the moment of awakening, the Zen-man is beside himself with joy to know that he has discovered THAT properly. This ecstacy will not last very long, maybe only a few hours, but after *satori* he cannot move outside its world whether awake or asleep. As you well know, Zen masters are in the habit of expressing in their verse their state of mind while in *satori*. The following poem by Yomoyo-Enju, a Chinese master, is among the best known. It may be helpful to know that he had his awakening at the instant of hearing a pile of firewood topple.

> Toppling over is none other than THAT:
> Nowhere is found an atom of dust.
> Mountains, rivers, plain—
> All reveal the Buddha-body.

Satori will make it possible for you to live constantly in a state of joy. But remember that one needs further discipline to rid oneself of this joy, for there must not be even the shadow of attachment, any kind of attachment, in Zen. In this way you can attain a genuine awakening.

IKEMOTO (after tea and a few minutes of small talk):   In principle, Zen masters should be able to read and utilize any kind of writing. Again with Westerners in mind, do you think that even the Bible could be read and commented on from the Zen point of view?

TAKAYAMA: Why not? If, that is, a talented master sets about it.

STRYK: Since Ikemoto-san brought up Westerners a-gain, in a recent article read by each of us the writer states that unlike Westerners, Japanese are Zen-minded, and for that reason Zen, as it is practiced here, is really inaccessible to someone like myself. Do you agree? To pursue this in a different way, were you more Zen-minded than your friends at the university? Would many of them have been able to undergo Zen training? And here I am perhaps repeating my-self: would a serious Westerner have a fair chance of understanding Zen, finding the true path? And if so, why do some Westerners known for their interest in Zen speak of the effectiveness of certain drugs in the attainment of *satori*? Is drug-taking compatible with Zen prac-tice in Japan?

TAKAYAMA: I'll take these questions up one by one. It is true, perhaps, that Zen may be somewhat inaccessible to West-erners. This is only natural. Of course, in itself, Zen has no such limitations: there's no East nor West in it. But in its most important manifestations, it has been characterized by geographical and his-torical features peculiar to China and Japan. Indeed, it may very well be these special features which most strongly appeal to the West. And maybe for that very reason, I should add, they stand more or less in the way of a Westerner's attainment of real insight, let alone Zen awaken-ing. Speaking of myself, I was not more Zen-minded than my fellow students in Kyoto, and I firmly believe that anyone should be able to profit by Zen discipline, though it is undeniable that some people, by reason of character and temperament, are more suited to the dis-cipline than others. If a Westerner can find a master willing to train him, he should be able to find the true path you speak of as quickly as a Japanese, always assuming of course that he understands the lan-guage. As you are no doubt aware, history offers many such instances. When Zen thrived in China, a number of Japanese went there to study and some of them attained true *satori*. It should be unnecessary to add that they already had, before leaving these shores, a proper know-ledge of Chinese culture in particular and Buddhism in general to make the experience profitable. Finally and most emphatically, drug-taking is not compatible with Zen.

IKEMOTO: Both of us are teachers of literature and are interested in Zen poetry. As you probably know, the contemporary poet Shinkichi Takahashi has undergone regular discipline and, it seems, is known as a Zen poet among his fellow writers. What do you think of the following poem, one of his most recent?

The Peach

A little girl under a peach tree,
Whose blossoms fall into the entrails
Of the earth.

There you stand, but a mountain may be there
Instead; it is not unlikely that the earth
May be yourself.

You step against a plate of iron and half
Your face is turned to iron. I will smash
Flesh and bone

And such the cracked peach. She went up the mountain
To hide her breasts in the snowy ravine.
Women's legs

Are more or less alike. The leaves of the peach tree
Stretch across the sea to the end of
The continent.

The sea was at the little girl's beck and call.
I will cross the sea like a hairy
Caterpillar

And catch the odor of your body.

TAKAYAMA: Most interesting, from both the Zen and the literary points of view. Let's begin with the former: an Avatam-saka doctrine holds that the universe can be observed from the four angles of (1) phenomena, (2) noumenon, (3) the identity of noumenon and phenomena, and (4) the mutual identity of phenomena. Now, whether he was aware of it or not, the poet depicted the world in which noumenon and phenomena are identical. Considering the poem with Zen in mind, the lesson to be drawn, I suppose, is that one should not loiter on the way but proceed straight to one's destination —the viewpoint of the mutual identity of phenomena. But from a literary point of view, the significance, and the charm of the poem lies in its metaphorical presentation of a world in which noumenon and phenomena are identified with each other.

STRYK: A very profound reading. I must confess that I

didn't see half as much in the poem, though I like it very much for the freedom of imagination and the harshness of tone. To continue with the arts, do you think Zen could be "used" by artists, as might have been the case with the master-painter Sesshu, to achieve, well, the proper state of mind for serious production?

TAKAYAMA: Zen is not something to be "used." Its art is nothing more than an expression of Zen spirit.

STRYK: I see. Well then, how would you describe that spirit, as it relates, that is, to the artist and his work? And though here I may be asking too much, would you say that artists—painters, writers, composers—might gain by periods of discipline? And if so, what have they to gain that drink or, to be more consistent, prayer and the seeking of vision might not be able to afford with far less difficulty? Finally have you yourself felt, however vaguely, creative while meditating? I ask because I have always thought of creative activity as being an assertion of self and can't imagine its taking place in a state of "non-being."

TAKAYAMA: In a sense, I have already described the Zen spirit or state of mind. Doubtless there are artists who try to achieve through Zen the proper spirit for serious production. Well, I'll try to relate the Zen mind to the artist and his work, though I should mention at once that I, myself, am not an artist and, to answer one of your questions, have not felt even vaguely creative while meditating. Let's put it this way: it is a state of mind in which one is identified with an object without any sense of restraint. In this connection one could mention the wakefulness of Zuigan, the Chinese master, who had the following dialogue with himself every day:

> Master!
> Yes, sir!
> Be wide awake!
> Yes, sir!
> And from now on don't let anyone deceive you!
> Yes, sir! Yes, sir!

When an artist, in this state of mind, depicts an object in words, he has a fine poem; when in lines, a true picture. Fundamentally, however, Zen offers nothing to gain, but there is something in this non-gaining which quite naturally becomes part of the Zen-man's whole being. As Rinzai, the founder of our sect, put it, you gain worthiness without seeking it. No, after all, I suppose it is possible to say that artists would gain by Zen. As to what it offers the artist who seeks inspiration from it that drink, say, cannot hope to give him, well, try it and see.

STRYK: You tempt me, but I'm sure to find the discipline too strict. By the way, have you yourself ever found it to be too strict? I ask this from a rather special point of view, from that of one who might find it too difficult, even impossible, to accept discipleship in an order so authoritarian, but who is very willing to concede that the authority must be imposed for the good of the initiate.

TAKAYAMA: No, I have never felt the discipline to be too strict. Indeed it is a very tough mental job at times, especially during a period of *sesshin* when for seven days, all day long, one is trained in devotional matters. But I am simply grateful for all this.

STRYK: Our time is almost up and Ikemoto-san, out of his usual courtesy, insists that I ask the final questions. You have heard of the great interest in Zen in my country. I understand that while in Kyoto you were sometimes approached by Americans seeking explanations. From your reading and observation, do you think it likely that those Americans who think of themselves as Zen-men, and there are a fair number, know what true Zen is? Is not the taking of drugs, upon which you have commented, a simple confession of defeat? And what about those who think that *satori*, or something like it, can be gained through drink or strenuous love-making? Last of all, does Zen have anything to offer the serious Westerner who, though he may not wish to undergo discipline, feels himself in search of a truer way?

TAKAYAMA: Well, I would have to meet those Americans you speak of before passing judgment. But, yes, drug-taking as it relates to the seeking of an awakening, could very well be described as a confession of defeat. By the same token, those given to excessive drinking and woman-chasing and who still hope for Zen are no doubt deluding themselves. Certainly they have never heard the old Zen saying: "A man of consummate activity knows no rules to follow." Zen offers Something to everyone, Westerner or Oriental, but just what it offers is beyond conceptual understanding. Indeed, Zen is always offering that Something and offering it directly. People just can't seem to grasp it.

RINZAI
ZEN MASTER
—WABI

The Joei Temple in Yamaguchi City is known throughout
Japan for the rock garden laid behind it by Sesshu (1420–1506),
Zen master and one of the greatest painters in the Chinese style.
The garden has been lovingly preserved by generations of Zen
priests who doubtless were chosen to serve at Joei for their personal qualities. Yasuda-Tenzan-Roshi, the present master of
Joei, possesses such qualities. He is very well known, even revered, in Yamaguchi as an expert in the art of tea and one who is
familiar with the other arts historically associated with Zen.

From all over Japan people converge on Joei Temple, usually
on Sundays and often in large tour groups. But on weekdays it is
possible to feel isolated there and, apart from the pleasant sound
of ducks paddling in the garden pond and, alas, the occasional
blare of a loudspeaker giving a description of the garden when
such is requested, there is silence.

The garden lies at the foot of one of the many fair-sized mountains circling the city, and the impression made on the visitor is
that of a perfect unity of art and nature, a Zen ideal. One is at a
loss to define where the garden ends and the mountain slope begins, so well did Sesshu's genius achieve this desired unity. The
mountain is thick with pine and bamboo, through which a path
winds from the garden, and at times the whole appears to be one
gigantic various tree. Wandering up the path alone, one may
find oneself having some rather strange, bird-like illusions.

It is autumn, the most beautiful season in Yamaguchi, and Takashi Ikemoto and I are looking forward to the exchange on Zen with the *roshi*. The appointed day is a fine one, and though, as in the case of our first interview with a master, we haven't prepared questions, we feel confident that the meeting will be a fruitful one. We bicycle out to Joei and are met at the gate by the *roshi* himself. Our greetings are very informal, and the *roshi* leads us to a room with a fine view of the garden, which I have grown to love, and immediately begins preparing green tea on a brazier. It has been decided that this time, in the interest of consistency, we ask our questions separately (if I know him as well as I think, Ikemoto-san will insist that I ask most of them). At his insistence I begin.

STRYK: Roshi, it is very good of you to take the time to answer our questions, but please, if you find any of them too sensitive, say so.

ROSHI: Open-mindedness, I like to feel, is characteristic of Zen masters, especially when you compare them with those of other Buddhist sects. I've nothing to hide, though of course I can't promise to answer questions that are too personal.

STRYK: I have heard that *wabi* (the spirit of poverty and self-denial) is rarely to be found in modern tea ceremonies, and that most people attend them to show off their finery. As a well-known master you are in a position to know; is this true? We know that everything in modern society would tend to make a mockery of seeking *wabi*. Is the tea ceremony, as it was originally performed by masters like Rikyu (1521–1591), doomed because of this?

ROSHI: I agree with what you say about *wabi*. You find all too little of it in tea ceremonies these days, something I'm always complaining about to those who attend the monthly ceremonies here. But you must bear in mind that though *wabi* is a state of scarcity, it doesn't mean lacking in things. Rather, they should be cast aside, or at least not used, nor even seen, during the ceremony; the ideal is to minimize life's essentials. Suppose you live in a mansion. You should have tea in a room of four-and-a-half mats or less. After all, the spirit of tea is the spirit of Zen itself and can be described with the words, simplicity, conciseness, intuition. I'm afraid that ceremonies today are like those in the feudal castles before Rikyu's time. People prize, as they did then, expensive utensils and what not. It was from the time of the master Enshu (1579–1647) that the cult began to introduce artistic elements. Needless to say, in the old days women did not take part in the ceremonies. Nowadays the ceremony is not serious enough for my taste. It's like a social gathering, a recreation for well-to-do women. Yes, I feel with you that tea as conceived by masters like Rikyu may be doomed, though, I hasten to add, there will always be a core of traditionalists.

STRYK: While we're on the subject of tea and Rikyu, in reading accounts of his last ceremony with his intimates, at the end of which he was on Lord Hideyoshi's order to commit suicide, I have been disturbed by a few of the things that are supposed to have happened. You'll recall that after breaking the cup with the words, "Never again shall this cup, polluted by the lips of misfortune, be used by man," and then dismissing his friends, save for the most intimate of them all, he killed himself "with a smile on his face." Now, it seems to me that the breaking of the cup and his expression of self-sorrow, however justified in the human sense, were neither in keeping with the spirit of tea nor the famous stoicism of Zen. When we compare Rikyu with Socrates, who died by poisoning himself in almost exactly the same circumstances, Zen does not come out as well as Greek stoicism. Have you yourself ever been disturbed by what I have sensed to be an inconsistency in Rikyu's final act?

ROSHI: I'm not certain that the breaking of the cup is a historical fact, but if it is a comment must be made. First of all, you must understand that Rikyu, though a great tea master, was very far from attaining perfect Zen, which is clearly revealed in his death poem, a most unsatisfactory one from the Zen standpoint. Take, for example, the line, "I kill both Buddhas and Patriarchs." I'm afraid that contains very little Zen, and it shows that he failed to reach the state of an "old gimlet," or mature Zen-man, one whose "point" has been blunted by long use. The Zen title "Rikyu" had been given him by his teacher Kokei, in the hope that it might help him soften his temper, but all that was in vain. Kokei once praised Rikyu in a poem, speaking of him as "an old layman immersed in Zen for thirty years," yet one can surmise, Rikyu was unable to discipline himself through use of the *koan*. Incidentally, as you probably know, it was Sotan, Rikyu's grandson, who created the *wabi* tea cult. Sotan had taken a regular course of Zen study. From what I've said, I hope you see that Rikyu was not a true Zen-man and for that reason cannot be compared, at least as a representative of Zen, with a great sage like Socrates.

STRYK: That's most interesting. Now, if you'll permit me to change the subject and ask one of those sensitive questions I threatened you with, I'd like to begin by saying that I'm troubled by two seemingly minor things in contemporary Japanese culture, as it relates to temples, gardens, and monuments. And, if you don't mind my saying so, both are to be encountered right here at the Joei.

ROSHI: Don't hesitate to ask your questions.

STRYK: Thank you. Well, the first concerns the use of that loudspeaker out there. I realize that it is used to inform visitors of the very interesting history of your temple and Sesshu's garden, and that loudspeakers are used in exactly the same way at all the famous places in Japan, yet because of the blaring it's not really possible to feel the calm which, among other things, one comes to find. As loudspeakers serve merely an educational end, could not printed information suffice? The other, more important thing I have in mind is the apparent need to supply obvious "comparisons" for visitors. In Akiyoshi Cave we are informed that certain formations resemble mushrooms, others rice paddies, etc. Here at your temple some of the garden rocks out there are supposed to look like mountains in China, and of course both Akiyoshi Cave and Sesshu's garden have their Mount Fujis. Even the world-famous Ryoanji rock garden in Kyoto is spoken of in this way. It all amounts to an aesthetic sin, I'm inclined to feel, and I use a word as strong as that because such naive analogizing runs strongly counter to the genius of Japanese art, which, most would agree, consists of great subtlety and suggestiveness, as in Basho's poetry. Finally, isn't it true that Zen, being very direct in all matters, would insist that a rock is a rock? I have it on good authority that masters like Sesshu did not themselves make these curious comparisons. Why not leave it to the visitor to imagine for himself, if he is so inclined, what such things look like?

ROSHI: Fundamentally, no information about the garden is necessary, I suppose; but really, you know, in order to appreciate his garden fully, you must have almost as much insight as Sesshu himself. This, needless to say, very few possess. Ideally, one should sit in Zen for a long period before looking at the garden; then one might be able to look at it, as the old saying goes, "with the navel." But to answer your questions, one at a time. As things stand, I'm obliged to resort to such devices as the loudspeaker, especially when a large, hurried group of tourists comes, because, frankly, most of them would scarcely bother to read printed information. The "blaring" you hear out there, unpleasant as it may be, serves an end, you see. After all, it's important to me at least that as many people as possible are informed of the essentials of Sesshu's gardening. Next, the problem of supplying "comparisons." Sesshu, it is true, left no written record of this type. The description of the garden given today seems to have started in the Meiji era (1867–1912). Nevertheless, it's most important to keep certain things clear. Sesshu was the first Japanese painter to adopt the technique of sketching, which in his hands became something like abstract painting. As the Zen method of expression is symbolic, it is likely that Mount Fuji out there (and you'll have to admit that the rock does look like it) represents Japan, while some of the other mountain-rocks represent China, and so on. In other words the garden is an embodiment of the universe, as seen by a Zen master. In short, those are symbols you see out there, not naive resemblances.

STRYK: I understand, but perhaps what I have in mind is the tendency itself. For example, last Sunday I visited a Zen temple in Ube, and the priest was good enough to take me around the back for a look at the garden. A very beautiful one, I should add. Well, without even being asked, he began pointing to the rocks and shrubbery and offering comparisons. As the garden is laid on a slope, it appears that the azalea bushes which fringe the foot of the slope (they're not in bloom now, of course) represent clouds. Frankly, I wish he had simply permitted me to take a look at the garden. But perhaps we've spoken enough about the few things that have troubled me, and I must say that you have answered my questions about them with the greatest forbearance. Something I saw inside the temple at Ube leads me to my next question. A group of men were sitting inside having tea, and when I asked the priest about them, I was informed that they had come to consult him about the traditional Zen-sitting for laymen, which, I understand, usually takes place twice a year, at the hottest and coldest times. These men formed a very mixed group, it seemed to me, and I've heard that those who come to temples for *zazen* represent all walks of life. Is that right? What is it they seek? Are they troubled? Do any of them succeed in attaining *satori*? Do you preach to them in a special way? As you see it, is the *zazen* session as necessary in these days of psychoanalysis, and so forth, as it was in the past? What, in short, has the layman to gain by lodging in a cold Zen temple, eating only rice and vegetables, and while sitting in Zen, being whacked if he so much as dozes? Finally, among those who come to your temple for the sessions, are there some who work, in one way or another, in the arts?

ROSHI: Most of the people who come here are students who, for the most part, are merely restless. They want *hara* (abdomen, or Zen composure). Then there are the neurotics, who come accompanied by their protectors, and older people who are troubled in one way or another. Many come simply for the calm, others, university lecturers, for example, because they are not able to find as much in other religions. I'm afraid that very few of them, whatever their reason for coming, attain *satori* worthy of the name. They may or may not be given *koan*, but after all one's problem can be *koan* enough. I give a *teisho* (lecture on a Zen text) on such books as *Mumonkan* or *Hekiganroku*. Additionally, and this is a feature of the Rinzai sect, there is *dokusan*, or individual guidance. Whether the session ends in success or not depends on the temperaments of the participants and on the efforts they make. On a slightly different subject, perhaps you know that Professor Kasamatsu of Tokyo University has conducted experiments, through measuring brain waves, on Zen priests engaged in *zazen*. He's found that even those who've been sitting for as long as twenty years do not have "tranquillized" brain waves. But I seriously doubt the importance of such experiments. As to whether those who come here for *zazen* are in any way connected with the arts, I suspect so, but really we don't go into such things.

STRYK: You are aware of the great interest in Zen in the West. Some feel that it is due to the same needs that made Existentialism and phenomenological thinking so popular in the years following World War II. Briefly, this might have been due to a kind of enlightenment, a sudden need for simplicity, directness, and the formation of a world of real things and manageable experiences. In other words, the disillusionment with high-sounding phrases, idealistic concepts, and intellectualism generally, forced men to search out something radically different. In some measure Zen seems to offer an adequate substitute for the unrealizable promises of idealism. Is this your feeling too? Finally, do you think that, given the major reasons for the need of so great a change in the way men view living, as far as the West is concerned, Zen can, among other things, teach us how to achieve peace?

ROSHI: It appears that the great interest in Zen in the

West is motivated by utilitarianism. This may be good or bad, but it's important to bear in mind that Zen does not aim directly at simplicity. The Zen-man's chief aim is to gain *satori*, to which simplicity, directness, and so forth, are mere adjuncts. Indeed, it is quite impossible that there be an awakening without such mental tendencies. In this respect, I gather, Zen seems to be able to satisfy the new spiritual needs of the West. Really, you know, in one sense Zen is the only religion capable of helping the world achieve peace. Its fundamental teaching is that all things are Buddhas—not men alone but all things, sentient and non-sentient. And not merely the earth, but the other planets as well. Universal peace will be realized when men all over the world bow to the preciousness and sacredness of everything. Zen, which teaches them to do this, is the religion of the Space Age.

STRYK: My final question deals with the arts and touches on Sesshu and your temple. What would you say are the chief qualities of Zen art, be it painting, poetry, drama, or gardening? To put the question another way, and to narrow it considerably, when you look at a scroll by Sesshu, when you look out at this marvelous garden, in what way do you feel his creations to be different from those works of Japanese art which, though perhaps equally important, have no connection with Zen? Last of all, what is there about Western art, if anything, that might leave you as a Zen master dissatisfied?

ROSHI (returning from a back room with an album of Sesshu reproductions): What expresses cosmic truth in the most direct and concise way—that is the heart of Zen art. Please examine this picture, "Fisherman and Woodcutter." Of all Sesshu's pictures, this is my favorite. The boat at the fisherman's back tells us his occupation, the bundle of firewood behind the woodcutter tells his. The fisherman is drawn with only three strokes of the brush, the woodcutter with five. You couldn't ask for greater concision. And these two men, what are they talking about? In all probability, and this the atmosphere of the picture suggests, they are discussing something very important, something beneath the surface of daily life. How do I know? Why, every one of Sesshu's brush strokes tells me. I'm sorry to say that I'm not very familiar with Western art, though occasionally I'll drop in to see an exhibition. To be sure, Western art has volume and richness when it is good. Yet to me it is too thickly encumbered by what is dispensable. It's as if the Western artist were trying to hide something, not reveal it.

STRYK: Thank you for answering my questions so frankly and thoughtfully. Now it's Ikemoto-san's turn.

IKEMOTO: Thank you. My questions will be of a more personal nature. To my knowledge, Roshi, you are the only qualified master in this prefecture. Please tell us about your career from the beginning.

ROSHI: I was born of peasant parents and went to live in a temple in my sixth year. In those days it was customary for one of the children of a religious family to enter the priesthood, and an uncle of mine was a Zen priest. I began to study Zen in the second year of junior high school, but it was only after the university that I underwent serious training. The temples I chose for this purpose were Tofukuji, Bairinji, Yogenji, and Engakuji, which are located in different parts of the country. I obtained my Zen testimonial from Ienaga-Ichido-Roshi, chief abbot of Tofukuji. I learned from him how to handle *koans* in the way favored by the Takuju school of the Rinzai sect, but I also desired to know how to deal with *koans* according to methods used by the Inzan school of the same sect (it seems a pity to me that few students of Rinzai Zen nowadays desire to know about both schools), so I went to Engakuji in Kamakura. There, under the master Furukawa-Gyodo-Roshi, I succeeded in my purpose. His strictness impressed me. His own teacher, by the way, was the famous Shaku-Soen-Roshi, one of whose lay disciples is Dr. D. T. Suzuki of Western fame. Soen-Roshi, a scholarly master, was very different from Gyodo-Roshi, of course, but both were great masters.

IKEMOTO: Could you tell us how and under what circumstances you achieved *satori*? I ask you to do this because reading an account of your experience may encourage students of Zen.

ROSHI (his face brightening):   It happened on the fifth day of the special December training at Yogenji, while I was engaged in what is called night-sitting. As is sometimes done, a few of us left the meditation hall and, choosing a spot in the deep snow near the river, began our Zen-sitting, each of us engrossed in his *koan*. I was not conscious of time, nor did I feel the cold. Suddenly the temple bell struck the second hour, time of the first morning service, which we were expected to attend. I tried to get up, but my feet were so numb with cold that I fell to the snow. At that very instant it happened, my *satori*. It was an enrapturing experience, one I could not hope to describe adequately. This was my first *satori*; now about my second. But you may be wondering why more than one *satori*?

IKEMOTO: I understand that it often happens to true Zen-men.

ROSHI: It was the second *satori*, experienced at Enga-kuji, that gave me complete freedom of thought and action. As I've already said, Gyodo-Roshi valued activity above all else. He gave me Joshu's Mu as *koan*. Well, for a whole year, every view of it I offered was curtly rejected by the master. But this was the Inzan method of dealing with the *koan*. At any rate, one day on my way back from *san-zen* (presenting one's view of a *koan* to the master) and while descending the temple steps, I tripped and fell. As I fell I had my second *satori*, a consummate one. I owe a great deal to Gyodo-Roshi, for without his guidance I might have ended up a mere adherent of *koans*, a man without insight into his true nature, which is afforded only by an awakening.

IKEMOTO: Most interesting, Roshi. By the way, this is the so-called instant age. I wish there were a special recipe for gaining *satori* instantly.

ROSHI: Well, the master Ishiguro-Horyu is said to have devised a way of training toward that end. It's rather easy to get Zen students to have special experiences, such as hearing the sound of falling incense ash or feeling themselves afloat. But that's not *satori*. *Satori* consists in a return to one's ordinary self, if you know what I mean—the most difficult thing in the world.

IKEMOTO: I understand. Finally, may I ask whether you are training successors?

ROSHI: A Zen master is duty-bound to transmit the nearly untransmittable truth to at least one successor. But everything depends on circumstances. You see, it's not a matter of five or six years. A training period of fifteen to twenty years is necessary. I am awaiting the appearance of earnest seekers after the truth.

RINZAI
ZEN MASTER
—TEACHER

Roshi Gempo Nakamura, master of Jishi-in, a sub-temple on the grounds of the important Rinzai temple Nanzenji in Kyoto, is a graduate in Chinese philosophy of Kyoto University. Expert in Chinese literature, especially early Zen poetry, he is a disciple of the late Shibayama Roshi, one of the great modern masters known in the West for his writings and lectures, particularly in the United States which he visited several times. Shibayama Roshi, who died in 1974, was once master of Jishi-in, and his tomb lies behind the temple. Gempo Nakamura studied with him many years, receiving *inka* (testimony to his enlightenment), one of few so honored by the master, another being Taigan Takayama, a co-translator of *Zen Poems of China and Japan: The Crane's Bill*. Shibayama honored these men, calling them his rarest disciples.

On this brisk October afternoon, maples on the temple grounds beginning to take on color from the sun, I look forward to my talk with Gempo Nakamura. Master of Jishi-in for thirteen years, since Shibayama Roshi left to serve as chief abbot of Nanzenji, he has tended it well, judging from the garden, one of the most renowned in Kyoto. Rocks placed harmoniously on raked sand, a touch of vivid shrubbery—so beautiful, that it's no wonder many come to visit. Such places resemble, in some ways, colleges of Oxford and Cambridge, a great temple like Nanzenji having a number of small temples circling its main building. The sub-temples use the large refectory in common, and the *Sodo* (meditation hall), each sharing the upkeep of a united whole. From them abbots are chosen to lead the main temple and, as with Nanzenji, its subordinate temples throughout Japan. Rinzai, one of the three chief schools of Zen (the others being Soto and Obaku), has sects, the Nanzenji of Rinzai being one of the most important of these. One day Gempo Nakamura, as his master before him, may be chosen to guide the Nanzenji complex of temples and subordinate temples.

Before our meeting, I wander through Jishi-in with a young disciple studying for the priesthood, who, in turn with fellow disciples, assists the master greeting visitors, and so on. He seems happy to be showing me the temple, which he clearly loves, his home for years to come, while I am awed by the openness of Jishi-in, whose garden can be readily viewed by all (most temples these days take entrance fees). The young disciple has been instructed to take me on to Shibayama Roshi's tomb, for which I am grateful. The dedication in *The Crane's Bill* shows our respect for the late master. His tomb, a simple white stone in the heart of the garden, is destined to be a pilgrims' resting place for Zenists throughout the world. Now I go in to meet Gempo Nakamura, whose welcome is informal in the large reception room overlooking the pattern-sanded garden. Slight, not too carefully shaven, like all Zen masters disciplined in movement, he begins preparing tea—among many accomplishments, he is an expert in this art. So we sip the aromatic tea, speaking casually of common friends. Now, he informs me, he is ready for my questions.

STRYK: As you know, I am interested in the different branches of Zen. Could you give me your idea of the three major sects?

NAKAMURA: The differences, alas, are better known than similarities: Rinzai's insistence on *koan* interpretation, its often-misunderstood austerities, its indifference to scripture. Yet, like the others, its chief concern is Zen itself. Really a matter of temperament, each offering a unique something to the seeker. The young, feeling need for what Zen offers can, this day and age, choose, and it's by no means uncommon for students to change sects, in mid-stream, so to speak. That is, begin with a Rinzai temple or monastery and, for whatever reason, on discovering its ways are not for him (or *her*: you know we have our nuns in Zen), can approach a master of Soto or Obaku, asking to be taught by him. Finding the right master, you see, may be the most important thing of all. Dogen spoke of the danger of dwelling on divisions, maintaining Zen itself the one concern. There—here I am, a Rinzai quoting a Soto master!

STRYK: What is your hope for those who come to train here?

NAKAMURA: That as the result of discipline they are able to live as Zenists—nothing less, or more.

STRYK: What does that mean to a young Japanese?

NAKAMURA: What it has always meant to young Japanese, always. Zen views, after all, are highly distinct.

STRYK: How many working with you are likely to achieve *satori*?

NAKAMURA: As you've no doubt discovered, there's great reluctance to talk of *that*. What, after all, does it mean?

STRYK: You surprise me. What *satori* means is surely no secret.

NAKAMURA: Very rarely, however, do we think of it in an absolute sense, and I believe that's what you have in mind. Such awakening is the rarest thing in the world, now as in the past.

STRYK: But the literature is alive with accounts of *satori*. Surely that's the whole point of discipline. When a master gives *inka*, when you received it from Shibayama Roshi, there's a very definite experience in mind, is there not?

NAKAMURA: Yes and no. You see, one works under a master for years—there are many ways of demonstrating attainment. *Inka* is given only when the master is assured, over a long period, that transformation, sudden or gradual, has occurred. The literature you speak of—and I admit it tends to emphasize awakening—usually concerns a specific event, proper to such literature. But all those things which came before and happen after are, if anything, more important. The daily life of the disciple, the way he conducts himself in and out the temple, is everything. The master's always sizing up, quite unconsciously: the young man who took you to the *roshi's* tomb, for example, was, I'll confess, observed. Also I wanted to look at *you* before our meeting! In other words, not quite the drama that the literature, especially all those anecdotes about sudden enlightenment, would make it seem. *Inka* is given after many years of close judgment and, yes, friendship. In giving it, the master testifies in no uncertain terms a disciple's training has been satisfactorily completed, that in his judgment he is now able to teach himself. That's almost the prime consideration, for there must be successful transmission if Zen is to be kept alive.

STRYK: Very illuminating, even to one who has lived the literature for years! Attainment, whether leading to a clearly recognized *satori* or not, is measurable then?

NAKAMURA: Observable may be a better term. All involved in the discipline gain immeasurably, and from the first days of training, it is possible to determine who is likely to succeed. You must understand that only those showing great capacity for sacrifice and hard work are received for training in the first place. This may be during *sesshin*, a few weeks in the coldest and hottest times of year, when those not able to cope with the regimen are noticed and informed that they should not continue. Indeed, only a few expect to give up their conventional life for temple or monastery. Yet things aren't as clear-cut as all that. Often one, unable to cope at first, returns to find he can.

STRYK: And he is permitted to do so?

NAKAMURA: Of course—such people often make the best disciples.

STRYK: Was Shibayama Roshi a strict master?

NAKAMURA: The strictest, and we revered him for that. He encouraged us to think of Zen life as made up of two phases, the attainment of true self, followed by a life of service.

STRYK: Our friend Taigan Takayama would seem to be a good example, wouldn't he? I have in mind the way he serves his community together with his work as priest. I recall he is director of the council for social welfare of Yamaguchi, as well as that of the prefectural association for the protection of cultural properties. And to top it off, he directs the Yamaguchi orphanage, on the grounds of his temple, Toshunji. I remember how dear he was to those children, a father. Then there is his great interest—one you share, I know—in Zen poetry.

NAKAMURA: Yes, Shibayama Roshi, all of us, were inspired by his dedication. Often Takayama returns for meditation in our *Sodo*. A remarkable man—who does not think himself that at all. Things of little merit, he always says.

STRYK: Is it usual for an enlightened man to come to his home temple for meditation?

NAKAMURA: For meditation, and friendship. Shiba-yama Roshi encouraged the practice. Without it, one gets caught up in activities, forgetting gradually the primal experience which led to all in the first place. Taigan Takayama believes firmly in the necessity of *zazen*, at which he always excelled.

STRYK: Excelled?

NAKAMURA: Yes. There are differences even when it comes to so basic a part of our life. Takayama sat perfectly while a disciple, everything he did, the humblest task, was performed in the spirit of meditation. He lives as he does today, doing all those things you mentioned, because his meditation was deep and lasting. A true Zenist.

STRYK: Like Takayama, you are interested in the arts, especially Chinese Zen poetry. Could you give me some idea of the way the arts of Japan have been conditioned by Zen?

NAKAMURA: A tall order! Well, I know of your interest in Zen art, and am aware of the way most Westerners associate Zen and art. I would caution against assuming that the connection is absolute. Far from it. There's nothing intrinsically Zen in any art, in spite of the way some seem to reflect Zen principles. It is the man who brings Zen to the art he practices.

STRYK: I see, but surely some arts would not have developed as they did had it not been for Zen. *Haiku*, for example. Basho was profoundly Zenist, an enlightened man, and quite possibly for that reason *haiku* became an important art.

NAKAMURA: There is, to be sure, a strong taste of Zen in his best poems, and it's true he studied Zen with the master Butcho. Perhaps he best illustrates the point I'm making. He brought Zen to the art of *haiku*, which was well-established before he came onto the scene. It was not really there before him.

STRYK: It might equally be said, would you agree, that there was not true *haiku* before him? Surely, from Basho on, there's something characteristically Zen-like in the form itself. The greatest *haiku* contain the sense of revelation we associate with Zen, and there's compression, which resembles that of *sumie* (ink-wash) painting of artists like Sesshu.

NAKAMURA: Such art is the expression of Zen spirit, whether painting or poetry—and all types of poetry, *tanka* as well as *haiku*. Many *haiku*, those of its finest practitioners, have no Zen whatsoever. No, it is man who fills a poem with Zen. Always man.

STRYK: As that's a problem which most interests me, may we pursue it? I have in mind the various *dō* (Ways)—*Kadō*, the Way of poetry, for example. As I understand, one follows a particular Way to the heart of Zen. For Eugen Herrigel, it was the Way of archery. Coming to Japan to learn something of Zen, he was informed the best way to grasp it might be through an art, working with a master. It seems he succeeded.

NAKAMURA: I'm familiar with Herrigel's book; it is very convincing, but you must bear in mind he was following his natural bent—since he was deeply interested in the bow. And of course he was fortunate working under one of its greatest masters. I would insist it was he who brought his growing sense of Zen to archery, for there's absolutely nothing in that activity itself which leads to achievement in Zen.

STRYK: Isn't that rather like the old question—Which came first, the egg or the hen?

NAKAMURA: I am being adamant on the point because I feel strongly that Zen is done a disservice by the easy association many make, here as well as in the West, between it and the arts. The problem is more complex than one would suppose. I'm simply maintaining that few works of so-called Zen art, including *haiku* and *sumie*, have true Zen. It's precisely the feeling that led Professor Awakawa to publish, a few years ago, his remarkable volume *Zenga* (Zen Painting) where he isolates the *sumie* that are true *zenga*, giving reasons, making distinctions. The same might be done with poetry and all other arts. Awakawa quotes, by the way, a fine story concerning one of the Kano School painters who would always tell disciples they must be in a constant state of enlightenment. One day, it appears, while the master lay sick in bed, though it was raining hard, his disciples came to visit. Suddenly the conversation was interrupted by loud singing in the street. "An interesting man," the master said. "Do you understand his state of mind as he walks singing in the downpour? *That's* how you should feel when painting?" The greatest practitioners of the arts we're discussing were profound Zenists—none would deny that. It doesn't follow, however, that when a man lifts brush or pen he is automatically engaging in Zen activity. He may not be the kind to sing in the rain!

STRYK: What, then, if he is in fact a Zenist, meditating, following principles?

NAKAMURA: Wouldn't matter in the least—though perhaps it should.

STRYK: Thus it may be possible for one without knowledge of Zen, even antagonistic to it—I'm being very hypothetical—to produce a true Zen work, something perhaps superior to work of a practicing Zenist.

NAKAMURA: It happens constantly, though I must add at once that, here in Japan at least, there's little of what you call antagonism. We are not a dismissive people, except in politics! Nevertheless, it is certainly possible that one without active interest in Zen might very well produce a superior work.

STRYK: Could it then be truthfully claimed as Zen art?

NAKAMURA: Why? One knows at once whether work has Zen dynamism balanced by composure. One doesn't consult a biography to determine the artist's qualifications. There is *zenki* (Zen spirit) or there isn't, whatever the man calls himself.

STRYK: You put your argument strongly.

NAKAMURA: With good reason. For too many years such associations have been casually made, often by people who should know better. Ours is a distinct Way, its expression in any form unique, rare. Just as attainment is.

STRYK: It must be irksome then to hear people claim to have discovered the truth of Zen?

NAKAMURA: Irksome? Hardly. In any case, I would have to know the people before passing judgments.

STRYK: Does the rebirth, East and West, of Zen give you much satisfaction?

NAKAMURA: As Shibayama Roshi's disciple, how could it fail to? You know how important it was to him.

STRYK: Yet you seem skeptical about the nature of Zen experience?

NAKAMURA: I am a teacher, my life work is to assure the spread of Zen, guiding others to its truth. The claims you speak of do not distress me, so long as those who make them benefit to some degree.

STRYK: That would be enough?

NAKAMURA: Considering what life is for most, more than enough.

STRYK: That makes the master's role very special, doesn't it? Like that of psychoanalyst.

NAKAMURA: No, for we do not treat the ill. Our assumption is not that those coming to us need such attention, but that they seek as conscious beings something beyond self, thus finding the true self. There is an overabundance of analysts in Japan; we do not compete with them. You must bear in mind we accept for training only those who, in our judgment, are clear-visioned, able to train successfully. For the most part, superior persons who might do well at most things.

STRYK: Superior? Surely they must feel some lack to take on discipline arduous as Zen.

NAKAMURA: Precisely, because they *are* superior. They feel restless, uncertain, things all feel—but they take action. What they seek, however, is not help with personal problems, of whatever kind, but a Way to truth which makes all such things unimportant. Until they know that Way, they grope in darkness. Yes, what the Zen aspirant seeks is light.

STRYK: And sometimes it flashes suddenly before one?

NAKAMURA: More often it is a small light at the end of a tunnel, approached gradually, becoming larger, brighter, as one nears.

STRYK: To the layman that sounds more like Soto than a Rinzai point of view.

NAKAMURA: Less a lay than Western misconception, I'm afraid. Zen seems so easily understood when such distinctions are made—Soto's gradualness, Rinzai's suddenness, Obaku's middle-of-the-roadness. In reality there are no such distinctions, or at least they are not so profound as some assert. As I've said, there is only Zen and the temperaments of those seeking it. I'm very much afraid most Western books on Zen, many of which, with Shibayama Roshi's help, I've read with care, too often stress dramatic differences. Simple, colorful, but far from truth.

STRYK: That's very humbling, especially to one who writes on Zen! My final question concerns something which interests us both so much, Zen poetry. Would you agree enlightenment and death poems of the masters, Chinese and Japanese, are the most important expressions in the literature of Zen?

NAKAMURA: I would indeed. Especially the death poems, which give the very essence of a life, a brush of wind, and are often pondered like *koans* by students of Zen. We have always learnt from them, they are infinitely precious. You are right to be interested in them.

PAINTER AND
POET

Koichi Awakawa, seventy-six, one of Kyoto's most distinguished painters and poets, is a legendary figure whose work is esteemed in Japan and highly regarded in the West. I have wondered at his remarkable *sumie* scrolls in museums and galleries, known for years of his collection of art works, often referred to in books on Zen. Entering his house, virtually a museum, I stand in the largest room filled with painting and calligraphy hung behind glass. Works by masters like Ryokan and Sengai, the latter being his favorite, Awakawa informs me, of all Zen artists. On the wall there is a photograph of the artist next to Sengai's tomb in Hakata, where Sengai had served as Zen master in the last half of the eighteenth century and well into the nineteenth, dying in 1837. Near the photograph, in Sengai's very distinctive calligraphy, hangs his death poem.

Koichi Awakawa greets me warmly and immediately begins to show me his house. He is taller than the average Japanese, thin, delicately-featured, slightly stooped, and like all the Zenists I know, moves and speaks vitally. He is clearly proud of his collection, and has for many years kept his house open to those interested in Zen arts. Admirers have come from America, where he himself lectured at universities like Harvard and Stanford, also giving demonstrations of *sumie* technique. In telling of these experiences, he becomes highly animated, offering to do a *sumie* for me on the spot, on any subject. I tell him Daruma (Bodhid-harma) would please me greatly. Without ado, he kneels, mixes some ink wash, and in minutes brushes a fine one, very much in the manner of Sengai. I am thrilled and honored, for though I do not tell him, I have longed for some time to own one of his works, of which I've seen a number at an art shop near my room in central Kyoto, but they are far beyond my means. When finished, he holds up the Daruma for inspection, very pleased at my response. I am overwhelmed receiving such a gift. Placing it in a large folder of fine paper, he hands it to me with a slight bow.

I feel he is anxious to tell me of his life and work, but kindly offers to take me to the other rooms before we start. In the handsome study, books are everywhere, many volumes of poetry, which, since he is also a fine poet, he esteems. Toward the back of the house, we enter a room with many precious ceramics, then a storehouse-room for works not currently displayed. There he hands me tea bowls to examine, and each time I express delight, for they are very beautiful, he beams, speaking briefly, lovingly of each piece. He tells with reverence of his Zen master, Mumon Roshi, a very wise man, some of whose writing I know. After we have had refreshment, we return to the museum-room where, crosslegged on cushions, surrounded by his glorious collection, we begin our conversation.

STRYK: Sengai must be very dear to you. The fine Daruma with which you have honored me is very much in his spirit—he happens to be one of the masters whose poems I have translated. I see the photo of you at his tomb, and notice you also have his death poem displayed.

AWAKAWA: Yes, he is my favorite—in painting and in poetry. His genius was inexhaustible.

STRYK: You must be aware of the great interest in him in the West?

AWAKAWA: Indeed, I was often asked about him in America. As you may know, the British critic Herbert Read spoke of him as one from whom all Western artists might learn.

STRYK: As a painter, do you consciously follow him?

AWAKAWA: I suppose I do, yes—one could do worse!

STRYK: Do you ever have misgivings about that? I mean, do you feel at times your interest in him might inhibit the development of something personal?

AWAKAWA: I have been asked that before, always by Westerners. Perhaps we have a different conception of originality, or perhaps it is not the ideal for us. I'm not sure. I would rather be a good painter following Sengai, whose work has spiritual meaning, than a mediocre painter working without inspired guidance. The main thing surely is to preserve a priceless spirit, something we must not permit to disappear.

STRYK: I see what you mean. It may be true, what you say about the Western view of originality and the very high store placed in it. Is your attitude peculiar to Zenists?

AWAKAWA: I wouldn't say so. The history of our arts demonstrates from the very beginning transmission of certain insights, and methods employed expressing them have been all-important to our artists from the start. Gives us something to strive for, much more difficult than you would imagine.

STRYK: You are not concerned, then, when your work is described as being like Sengai's?

AWAKAWA: Humbled, rather. But you must bear in mind that working as I do, in so definite a tradition, I will achieve something personal by the use of that tradition to depict my world, one quite different from Sengai's.

STRYK: In the things that make it up?

AWAKAWA: Partly—in pace, tone, coloration.

STRYK: Recently, I spoke with some *haiku* poets, some of whom reject outright the old *haiku*, even Basho's, claiming they have nothing to do with the present day. These poets consciously introduce the modern—writing of factories, automobiles, such things. Is that what you have in mind when speaking of our world being different from Sengai's?

AWAKAWA: I would not like to make comparisons with that view, since I find deplorable such rejection of the old. I don't know what kind of *haiku* they write, but I'll venture they have little sensitivity if they dismiss Basho. One simply cannot be a serious poet and do that. Would a poet reject, for whatever reason, Shakespeare? I am certain fine poets think of Basho as I think of him and Sengai: there could not be good poetry today without their example, simple as that. I don't think it necessary, in order to be modern, to write of machines. Far from it. One has to be more subtle than that.

STRYK: You are a traditionalist in painting, using ink and brush exclusively. What of your poetry, while we're on that subject? Do you write *haiku*?

AWAKAWA: Ha, when it comes to poetry, I'm even more traditional! I write Chinese poems, using *kanji* (Chinese characters) and classical forms. Perhaps it's because I am also a calligrapher, and of course a Zenist. The great Zen poems, Chinese, Japanese, were written in the old Chinese forms. But you know all that.

STRYK: Could you tell me in detail what makes *kanji* so special for the calligrapher?

AWAKAWA: The Chinese character has great expressive power. There's nothing to compare with it for that.

STRYK: Could you give me an example?

AWAKAWA: In classical Chinese poetry nothing is left to chance, all is harmony, created in part by choice of characters, their graphic compatibility. There's balanced structure, and careful rhyming, among other things, including a very special form of parallelism. Our greatest masters—Dogen, Hakuin—wrote strictly according to Chinese rules of versification.

STRYK: But they also wrote *tanka* and *haiku.*

AWAKAWA: Yes, but their finest poems are in Chinese, those giving the profoundest sense of Zen. Natural enough, for their works were deeply influenced by those of the Chinese masters.

STRYK: You spoke of the expressive power of *kanji.*

AWAKAWA: When the brush is used, of course, not printing—but even there, what I have in mind can be suggested. Surely attempts are made by the best printers. Yet it is possible for a character to say a great deal more, when brushed, than it normally means.

STRYK: That's puzzling.

AWAKAWA: The best kind of example might be the character for wind. Now the calligrapher, without using a modifying adjective of any kind, can give not only the intensity of wind, through the thickness of his stroke, but even its direction through slanting or dripping ink. And this is true of most such things. The effect of fine calligraphy can be extraordinary.

STRYK: Like painting?

AWAKAWA: Precisely, the relationship between the two is intimate.

STRYK: Can one in a limited sense do the same with Japanese?

AWAKAWA: Of course, but the nature of a syllabic language—and as you know Japanese has a syllabary—makes constant expressiveness of the kind I've described far more difficult. Still there are great Japanese calligraphers, great because they turn such disadvantage to strength.

STRYK: Please explain.

AWAKAWA: Well, the calligrapher, in taking account of the non-*kanji* elements, can, if he's very skillful, create an even greater sense of intensity through pacing and contrast. In any case, he never seems to be inhibited by them; our best work rivals in every sense fine Chinese examples.

STRYK: Is not the writing of Chinese poems very difficult for a Japanese? Where is his audience? There can be only few able to read and appreciate such poems.

AWAKAWA: When have such considerations ever proved deterrents? One writes Chinese poems because one loves the art, thrills to its depth and harmonies; and because Li Po, Tu Fu, Wang Wei wrote such poems. Where is their equal, anywhere?

STRYK: For you as Zenist the fact that the great masters wrote such poems must be an added inducement. Could you tell me something about that?

AWAKAWA: Yes, overwhelmingly inspiring, for greatest insights, especially in enlightenment and death poems, were expressed through them. When I read them I feel that I am standing in the presence of the masters, their voices are so clear. Naturally my poems, written in the same spirit, according to the same aesthetic, take strength from theirs; a feeling far more mysterious than I can hope to express.

STRYK: Your paintings are exhibited and sold in galleries. What of your poems? It must be difficult to print Chinese poems. Is there much interest in them?

AWAKAWA: Limited, I'm afraid, to fellow Zenists, perhaps scholars. We have our magazines, few to be sure, but they are good. Then, of course, I exhibit calligraphy of my poems along with paintings—that's my chief interest as artist.

STRYK: Have any contemporaries writing exclusively such poems won fame? Are their books bought and discussed?

AWAKAWA: Hardly! No, we're a small group—not that it matters.

STRYK: You have some Daumier reproductions. Do you like Western painting?

AWAKAWA: Some—obviously Daumier, his simplicity, directness, the strong linear quality. Such things attract me strongly to him.

STRYK: There are others like Daumier.

AWAKAWA: I beg to disagree, though admittedly I've not made a deep study of Western art. Many in Japan think Daumier supreme.

STRYK: Impressive as Sengai?

AWAKAWA: Not to me. Even at his best, he does not give essentials in the way that Sengai does. You see, a Zen painter works swiftly, captures the essence of a moment, therefore the absolute. No thinking, no deliberation, no mind-work to cloud the image. Painting like Sengai's is pure *zenki* (dynamism), a combination of lightness and depth, that's what makes it unique.

STRYK: Nonchalance?

AWAKAWA: That's often the effect, to be sure, but only through careful preparation lasting years. Discipline is always part of it, making possible the freedom you admire, the nonchalance. Such quality can't be found elsewhere.

STRYK: When you lectured and demonstrated in America, did you encounter any skepticism?

AWAKAWA: Little, if any. No, those who came to listen and observe seemed very sympathetic.

STRYK: Did that extend to Zen itself? Was the interest serious?

AWAKAWA: Strangely enough, more so perhaps than in Japan at that time. Bear in mind I speak of twenty years ago. Now the interest here is very strong again, stronger than ever before.

STRYK: To what do you attribute that?

AWAKAWA: The need is greater today. Look around you: most have gone mad with desire for material things. Zen reaches inside them when they are off-guard, revealing something precious which they know must be preserved. It is, after all, their heritage. In recent years that need, that realization, has intensified. Zen painting and calligraphy have never been more in demand.

STRYK: The prices bear that out. When living here in 1962, it was possible to find treasured *sumie* selling for $100. Today the same scroll would sell for $1,000, and one would have to be lucky to find a truly good one.

AWAKAWA: All that began about ten years ago, when suddenly the Japanese woke up to find themselves among the wealthy of the earth. What a surprise, when you consider what happened to us. People began buying feverishly back into their past, especially the old scrolls.

STRYK: Most Japanese painters though are as ultra-modern as their contemporaries elsewhere, and their works often command high prices. What of traditional modern art?

AWAKAWA: There's no comparison. People like myself find it impossible to live by painting alone.

STRYK: Are you troubled by the way so many work today? I mean advanced painters, whose works resemble in every way those of Westerners.

AWAKAWA: Troubled? Should I be?

STRYK: Well, do you value what they do as art?

AWAKAWA: A better question may be, Do they think it is? If so, why shouldn't they work that way? So long as there are those who appreciate what they do.

STRYK: Very little of it, I feel, is good. Recently I went to an exhibit of contemporary works at the Modern Museum at Ueno, Tokyo: acres of sameness plastered the walls.

AWAKAWA: Ah, *you* seem to be troubled by the fact.

STRYK: Puzzled, certainly. I found nothing distinctive in their works, certainly nothing of Japan.

AWAKAWA: Quite the contrary. Much of contemporary Japan, I'm afraid, a new Japan which for the most part has little interest left in things concerning me. But it, too, is Japan—that's reality.

STRYK: What do such artists think of tradition, as upheld by you, by Zen communities?

AWAKAWA: You'd have to ask them. I suspect they tolerate us, I doubt they despise us. Most are young and very tired of what they think is past.

STRYK: I find such tolerance remarkable. You feel no misgivings?

AWAKAWA: None, truly—were I to, what good would it do? What interests me has never had broad appeal, for it concerns enlightened vision, something few attain. Yet there is interest enough. Works like mine, after all, are exhibited, drawing some—if only grudging—attention from the critics.

STRYK: For you, then, painting is *Gadō*, the painter's Way to truth?

AWAKAWA: That I cannot claim, such claims cannot

be made. If my painting leads to insight, revelation, then perhaps *Gadō* may be my Way, but it could equally be *Shodō* (calligraphy) or *Kadō* (poetry)—or a combination of the three! All that is for others to decide. You see, ours is a language of honorifics. One does not call oneself poet, for example. If one is gifted and fortunate in poetry, others may call one so. As you can see, your question is somewhat embarrassing.

STRYK: Yet art is your whole life, and even in these times your work is much admired.

AWAKAWA: That should mean nothing to a Zenist.

STRYK: That reminds me of something the master Taigan Takayama said in his foreword to our volume *Zen Poems of China and Japan*. He spoke of our translation of the poems, with Takashi Ikemoto, as a thing of no merit. He was right, in the strict Zen sense, but I'd like to feel it is good to see one's endeavors having merit. Else why engage in them? Is that a Western attitude, a form of attachment?

AWAKAWA: All such things are relative. One should of course regard one's work as the most important thing in the world for oneself, which indeed it could well be, yet in the grand scheme of things, it truly may be of no merit. In any case, it might be dangerous to think otherwise.

STRYK: Dangerous?

AWAKAWA: The Zenist, you see, learns early in his career—whatever it may be—that the only worthwhile pursuit is the discovery of the original man, which takes a lifetime's effort. All those things we do—paint, make poems, whatever—should serve that effort.

STRYK: So that's what's meant by a *dō*, a Way?

AWAKAWA: Yes, though it's a bit more complex than I put it. On such matters we expect our masters to pass judgment— *they* decide whether a man's art may become his *dō*.

STRYK: Have you felt over the years, through your activities, a discovery of the original man in yourself?

AWAKAWA: The masters with whom I've worked from time to time advised me to continue my work in the arts. They seemed to feel it helped in my endeavor.

STRYK: Have they been competent to judge your work?

AWAKAWA: More competent, I can assure you, than many so-called art experts!

STRYK: Because of knowledge of the arts?

AWAKAWA: Rather because of their knowledge of man, of me, and all those things historically true of Zen. None of them have been practising artists.

STRYK: But such spiritual qualifications, important as they are to Zen itself, would not assure competence in judgment of art works. I'm a bit puzzled when you speak of seeking their approval over that of qualified critics. Indeed, it's that kind of mysticism which troubles many interested in Zen.

AWAKAWA: Why mysticism should be troubling, I can't fathom. Perhaps such a person should look elsewhere for intellectual stimulation. I have never known a Zen master less than unerring in his judgment of such matters. For one thing, all are expected to excel, if not in actual making of art works of one kind or another, then in the appreciation of the aesthetic on which they are normally based. That should not surprise the student of Zen.

STRYK: Yet it does surprise me in a way.

AWAKAWA: Let's put it this way: a master's main concern is the enlightenment of those who come to him, whatever they bring him in their hands. His assessment of what's offered, whether the solution of a *koan*, a poem, a painting, is based on a clear aesthetic of Zen. He knows instinctively whether a work touches on essentials. It's for that reason he is the best possible evaluator. Were you to hand him a *haiku*, he would take for granted it's composed of seventeen syllables, and so on. That need not be discussed. What would interest him would be whether the poem reveals, brings light to darkness. It would be revelatory, by his high standards, only if finely done, yet, technique taken for granted, he would only discuss content.

STRYK: Whereas an art critic might discuss method at the expense of spirit?

AWAKAWA: Naturally, he would see that as his job. His judgment would have a limited kind of importance to his readers— but that's as far as it would go.

STRYK: Are there not masters indifferent to art, feeling it a waste of their disciples' time?

AWAKAWA: There are some less involved than others. Zen artists naturally show their works to masters whose interest is strong, perhaps practitioners themselves. Just as there are different sects appealing to distinct temperaments, there are masters right for some, wrong for others—though sometimes he who appears the wrong one may be just the right one! His lack of sympathy or natural interest spurring the disciple to greater effort, whatever's being done. There are many such examples.

STRYK: Art for you, then, is a way to understanding?

AWAKAWA: That's the intention behind everything I undertake.

STRYK: That in itself sets a very high standard.

AWAKAWA: In things of spirit—can any standard be too high?

STRYK: What I have in mind is the personal quality of works made in that spirit. How can one determine, whatever the response, whether in producing a work its maker experienced revelation?

AWAKAWA: Simple enough: if we are moved by it, he must have been, if a truth is revealed, it was revealed to him in making it.

STRYK: That *sounds* simple, but is it? Life even for the enlightened isn't always intense. Surely there are times when one feels very ordinary yet is able to produce impressively.

AWAKAWA: An enlightened man *must* feel ordinary at all times, but this ordinary state is, comparatively, on a high plane of awareness. No, I don't mean to suggest the artist creates in a state of excitement—he would not work well that way. Rather as a result of certain experiences, usually coming early in his career, his mind has a certain cast, everything seen in a certain light—where perhaps there would be darkness for others. He may not even be conscious of that light, but we are, standing before his works. Sengai's nonchalance, as you call it, everywhere present, in the most casual of his efforts, was surely the result of his awakening, gained early in life. From the very start he was unique, thus he is unique in our culture.

STRYK: Because of his art do you place him above other masters?

AWAKAWA: Strictly as Zenists?

STRYK: Yes.

AWAKAWA: Well, we must remember Sesshu too was a Zen master—and there's Hakuin. But, yes, Sengai is my favorite, and he was a very important Zen master. Fortunately there are records, anecdotes, concerning him as priest. They verify the spirit every one of his paintings and poems suggests—vivacity, extraordinary perception.

STRYK: If there were no such records?

AWAKAWA: The works themselves would tell. Whenever I consider one, I envy those who knew him, whose Zen came to perfection under him. They were blessed!

STRYK: Yet there must be fine artists who would make poor spiritual guides.

AWAKAWA: Undoubtedly, but not Zenists. No Zenist could possibly be such a one. The works of such men, however valuable, would probably not appeal to Zenists.

STRYK: It must be wonderful to live, work with so clear and exalted an idea of art's meaning.

AWAKAWA: That's what *Zen* means to me.

NOH ACTOR

After two hundred years the Kongo *Noh* Company remains one of the most active and highly respected in Japan; the original hall in the heart of Kyoto well-preserved. Its seasonal cycle of plays is attended for the most part by subscribed connoisseurs, from all over, many of whom devotedly follow the action with one eye on the text, like music lovers listening to a favorite score. This is especially true when classics like *Miidera* are performed, one of two major offerings on this afternoon. Later, I am to meet Mitsiharu Teshima, the actor who will play the leading role, that of a mother crazed with grief over a lost child. Mitsiharu Teshima is son of the "Living National Treasure," Dazaimon Teshima, who will also perform this afternoon, giving a remarkably moving interpretation, undistracted by a filming of the performance—a not uncommon practice, I am told. Flashbulbs flick among the audience, even at the highest moments of the drama, but most are very calm, clearly absorbed. A field-day for enthusiasts: the richly-colored, patterned costumes, the stark but brilliant setting dominated by a painted pine tree, the ceremonious grace of actors, musicians, chorus, the panorama of the long ramp over which all enter. Once *Miidera* is underway, I sense once more why *Noh* is thought the perfect art, using music, chanting, gesture, dance, and, above all, poetry, with absolute harmony. The play lasts a little over an hour, yet the impression is of great length, transporting one into a timeless realm. Intense experience, some are so overcome they leave the hall briefly to recover with warm tea, usually when the chorus takes over from the actors to relate in most expressive chanting the story, for only the highest moments are enacted.

Deeply stirred by the artistry of Mitsiharu Teshima's style, I can hardly wait to talk with him about his art, the way in which it has been affected by Zen. *Noh*, preserved, developed for centuries by its masters and priests, has long been considered Zen art. This being my first meeting with a *Noh* actor, I have strong expectations. His performance in *Miidera* overwhelms me. I find myself relieved that it comes early, giving me the chance to compare his work with that of other actors, including that of his famous father, the principal in the other of the two major offerings, *Tenko*. The acting of the "Living National Treasure" is what one might expect, there is a great hush at his every entrance—such men are greatly honored by the Japanese. But his son is no less impressive, every gesture, every subtle turn of head so that the light on the mask alters expression, the heartbreaking voice. A half-hour after the last play, we meet backstage: his room, large, dimly lit, is filled with packing cases, small silk-lined wooden boxes holding masks, and costumes. Mitsiharu Teshima sits, head bowed, at a small table in the center, and when I enter rises, bows deeply, lifts his fine head. His face, hidden until this moment behind a mask, is beautifully expressive. I am surprised to find that he is not tired, rather elated, all having gone so well. His voice, which on stage echoed like a singer's, is deep and calm, his smile most welcoming. I begin by asking about the dance in *Miidera* (dance is the climax of all *Noh* plays), which he performed magnificently.

STRYK: One of the many things which interest me is the idea of variations on what I assume to be a set dance, in movement, speed, and gesture. Are any possible?

TESHIMA: Yes, and no. That is, variations, if I get your meaning, are always themselves set or prescribed, nothing impromptu permitted. That surprises you. Well, I can assure you if an audience detects any such attempt they walk out as a man—or worse. Yet prescribed variations are known to all lovers of *Noh*, and an actor who could not use them would not be taken seriously. But great care must be taken—always is. There is no place for the ambitious amateur, out to shock, in our theater.

STRYK: Do such variations differ from one *Noh* school to another?

TESHIMA: Schools differ in all things. I speak only of ours, the Kongo. Were you to see another school's *Miidera,* you'd find many differences. We are a Kyoto school, our interpretations reflect life and taste here. Costuming, chanting, pacing, atmosphere, everything. In some schools the mother's dance in *Miidera* may be, shall we say, more vigorous, but perhaps lacking in the refinement we aim at.

STRYK: Would that make it less effective?

TESHIMA: Far from it. As one might expect, Tokyo dancing is more vigorous, like the place itself. I've been formed not only by our *Noh* tradition but the very tempo of Kyoto life, the ambiance of all that makes this city unique—temples, gardens, weather, everything.

STRYK: I was so much affected by your voice, resonant, even behind the mask. Could one become so fine a performer without such natural delivery?

TESHIMA: "Even behind the mask?" Rather because, in part, of the mask, knowing how to use it. Yes, it's doubtful one could achieve the same result without an expressive voice, simply because voice delivers the poetry—most expressive in *Noh.* The voice need not be deep as mine, a purely physical matter, like the shape of an ear. Without depth of voice one could still be very expressive, so long as feeling's there and the voice pointed properly from behind the mask. The same must be true in the West—surely all your great interpreters of Shakespeare don't have deep voices. One knows the expressive possibilities of words, understands the author's intention. Besides, when a voice is not naturally rich, there may be compensating qualities: grace, poise, delicacy of gesture, a thousand and one things.

STRYK: It must be gratifying to have given so much pleasure to so many this afternoon. The audience seemed electrified. There may have been some critics among them. Do you read what they write of your performance? Can you learn from them?

TESHIMA: Not at all. Usually critics of *Noh* are men with much time and minor literary skill. Their praise is often effusive, and always very general—always the same adjectives—one article echoing echoes of echoes. You know well, as a writer, what I mean. The same things must be true in all the arts all over the world. I don't mean to sound ungrateful—I've been very generously treated —but as a group, despite a handful with talent, their taste generally saddens me. They seem to care only for the more sensational things. It would take the most sensitive poet to deal adequately with these things. The poets are of course busy writing poems. Most critics seem to feel they must appear in print for one reason or another, in order to hold jobs, writing on cultural matters in very general terms, no matter whether it's on flower arranging, pastry making, or a performance of *Noh*. Learn from them? Hardly.

STRYK: At times it must be difficult to be son of a "Living National Treasure"—so much to live up to. Watching your father perform *Tenko*, watching the audience respond to him, I felt something awesome unfolding. Did you begin training very young? Was your father strict? Are you still learning from him?

TESHIMA: I began training when seven or eight, the usual age in *Noh* families, and, yes, my father is known to be a disciplinarian—with everyone, not only me. Always with himself. But of course I have learned from others, as you might expect—some very different from my father in their approach to the art. Perhaps more than through technique, he taught and inspired me through the quality of his life. He has given me what he has always had, something important to live for. That's the important thing, isn't it, whatever the pursuit? *Noh* is my world, but I'm interested in all arts.

STRYK: Ballet, opera?

TESHIMA: Among others. Anything that's touched with poetry, for that's what *Noh* is—poetry. Nothing less. In whatever art, that is what matters to me. Work without it would be worthless.

STRYK: I know *Noh* texts are read more as poems than plays. Are you especially affected by the text? Is a fine *Noh* play without an impressive one imaginable?

TESHIMA: No such play exists: text is everything. I could not possibly perform a play whose text does not move, even exalt. I act out poetry, the greater the poem the better my acting—if I am up to it. That's the main thing, being worthy of the poetry. It takes a lifetime.

STRYK: *Miidera* is renowned for splendid poetry. Could you have performed it as well as you've done today, say, ten years ago, when around twenty?

TESHIMA: I would not have been given the chance! I could not have done well, had I been: ten years make all the difference when it comes to the interpretations of words so profound. Life teaches, life prepares.

STRYK: What are the conditions of ideal performance?

TESHIMA: Well, assuming such performance possible, everything—musicians, timing, what we refer to as *yugen*, a depth of mystery which has to enter the audience itself.

STRYK: Audience?

TESHIMA: Oh yes—they vary, time to time, place to place. Some watch very keenly, like participants. One always does better for them.

STRYK: How was today's?

TESHIMA: For Kyoto, these days, not bad, but surely you must have felt as strongly as I up on the stage something profoundly wrong with all that filming and so on. Appalling. Yet it's something we have grown to expect, must live with. However, it doesn't happen always, or everywhere. Tokyo audiences are better, we find. Perhaps we do our best work there.

STRYK: That's hard to believe. Though the filming was at times distracting, I felt the audience very much in harmony. They certainly seemed moved.

TESHIMA: What we feel from the stage is often very different. I'm simply trying to give frank answers to your questions. The truth is, need, when it comes to audiences, is a major factor. In Kyoto, culture is everywhere. People living here hardly distinguish between its various manifestations, visiting a famous garden in the morning, going to a performance of *Noh* in the afternoon, in the same spirit in which they attend a fashion show of new kimono at Nijo Castle. Perhaps I exaggerate, but not much! In Tokyo where the sensitive often feel brutalized by the city, they truly need the poetry of *Noh*. When given the chance, they rush to it with a kind of hunger. The actor feeds their hunger with his best and gives it gladly. Don't judge *Noh* audiences by what you found here today.

STRYK: One thing which intrigued me was the way so many looked on at the text, like music students at the playing of a great quartet. Yet it might be disconcerting to you that every word is not only being listened to but read?

TESHIMA: I neither approve nor disapprove the practice. Still I can't imagine those who come to follow texts are responsive to the whole, though they must have great appreciation of

the *text*. What of the unwritten poetry, gesture, harmony of movement? That takes both eyes to appreciate.

STRYK: Though small, the hall was filled today, yet
numbers were scant compared with the great gatherings at *Kabuki*.
Is *Kabuki* so much more popular?

TESHIMA: It would seem so. Obviously it gives more
pleasure—simple as that.

STRYK: What do you think of *Kabuki*?

TESHIMA: The finest performers are wonderful. Un-
like many fellow artists, I don't find *Kabuki* vulgar because it is flam-
boyant. Yet I think it a lesser art, by far. To sense the difference, you
must see a play like *Kanjincho* done first as *Noh*, then as *Kabuki*.
Historically, as I'm sure you're aware, the *Noh* came long before the
Kabuki version. The *Kabuki* is very colorful, emphasizing the sensational part of the story, the *Noh* is very subtle and yet, at the same
time, building in intensity. Well played, the *Noh* is far more dramatic. The difference between *Kabuki* and *Noh* is essentially that between prose and poetry, and the prose of *Kabuki*, though wonderfully vigorous at times, is always prose. As I've said, *Noh* is poetry.
The difference lies in the texts themselves.

STRYK: A very tolerant view of an art form that seems to
threaten the survival of one's own!

TESHIMA: *Kabuki* has never threatened the survival of
Noh. When has prose threatened the survival of poetry? Never—not
in a thousand years!

STRYK: Could you speak a little of the use of mask in
Noh?

TESHIMA: The mask is all-important, having a force of
its own, as the actor feels putting it on.

STRYK: The great poet W. B. Yeats was strongly affected by *Noh*, basing his own dramatic work on its principles—plays
very much admired. In an essay dealing with *Noh*, he spoke of the
mask as assuring the gravity and depth of performance. He thought it
a constant, superior to the living face in its expressive range—a shock
to those brought up to value Western theater.

TESHIMA (gently lifting with a cloth the mask of the old
woman he had worn in *Miidera*):   This mask, my friend, is two hundred years old. For generations it has served our theater, its tradition.
Wearing it, I step outside time; what in Buddhism we call *Samsara*. It
fills me with confidence I couldn't possibly feel without it. My face,
changing from minute to minute, registering the whirl of self, is in-

capable of expressing what it expresses, what it always has and always will, the absolute. I would feel naked, vulnerable without it.

STRYK: I am beginning to see. Tell me, did the wearing of such a treasured object take a long time to get used to?

TESHIMA: Almost as another self. There is great art in wearing it. Pointing it to take the light just so, at precisely the right moment. Using voice so that it emerges just right, for the mask is a kind of echo chamber and plays tricks.

STRYK: Do you always handle it so gently with a cloth?

TESHIMA: Yes, that's why the lacquer is unfaded. It has been handed down respectfully, just so, for a very long time.

STRYK: When you say that you have learnt from many, do you mean you find yourself learning constantly, and as you develop in the art, do you find your life changing?

TESHIMA: There's no end to learning. My father claims to learn each time he sets foot on the stage, and that at over seventy and having attained, as you know, the highest possible recognition. I am only just beginning to grasp his meaning.

STRYK: What importance has Zen in your life?

TESHIMA: *Noh* has always been associated with Zen, and many of its finest artists have been priests. In fact the young man who played my son in *Miidera* is studying for the priesthood. I have been a Zenist by family tradition and by necessity—it is my Way. For most of us the writings of Zeami, the greatest figure in *Noh*, author of our greatest plays, are sacred, read like a bible. As you may know, he based the *Noh* aesthetic on Zen ideals.

STRYK: Do you practice *zazen*, attend a Zen temple?

TESHIMA: I have done, but I am now so fully into my career that it takes all my time, energy, and imagination. Yet all that I learned of the Way has carried over into my work.

STRYK: In a few weeks, I have been told, your company will appear on NHK Television. Are you excited?

TESHIMA: Excited? No, but pleased, since it's our hope to share *Noh's* beauty with as many as possible. More than hope, responsibility. It could enrich the lives of many, were they to give it a chance.

STRYK: In preparing for television, do you contemplate doing anything which might make the performance more appealing, less difficult?

TESHIMA: What a thought! No, of course not. That would destroy its spirit altogether.

POTTER AND POET

That he is a wonderfully vital eighty-three, Hokuro Uchijima attributes in part to a spare Zen diet, which he began when undergoing discipline some fifty years ago. He was one of three chief disciples of Kenzan Ogata (another was Western potter Bernard Leach, whose work is represented in ceramics collections throughout the world). He was also student of the great *sumie* painter and follower of Sengai, Kasen Tamita. All of these associations are greatly valued in Japan. For years he practiced *zazen* at Shokokuji Temple in Kyoto, his last master being the respected Mumon Roshi. Telling of his friendship with Mumon, he leads me into the guest room of his beautiful house, near the Kyoto National Museum, where his works are in the permanent collection. To the right of the alcove is a superb Buddha figure and a fragment of Gandhara sculpture given him by Mumon, to whom it was presented by the Indian government—a token of great regard for the artist. Their friendship, Uchijima says, has been the greatest influence in his life.

Like most Zenists, Uchijima is informal. After looking at splendid tea bowls and pots, many his own work, we wander into other rooms, one exhibiting works of fellow potters he admires. Some magnificent examples are the late works of Kenzan Ogata and Bernard Leach. He handles them quite casually, passing delicate cups to me for close examination. I hold them gingerly, sharply conscious of their pricelessness. I feel honored, but wonder at his trusting me this way. We end up back in the guest room where he invites me to sit, back to the alcove, gesture of respect, and serves tea in his own lovely bowls. Like most Zenists, he is a *chanoyu* (tea ceremony) devotee, and tea is taken in the formal way—three long sips, while turning and admiring the bowl.

Hokuro Uchijima collects *sumie* scrolls and calligraphy, particularly of *haiku*, in which he is a leader of the So-Un *Haiku* School. These days he spends his creative energy on *haiku*, as, he informs me, he is getting too old to work much at his wheel. His schoo , one of the most unusual in the history of *haiku*, is very controversial. Among other things, it is a free-verse school, not bound by the most important formal elements, including the seventeen-syllable limitation. I want to know about So-Un, since in translating *haiku* I have heard much of the school in recent years. Well-known as *haiku* poet, it is as potter he has won most fame, works exhibited everywhere, including France, where he won an international prize. In recent years his home has become school for his disciples in *haiku*, and he edits the So-Un magazine of which he shows me copies. Beautifully printed and designed, it puts most poetry magazines to shame. After leafing through some copies, and some fine books where his works are illustrated and commented on by experts, I ask my questions.

STRYK: You have won distinction in so many things. How have you accomplished so much?

UCHIJIMA: By living eighty-three years!

STRYK: It is not unusual for Zenists to practice more than one art, but rarely with such success in each.

UCHIJIMA: Man is a flower with at least five petals. If you look hard enough, you'll discover them all.

STRYK: That's very humbling—I wonder how true it is. It must have been inspiring to be disciple of so great a potter as Kenzan Ogata. Did you work at his studio along with Bernard Leach?

UCHIJIMA: Yes. Leach and I were good friends, and we adored Ogata—though he was tough on us, so hard to please.

STRYK: Could you give some idea of your discipleship in pottery? How did you become apprentice-disciple of Kenzan Ogata? I ask because such an arrangement, common for centuries in Japan, is less known in the West.

UCHIJIMA: Really? Think of the great Italian masters of the past—but perhaps it is the significance which may not be as much appreciated. Important Western potters, men in all arts, have assistants who may surely go on to do work of their own. The expected way, everywhere. What you have in mind, I feel, is how much more is made of such associations here.

STRYK: Yes. The first time I heard of you, for example, I was informed you trained along with Bernard Leach under Kenzan Ogata. At the recent exhibit of your work here in Kyoto, again there was reference to that in the first paragraph of the brochure. I realize your relationship with Ogata must have been extremely important to your career, but . . .

UCHIJIMA: Because it was important to my life!

STRYK: Of course, but what I have in mind is the possible difference in the practice, East and West. An assistant of sculptor Henry Moore, say, may become a fine sculptor—I'm sure that has happened—but one is not likely to hear much, if anything, about it when his work is exhibited. Indeed, it may well be that the younger artist would rather that it not be dwelt on. Perhaps because he considers the association, however important to training, might prove detrimental to his career: he might be thought less individual, critics picking out the Moore in him, no matter if his work were highly individual.

UCHIJIMA: I see. Bernard Leach, very much a Westerner in all respects despite involvement in our arts, didn't seem to be like that at all. On the contrary. He was proud, as proud as I, to work with such a man.

STRYK: You trained in Zen under, among others, Mumon Roshi at the Shokokuji. Do you feel, thinking back, that your work with him resembled in any way that with Ogata?

UCHIJIMA: Interesting question, very hard to answer. Ogata was a Zenist, but no master. We talked chiefly of ceramics, yet my work with him did resemble that with Mumon. Hard to explain. In a sense, I suppose, I was trying to realize myself through both. Yet first things first: my work in Zen prepared me for everything—ceramics, painting, poetry were extensions of it, my way of attempting to attain the goals it defined. Everything Ogata taught me would have been approved by Mumon, and vice versa—of that I am sure. The principles underlying the arts I've practiced are naturally those of Zen.

STRYK: I wonder if you'd mind my asking what may be a somewhat sensitive question. Do you approve the way art objects, especially ceramics, are displayed and sold in galleries and department stores?

UCHIJIMA: Approve? Artists have to live!

STRYK: Again, what I have in mind is the way the artist's association with his master is always mentioned, indeed made much of. Works of a famous master potter you would naturally expect to be expensive—that's true all over—but this is extended to that of his students. Yours, for example, are always associated with Kenzan Ogata and Bernard Leach. You've already explained it as the custom here, and results may be generally good, but isn't there an accompanying danger, a lessening objectivity in judgment of works?

UCHIJIMA: I'm frankly puzzled. What do you mean?

STRYK: Well, consider a gifted potter wishing to exhibit, someone who hasn't had the privilege of working under a distinguished artist, who may even be self-taught. There must be many such. Would it be possible for him to exhibit, earn adequately from his works? Would he be given a chance?

UCHIJIMA: I'm sure young, gifted artists in the West have similar problems. They wouldn't expect to earn as much as Picasso.

STRYK: True, nor would it matter if they had studied with Picasso. What disturbs is the suggestion of pedigree in such a practice—though, as in your case, there's no question of the value of the work!

UCHIJIMA: I see. Perhaps I should explain the great ones like Ogata do not have schools. Those working with them dare not even mention the association without their approval. It would be unthinkable, really.

STRYK: Ah, then it's rather like a Zen master's *inka*, formally acknowledging a disciple's study is successful?

UCHIJIMA: Yes and no. An artist doesn't do anything so formal, of course. He simply lets it be known that the younger artist has perfected works ripe for display. Always being asked to exhibit, sometimes he cannot, suggesting his assistants show things in his place. Most natural, hardly suspicious! The rest, as you can imagine, happens of itself.

STRYK: I see. Then an exhibit is arranged and the artist's association with the master referred to in publicity?

UCHIJIMA: That often happens.

STRYK: Is it possible for a potter, of whatever background, to make a decent living?

UCHIJIMA: Things are better these days, because of the new wealth, but it has never been easy.

STRYK: Is it still usual to make things on order?

UCHIJIMA: That's how it's often done once an artist becomes known. Before that he works as artists everywhere without too much expectation, developing whatever individuality possible. He will occasionally exhibit alongside others, only fairly late in his career can he expect a one-man show. What happens then makes all the difference to whether he receives commissions and so on.

STRYK: What sort of things are ordered?

UCHIJIMA: Tea bowls mainly, by people beginning to take interest in tea-ceremony. A father will order one for his daughter, say, as a birthday present—a son one for his mother. Then there are vases, all sizes, occasionally coloring specified. The kind of order one dreads, I'm afraid, but one must eat. Those who respect my work expect me to offer the best I have, but these days there aren't too many orders and I'm reluctant to sell my favorite pieces done over the years that aren't in collections. These I like holding onto—I'm not sure why!

STRYK: I suppose every artist hopes something will be preserved, there's a tradition of that kind. I'm thinking of those remarkable tea bowls, with names like "Maple Leaf," "Chrysanthemum," one sees at museums, some handed down for centuries, considered precious works. What has led to their preservation, their beauty or fame of their makers and owners?

UCHIJIMA: Both. Of course they would have to be beautiful to be chosen by men like Ikkyu, for example, but there's little doubt the fact they were held in such hands with great reverence makes them all the more valuable to us. If for the samurai the sword is envisioned as his spirit, for the tea master it's his bowl. Yes, we value such things above all others.

STRYK: Perhaps a hundred years from now a Uchijima bowl will be shown with such veneration.

UCHIJIMA: Who knows? One works with that kind of hope—like poets and all other artists.

STRYK: Is the fragility of what you make important to the way you think of it?

UCHIJIMA: All that's relative. From life on, what isn't fragile? If what I make is fine, it will be well taken care of.

STRYK: Even if it were cracked or broken, it could be restored?

UCHIJIMA: Sometimes that's fortunate! Some of the greatest works have been enhanced by restoration. That's an art in itself.

STRYK: As one successful in so many arts, you must have had to make choices of one kind or another—in how to portion out your time and energy, among other things. These days you devote much time to *haiku* and your famous So-Un *Haiku* School. Does this give as much satisfaction?

UCHIJIMA: Yes, altogether as much. Naturally there's a difference. When I fire my bowl, that's it. With *haiku* I must mold, tear down over and over till I get it right. I like that. There's less tension in the process, paper is so expendable! These days *haiku* is my chief interest.

STRYK: The So-Un School is perhaps the most unusual in the history of the art. In some quarters, I've discovered, it's little short of notorious!

UCHIJIMA: Has been for fifty years.

STRYK: That long? Then I assume it started with the interest in free verse, which caught on about that time.

UCHIJIMA: Yes, the first So-Un poets were clearly influenced by the writers of free verse, but, if anything, their innovations were more daring, as you can well appreciate. Never in three hundred years or so had anyone dared depart from strict *haiku* form.

STRYK: You mean the abandoning of the seventeen-syllable limitation?

UCHIJIMA: That was the most obvious break with the past, but not the only. The idea behind all of So-Un's departures from the norm was precisely that they had become the norm. Our first writers wanted to restore *haiku's* vigor: the art was in a bad way—little originality, less depth. They wanted to return the spirit of Basho to *haiku*, whatever the consequences. We're still trying to do just that.

STRYK: Were the first So-Un poets Zenists?

UCHIJIMA: Yes, above all they wanted their works to have *zenki*. That was behind all they did.

STRYK: Resistance must have been powerful.

UCHIJIMA: It was, of course, because *haiku* societies have always been deeply traditional. By most our school was dismissed out of hand, simply not to be taken seriously.

STRYK: And today?

UCHIJIMA: Things haven't changed that much, I'm afraid. You've met with members of other schools and should know.

STRYK: It's true they're skeptical of So-Un, regarding it as the "School of one-line poems," but they are nevertheless impressed with many of the works—especially yours.

UCHIJIMA: Good to hear! But really we go along in our own way, have our own ideals.

STRYK: How would you sum up the ideals of So-Un?

UCHIJIMA: To put it simply, significance.

STRYK: Significance? You mean seriousness of theme?

UCHIJIMA: That and depth of treatment, whatever the theme. I tell my students *haiku's* not a game, at least not in So-Un! We aren't a mutual admiration society—I expect my own work to be judged sternly.

STRYK: You have many students, most of them young. Are any Zenists?

UCHIJIMA: Nominally, perhaps all, but their youth must be taken into account, they could change. They are all interested in Zen culture—they would have to be, working with me. I'm always talking about it. I love working with the young—more than anything else perhaps, it keeps me young.

STRYK: Do you find your position like that of a Zen master?

UCHIJIMA: Oh no! Merely a teacher of *haiku.*

STRYK: But you do recommend your students sit in Zen, among other things?

UCHIJIMA: I recommend that to everyone! Additionally I ask them to read certain books, apart from collections of poetry—*koans,* for example, to sharpen their wits. But that's as far as I go and for good reason. We have to be very suspicious of those who set themselves up as Zen masters. Only the few have the right to do so—that shouldn't surprise you.

STRYK: What then qualifies a man to be a master?

UCHIJIMA: Enlightenment, testified to by a master, and the gift to guide others.

STRYK: That gift is rare, surely, even among the enlightened.

UCHIJIMA: So it is. There are of course differences among masters, some more successful with disciples than others. Just as one would expect, in all pursuits.

STRYK: Including *haiku?*

UCHIJIMA: Most especially in an art like *haiku*. There are many fine writers incapable of teaching well. If I do, it's for love of my students. I think of teaching as having very broad application, you see—the better the life, the better the poetry.

STRYK: Better? In the sense of deeper experience?

UCHIJIMA: Yes. I insist my students work and rework until the subject is given its proper significance. Everything must serve that end.

STRYK: I see. And the involvement in Zen makes the difference, leads to an awareness of significance?

UCHIJIMA: When the involvement is true, yes. You must bear in mind that those who work with me expect, come prepared, for such involvement, knowing the school's association with Zen has always been strong. My students, some of whom are quite old, by the way, come to me and other So-Un teachers knowing full well what's expected. The process, in its entirety, is a very natural one.

STRYK: When a student begins to take up Zen, is the effect on his work apparent?

UCHIJIMA: Usually, not perhaps at once. We must keep things in perspective: only serious people join us, and they are aware of our historic connection with Zen. In a sense, you see, they are Zenists from the start.

STRYK: What I have in mind is more specific. When you recommend a student begin *zazen*, for example, or *koan* study— then do his poems begin to change?

UCHIJIMA: Rarely in a dramatic way, but over the years very much so. Zen is not magic. What it offers is already in oneself, waiting to be discovered. For some the original self emerges quickly, for others slowly.

STRYK: Are the former better poets?

UCHIJIMA: I think I know why you ask that, and dislike disappointing you, but no, they are not always better poets. What Zen offers is simple and direct, however difficult of attainment, but art is the mystery. Who knows why some succeed when many fail? Obviously the question is of inner need, capacities which may be as much visceral as spiritual. Perhaps my work in ceramics and painting convinces me of this, or having worked alongside men of genius like Ogata and Leach. Some are simply more suited to a calling than others.

STRYK: Yet all your students advance in some way?

UCHIJIMA: I like to feel they do, yes.

STRYK: Some win fame?

UCHIJIMA: Fame? I couldn't claim that. Indeed I discourage such ambition, something I've never been concerned about myself. For years I refused interviews with journalists to talk about my work. I've a suspicion of those who actively seek notoriety, having seen what happens to so many. In spite of what you've heard of my work, the rewards it brings, I am a small flame. That it has never gone out is my good fortune—nonetheless it is a small flame.

STRYK: You are familiar with classical Zen poetry. Have you written any?

UCHIJIMA: As you know, classical Zen poetry is written in Chinese. I am a Japanese. I write for my people.

STRYK: Do you admire such poems?

UCHIJIMA: Who would not? But I admire more the *haiku* of Basho. He wrote for us, while possessed of as much Zen insight as the masters. We revere him for that. No, though I've the greatest respect for those differing with me on this point, I feel strongly that Japanese genius is best expressed in our own language.

STRYK: Since it greatly interests me, may we take that a bit further? I understand why you say that, and agree a people's genius is best expressed in its own language, yet your school more than any other group I know is Zenist. When you read the great enlightenment and death poems of Japanese masters, most of which were written in Chinese, aren't you tempted to employ those forms? Surely they contain great wisdom, Zen truths not normally found in *haiku*.

UCHIJIMA: I disagree! *Haiku* often have such wisdom, in a different way, of course. A sympathetic reader, lover of our art, finds in *haiku* written by Zenists as much wisdom as in classical poems. And though it's true our most illustrious masters wrote poems in Chinese, they also used Japanese forms—Dogen the *waka*, Hakuin the *haiku*—and are as profound in each. The important thing to me is that, written for everyone, all can understand them.

STRYK: Then the democracy of *haiku* is important?

UCHIJIMA: To me, profoundly, as it must have been for those who first wrote them. Though I believe talent very rare, I feel everyone should at least be able to appreciate an art. That's the ideal.

STRYK: Well, *haiku* is certainly popular. Would such poems as yours, so free of convention, be popular as those of traditional schools like Ten-Ro?

UCHIJIMA: We have fewer adherents, just as free verse, but there are some who value our work.

STRYK: Are you criticized for your freedom?

UCHIJIMA: Rarely. As you know, Japanese tend not to be critical of each other, at least publicly. I suppose there are a few who regret we exist. By and large there's appreciation. These days few sophisticated readers stop to count the number of syllables in a poem. Admittedly there are some, among them influential critics, but I sometimes wonder whether they are interested in poetry in the first place.

STRYK: In what are *they* interested?

UCHIJIMA: In the maintaining of tradition, as they understand it in their limited way, not simply as past, but as something like a judge, or a god.

STRYK: Which to you is oppressive?

UCHIJIMA: Oh no—which does not exist, except as an accumulation of what is neither good nor bad.

STRYK: For you and your followers, then, *haiku* is a Way?

UCHIJIMA: One among others, but I hope a true one.

STRYK: For all members of So-Un?

UCHIJIMA: For most, and it's my hope eventually for all. That's what I strive for above all else—to make our poetry enhance our lives.

STUDENT

Over twenty years ago Hideo Kotaki was my student at Niigata University, serious, deeply involved in literature. Toward the end of my two-year stay he became ill with tuberculosis and was forced to enter a sanatorium for surgery and extended treatment. His family was too poor to help, and though my wage as visiting lecturer for the Japanese government was very meager, I did what I could, and by frequent visits to the sanatorium made it possible for him to continue his studies and complete my courses. All the time he was becoming increasingly interested in philosophy.

Of all this he reminded me when, to my joy, I found him waiting to surprise me at the Niigata railroad station when my train pulled in near 1:00 A.M. one mid-October morning. He had discovered I was coming to lecture at Niigata University that day and had decided to pick me up and drive me to my hotel. In spite of my fatigue from having lectured all week at universities throughout Japan, we had a wonderful reunion. His pretty wife, who had come along, said Hideo had talked for years in hope, one day, of our meeting once again.

He had fully recovered, and had been a high-school teacher for some time. Also, he had undertaken a most thorough study of Zen, and since he was aware of my involvement with it (he had purchased my books on a study grant in America some years before, at a time I was out of the country), he hoped when I had rested we would have time to talk. We arranged to meet later, next evening. As we parted, noting my concern for him, he joked about his former helplessness. Now he was fit, life had been good to him.

Later, former colleagues at the university told me he had indeed distinguished himself and won their lasting respect. In fact they hoped to help him gain a scholarship which would make possible an advanced degree leading to college teaching, possibly there at his Alma Mater. That evening I met Hideo at the Spain Coffee House, a favorite meeting place where I had often gone with students after classes years before. The Spanish decor and recorded *cante hondo* and *flamenco* were very pleasant, and he had suggested we meet there for old time's sake. He had enjoyed and benefitted from my lecture, he assured me, and was very much now in the mood to talk. So, sipping coffee, we began.

STRYK: When I was your teacher years ago, you were intensely absorbed in Western literature and philosophy. Besides that, you were at times a difficult young man, long before you became ill—difficult perhaps, for reasons beyond your control. I remember, for example, that you didn't like coming over to our house for conversation with the other students, always wanting my attention for yourself.

KOTAKI: I had little respect, I'm afraid, for all those who went regularly to your house, arrogantly thinking them glib. As you know, we Japanese tend to mistrust those who talk a great deal.

STRYK: I've never been able to understand why. Could you tell me a little about it?

KOTAKI: Probably not much you would find helpful. It's simply a dislike for what you call eloquence, possibly because a sensitive person distrusts words. There are other ways of expressing oneself, some more important.

STRYK: Gestures?

KOTAKI: More than gestures, though they're part of it. A person's air, the way he holds himself, his look as he listens. Such things mean more than all the words he uses.

STRYK: Each of my students must have felt his words important enough—did you find them superficial?

KOTAKI: Perhaps the way they could open their thoughts in public made me feel them weak, unmanly.

STRYK: You're an intellectual. You must realize that's what the rankest anti-intellectual might say.

KOTAKI: In the West perhaps, not here.

STRYK: In any conceivable way is the feeling, thinking of it now, connected with your interest in Zen—or Japanese art, perhaps, its restraint, economy?

KOTAKI: I don't know, but it is deep. People I most respect share it.

STRYK: What made you turn to Zen? I don't remember your concern with it in those days.

KOTAKI: My illness, perhaps, the realization that comes when at nineteen one is dying. I suddenly began seeking depths, answers to questions nothing else would answer—not that I was sure Zen could. Anyhow, I found no help in normal pursuits or in the subjects I had been studying.

STRYK: Did you begin doing *zazen* after leaving the sanatorium?

KOTAKI: While there. I had time on my hands, had always been a great reader. But school books became lifeless, the very thought of school. A fellow patient, a Zenist, handed me books on the subject. As I turned the pages, my thoughts went to my early years when Buddhism had played a small part in my life. When I started studying Zen, I was amazed to find so much in Buddhism which I hadn't seen before. Life became so simple, so real.

STRYK: And you began to meditate?

KOTAKI: Yes. Suddenly I knew the discipline was good, the literature began to fascinate me.

STRYK: Had you thoughts then of entering the priesthood?

KOTAKI: No, not a notion. I just felt I had found the way to make life livable, that was more than enough. I had become so bitter about my illness, felt so hard done by, desperately sorry for myself. Zen seemed to make it possible to find a deeper sense of what life was about—I had, after all, no more certainty that I would live, even the look of health in others disgusted me. Suddenly what time was left I wanted to be different. My study of English, all such things, became absurd; a stupid game, nothing to do with actuality.

STRYK: I remember we were reading poets like Tennyson. Did you turn from that kind of reading?

KOTAKI: It became very foreign, no longer interesting.

I began discovering Japanese poetry, especially *haiku* and the old Zen poems. But not only poetry. I began reading Dogen's essays, Hakuin's. A revelation! I think—and I'm quite serious—that such works saved my life. It was then I resolved to become totally Japanese in every way.

STRYK: When did you turn back to other literature again—you must have, resolutely, for you certainly distinguished yourself in it later.

KOTAKI: Slowly, as my recovery became certain. I returned to former interests with a vengeance! I found after leaving the sanatorium, studies became easier, that in many respects I was far ahead of my classmates.

STRYK: Politically those were active days—in fact many of your classmates were radical. I remember it took time and patience for me to win their confidence. Were you involved in such things?

KOTAKI: No, even then I had a hatred of abstractions— national interests, class war, "isms" of all kinds. I didn't argue, just went my way.

STRYK: Were you criticized for being that way?

KOTAKI: Not to my face! But it wouldn't have changed things. I knew what I was after; it had nothing to do with politics— only life.

STRYK: And Zen? Did the interest continue once you regained your health and came once more to studies?

KOTAKI: Formally, no, but by then Zen was so important it didn't have to be a conscious interest, or pursuit. I'm sure that often happens. It was just part of my life.

STRYK: How part of *your* life?

KOTAKI: Well, when young and taken on school trips to famous temples, I couldn't have cared less. I don't think I even found them beautiful—just old, historical. Now, well, when I visit a temple or view an exhibit of *sumie*, say, I feel so deeply. Those things speak a language that penetrates, one that I need. Same with poetry. Now I read *haiku* with keen appreciation; whereas the poems of Basho and Buson were once just things we schoolboys had to learn.

STRYK: Do your friends feel this as much?

KOTAKI: I've no idea—how can such things be measured? But I have my doubts. Perhaps one has to face the void, as I did, to feel this way.

STRYK: One hears the young are, for the most part, indifferent to the older culture, more interested in modern art, literature, and music. Even that some are hostile to things like *haiku*.

KOTAKI: I'm not aware of that, though as a high school teacher I should be. I only know what's important to me. In the long run, I don't suppose it matters how many people at a given time have similar interests. Basho's poems have been around over two hundred years, will be for centuries to come. At times they're ignored, at others revered—the main thing is they exist.

STRYK: Do you think that's true of Zen?

KOTAKI: Again, my approach is personal. The Zenists I know are serious about it, as men were at the time of Bodhidharma. Do numbers matter?

STRYK: Don't you fear there's danger, should few people care, that Zen culture will die out—unable to survive this world's increasingly materialistic trends?

KOTAKI: I really doubt it. Zen teaches constant evolution, change. Perhaps it too must undergo such transformations; perhaps a few hundred years from now it will be altogether different.

STRYK: Then it would no longer be Zen.

KOTAKI: So? What matter, so long as it serves the living?

STRYK: But unless it is very close to what it's been for centuries, could it possibly serve in the same way?

KOTAKI: To me Zen, progress, just is—neither good nor bad. It's hard enough to ever know what's good. When are we ever sure that what we think good really is? Why fret about what will be good in the future?

STRYK: Ah, you have understood the great Zen lesson, non-attachment!

KOTAKI: Not consciously, yet from the moment I got off my back and went out through the sanatorium gates, I felt something like that. A wonderful uplifting sense of freedom from all thought of time, of conventional morality, swept through me. All I cared to do was live, and though it's true I became a better student, I had very pragmatic reasons for becoming one. I thought, to hell with past, hell with future, make the most of now.

STRYK: You've always been a student of literature, more than philosophy. Has Zen changed that, have you been reading more philosophy?

KOTAKI: No, less.

STRYK: What of books on Zen?

KOTAKI: I no longer need them—that may be one of the results of my Zen studies. In the sanatorium I did quite a bit of reading of that kind—studies on Zen, Western philosophy, the phenomenologists, existentialists. Suddenly all that sort of thing, for whatever reason, became distasteful. So for years I've not touched such works.

STRYK: Discovering the truth of the old adage, not mistaking the pointing finger for the moon?

KOTAKI: I'm not sure I can put it that way. How easy it is to deceive oneself about the rightness of one's actions. Finger pointing at the moon: living in a relative world—can one escape the necessity of pointing that finger? Would one know what to do with that moon? No, it would be putting what I've found in far too favorable a light to make such claims. Philosophy bores me, it's simple as that. Whereas fine novels, poems—Asian, Western—seem to contain all wisdom, at least all I require. You see, I've no special philosophy of my own. In any case, you as poet would, I suspect, be inclined to agree fine literature reaches to truth.

STRYK: A poem or novel does it more interestingly?

KOTAKI: Yes, thus captures more of it.

STRYK: Though I can understand, I feel good reason for philosophy. Some are incapable of gaining the wisdom we speak of from art. For such people more explicit forms are necessary. Let's remember, few works of art contain the wisdom that helps us live—most being little more than entertaining. Surely you will agree?

KOTAKI: I admit I'm speaking personally, but that's the point of our discussion. Philosophy, including Zen, for me is something best discoverable outside its own terms, if I can put it that way. I'm not only bored but offended by writers who tell me, explicitly, this or that is good or true. Let me discover for myself, let those things which teach me appeal to the whole of me. They have to.

STRYK: Have you ever thought of working with a master?

KOTAKI: I don't see the point.

STRYK: Well, Basho did. Shinkichi Takahashi, the contemporary poet you admire, did for years.

KOTAKI: I'm not a poet. What could a master do for me that I can't do for myself?

STRYK: That's incredible. I don't think I've ever heard that from a Zenist.

KOTAKI: You see, my ambition, if it can be called that, is limited: it is to understand, appreciate the creations of others, and inspire students to the same thing. That's not so arrogant, is it? I want to be a good teacher above all, because I know a life can not only be enriched, but saved by art.

STRYK: Saved? Why—you're thinking still of your own illness?

KOTAKI: Who isn't ill? Blindness to reality is illness, isn't it? Indifference to beauty, unawareness of depths. Those things can be overcome by awareness of what gifted men have shown us.

STRYK: Among them philosophers, and Zen masters.

KOTAKI: Granted—but not for me. Philosophers explain everything for themselves ingeniously, cleverly to be sure: that's the extent of them. At his best an artist does not tell, he reveals. That's what interests me.

STRYK: Not all artists reveal, or to the same degree.

KOTAKI: Those are not artists.

STRYK: Hideo, you've been intensely affected by Zen studies, consciously or not, for the arts of Zen are meant to do just that.

KOTAKI: Not those of Zen alone. Zen would be false if it claimed otherwise. Artists with no knowledge of it accomplish what I have in mind when I speak of revelation. I've found some of their work to be altogether as revelatory as the works of great Zenists. It would be limiting one's world unnecessarily to confine one's search for truth to such works only.

STRYK: I feel with you in that, so long as one knows what's meant by revelatory. Could you tell me of that?

KOTAKI: In the presence of the revelatory, by definition, one knows that instant change takes place in one. Kawabata wrote a novel set here in Niigata, *Yukiguni* (Snow Country). When I put that book down, one of the most startling I'd ever read, this was a different place: mountains I'd often gone by on the train, villages I'd often passed and thought mere stations on the route to Tokyo, suddenly came alive. I saw them for the first time, the very air pulsed with their reality. That's what I mean by revelatory art.

STRYK: Interesting that you chose to make your point with the work of a Zenist! Kawabata's Nobel Prize acceptance address must be the finest tribute to Zen ever. I very much appreciate what you're saying, but I'm still trying to narrow down to something quite specific. Chekhov once wrote a friend that life without a definite philosophy is a nightmare, yet there's no direct hint of philosophy as such, except now and then by some of the characters in his plays, and other works: he never deals explicitly with issues in philosophical terms. The point is, though, he felt philosophy had to be there, directing him. More recent writers like T. S. Eliot have felt the same.

KOTAKI: True, but why speak of those men?

STRYK: Well, I'm puzzled. You feel you have benefitted so much through Zen, and at the same time have no use for philosophy.

KOTAKI: But is Zen philosophy? If it were, I doubt I'd have been affected by it. You suspect, I'm sure, that I'm something of an anti-intellectual. Perhaps I am—what's so special about intellection?

STRYK: Come now, Zen to be sure is anti-conceptual, suspicious of held attitudes, ideas, but from a distinctly philosophical point of view—paradoxical as that sounds. Once I was giving a lecture at a woman's college in America, and a teacher of philosophy accused me of trying to corrupt the minds of students with my anti-conceptual talk. She felt threatened, and plainly said so. Now I maintain the viewpoint of Zen, anti-conceptual though it may be, constantly challenging our abstractions, trusting only the moon itself and not the pointing finger, is not only philosophy but a most complete one, based very fundamentally on Buddhism.

KOTAKI: Our experience of it differs. You approach it looking for a system, from outside. I could not do so because it has always been near me, part of all I cherish in our culture since I awakened to its richness. Though closer admittedly than other Westerners, you still look on from outside. At times the Western interest in Zen not only astonishes but makes us feel guilt, since we're not involved in the same way. I'm trying to be frank as you would have me: I feel that seeking such a Way or system, even one so congenial to those who find contemporary values turn them off, is in itself a fruitless pursuit. I have a feeling you're asking provocative questions to draw me out, and I don't mind at all, but surely as an artist you agree that only the immediate can be trusted.

STRYK: The immediate is different for each of us; whatever it is can be approached in many ways. There are things, events, to be reckoned with day in, day out. What makes them special, revela-tory, is obviously the way we perceive them. That's what philosophy is meant to do for us. I can assure you that has been precisely my ex-perience, as artist. The hand, the eye, must be guided by the inquiring mind—if the work is to have depth.

KOTAKI: Well, as writer you are conscious of such things. You feel you have to understand the process of awareness: making poems, you have an aesthetic. Not being involved in all that, I give it little thought. Yet I suppose even for someone like myself, before appreciation can take place, there may be something like philosophical preparation. That much I'll grant. Zen art, after all, moves me—I had to learn to need it.

STRYK: Have you tried persuading friends to benefit from Zen? Your students?

KOTAKI: Never. Why should I? If they feel the need, they'll find it for themselves. No one will have to tell them, as Japa-nese, where to go. You must remember that we tend to be less eclectic than Westerners—there are fewer choices anyway.

STRYK: Yet at one time you were interested in Existen-tialism, that sort of thing.

KOTAKI: True enough, but always as part of study. Rarely—so far as I know—out of personal need. The difference is great.

STRYK: Are you content with life these days?

KOTAKI: Why not? I'm fortunate, in work, in marriage. Every day, for years, has been a kind of bonus—as my father, who survived combat, has told me, like a soldier. That's my feeling.

STRYK: Wonderful.

KOTAKI: I regained more than health, you see—a sense of what one should be healthy for.

STRYK: Has Zen lessened your ambitions in some ways? I mean do you strive less for things most would consider important?

KOTAKI: I don't understand.

STRYK: Where you live, for example. Are you content living in Niigata, do you regret not living in what some might con-sider a more beautiful and stimulating place—that sort of thing.

KOTAKI: Ah, perhaps in that sense I have been most affected, for truly I can't imagine better circumstances. With the proper attitude, one can make a great deal of what others might deem worthless. Nothing is worthless, nothing "better."

STRYK: What of the humble tasks that go with teaching high school, things many people do find thwarting.

KOTAKI: I am sorry for such people—their delusions! I'm very fortunate. I want no more than I have. Whether that's to be attributed to Zen, I'm not sure, but it's a fact of my life and whatever led to it was a good thing. Yes, it might very well have been Zen. That I'll concede.

POTTER

Takashi Sasaki lives in the small town of Uozumi, overlooking Akashi Straits and Awaji Island, a beauty spot made immortal by Japan's great painters, fifteen miles from Kobe at the beginning of the Inland Sea. At first glance the seventy-eight year old potter seems to blend into the scenery, firm as those small crooked pines dotting the hills and beaches far into the distance. At once he apologizes for the "blight" of jerry-built homes sprung up everywhere, none of which existed when he moved to Uozumi more than twenty years ago. Most of the new structures are owned by people out from Kobe, easily accessible by rail, and for the most part they are eye-sores.

His own old house with its fine garden stands superbly on a cliff facing the sea. Awaji, one of the large islands of the Inland Sea, is visited season on season by thousands who come to marvel, as I discovered on a visit there the previous day: it deserves its reputation. From Takashi Sasaki's front room one can't see the ugly buildings he despises. There are grape vines stretched along the windows, changing color every day. He observes from seeds on to flower and to fruit: now, early September, they are ripening along with the persimmons in the garden. His wife, a gracious lady, blind since the war, serves us sun-warm persimmons with our tea, moving with sureness, ceremonious and pleasant.

In the room are Picasso and Beardsley prints, and pots and tea bowls arranged next to the alcove, before which, as guest, I have the honored place. For many years Takashi Sasaki has enjoyed local fame, exhibiting chiefly in Kobe, occasionally elsewhere. He is proud his son is studying sculpture in far-off Rome, and has hopes for his future in the art. Among a fine collection of ceramics, there is much Western—Picasso, Chagall—, though some of the best is traditionally Japanese. Though he has been involved in Zen for years, one of the reasons I am anxious to speak with him is that he has so strong an interest in Western art. As I look over his collection, I find myself a bit uneasy about what appears to be a high degree of eclecticism in taste.

Takashi Sasaki shows me his fine kiln outside. Despite his age, he is an active potter, and many pieces wait the firing. Like most artists, he finds it impossible to live on art alone, and so for many years taught ceramics at a local college. He still teaches part-time, though now mostly art history, which might account for his strong interest in Western artists like Picasso. He mentions students who have distinguished themselves as potters, and is disappointed that I do not know their work. I find myself comparing him with other artists I've been meeting, since he alone among them claims to have been inspired by Western art while at the same time practicing Zen.

STRYK: How deeply into Zen are you?

SASAKI: At one time it was of first importance, but I haven't done *zazen* in many years—if that's what you mean.

STRYK: Most artists involved in Zen tend to be more traditional in their tastes than you. Have you always admired artists like Beardsley and Picasso?

SASAKI: Almost from the start of my work in ceramics.

STRYK: In your collection design and painting predominate, as in your own work. That seems especially Western—am I wrong?

SASAKI: Far from the truth, among contemporary potters. We're no different from Western artists in that respect. I'm also a painter, as are most my fellow potters, and many modern Japanese masters have excelled in painted ceramics. Though it may be true they were more interested in purely decorative possibilities of paint, whereas great Western artists, Chagall for example, try to make their surfaces more expressive. Perhaps that's why we think their work so personal.

STRYK: The result is very different from the more traditional Japanese schools like Tomba. I'm particularly fond of Tomba,
by the way, its simplicity and practicality, the sense of the usefulness.
Would you agree?

SASAKI: Tomba is one of the greatest schools. Who
would not admire its purity and strength? But few living potters work
in such modes: wonderful as it is, it is the past.

STRYK: You speak like an anti-traditionalist. Isn't that
unusual for a Zenist?

SASAKI: I'm far from being anti-traditionalist, as you
can tell from many works in my collection. But Zen insists we be ourselves, that the great treasure is original self. I like what I like, do what
I want, never bound by conceptions of what is proper or improper.

STRYK: There's something I very much want to ask. If
true that each art has a quintessential nature, then the beauty of fine
pottery is found in shape and texture, is it not?

SASAKI: To be sure.

STRYK: Then allow me to tell you what troubles me
about the Picasso and Chagall pieces. In such works painting dominates all else, hiding the essentials—the pot's shape and texture.

SASAKI: Does that matter, if the result is pleasing?

STRYK: Well, would such work be less, however fine
the painting, done on any other surface, even brick? One responds to
such work as to painting.

SASAKI: Theoretically that might be, but they are good
only because those great men were very much aware of painting pots,
not bricks. They would have painted very differently otherwise, of
that you can be sure!

STRYK: Perhaps I should explain that my concern is
the result of going to a recent show of Tomba pottery in Kobe. I was
so strongly affected by the beauty of work made to hold and use,
whereas when I look at so much modern work I'm affected by surface
alone. I wonder whether that's enough. In any case it would be fright-
ening to *use* one of Picasso's pieces in any way, though fine to look at
on a shelf. Traditional schools have this practical element which I
find true to life, and know to be important to Zen.

SASAKI: Not all arts done in the name of Zen are practical. Far from it. Some of its works are held precious, things to be displayed with caution from time to time, once in so many years, at the
temples which own them.

STRYK: Yet there's the truth that nothing should be revered to that point. Perhaps that's why Tomba would seem more satisfying. Some of the best-known contemporary pottery done in Kobe, though based on traditional methods and fired in ancient kilns, is in the light of such ideals, seriously wanting. Recently I visited one of the most famous red-clay kilns, of the Akahada School, in Nara Prefecture. I was disappointed not only in the works produced but by the very atmosphere—frankly it struck me as a sleazy tourist operation, almost all the work commercially designed. The day I went a group of ladies from a tea-ceremony school were being shown the operations generally. It struck me that the obvious intent of those in charge was to sell the very costly and for most part vulgarly designed tea-bowls, lacking personal distinction, done hurriedly, as for a supermarket—something in which the owner of the kiln took great pride.

SASAKI: I know the sort of thing—outrageous. But isn't that to be expected nowadays? I doubt that it reflects anything worth worrying over. Serious artists go their own way, hoping always to produce genuine works. How that's accomplished is always a mystery. One moves according to one's own lights, you see, whether producing tea-bowls for fashionable young ladies or following traditional ways, like Tomba. Or like myself trying something altogether new and personal. One must above all remain oneself.

STRYK: Is it not difficult to work contentedly in an art with so direct a market link?

SASAKI: Don't all artists, even poets, make things to be used, one way or another? Isn't that behind all art? The main thing is how it's used, in what circumstances.

STRYK: You make your pots with that in mind?

SASAKI: Not exactly, but one hopes for a buyer capable of appreciating his purchase, whatever purpose it's put to.

STRYK: I've always found that a problem. I mean even with a book of poems one fears it will get into the hands of one who will toss it onto a shelf and forget it.

SASAKI: Your view is idealistic. As potter I can hardly be expected to share it.

STRYK: I have asked others something that interests me very much: I wonder, are you concerned about the importance of artistic lineage? I mean the way pottery is displayed in shops, that being always stressed—the disciple of such-and-such a master, that sort of thing. The difference in value can be very great.

SASAKI: I'm trying to understand. I suppose you feel unfairness in all that?

STRYK: Frankly, yes, for some of the things thus priced don't seem superior. One may be paying purely for a name.

SASAKI: That's a practice, I suppose, in any highly traditional culture—one of the best reasons to challenge it! I have, all my life. Not that it's done much good!

STRYK: Have you always challenged tradition?

SASAKI: Not all that consciously, but I've certainly felt threatened at times. Yet I've not planned my career, so you see have never really taken such matters into account. I know what appeals to me, and couldn't care less about the nationality of artists producing things I love.

STRYK: Your son is studying sculpture in Rome. On your advice?

SASAKI: Not directly, but, as my son, he's been around art of the world. I suppose in a way I might have encouraged him. Why not—he's very talented.

STRYK: Would you have liked to study in Europe?

SASAKI: Would I indeed! But reaching maturity in the war years, there was no hope of that.

STRYK: Is your son interested in the great sculpture of Japan? The Buddhist sculpture and wood carving of Nara, for example.

SASAKI: Humans always seem to be stimulated by what is different—challenged by it. I have been, so has my son. Great as our sculpture is—and I'm first to admit that in certain respects it is supreme—there's something about Italian sculpture—Donatello, Michelangelo—inspiring to grandness of conception, with or without religious significance. Men, not Bodhisattvas, are celebrated. For some reason, to me, and certainly to young men like my son, that's very important.

STRYK: Is your son involved in Zen?

SASAKI: No! Forgive my laughing, but the thought of my son doing *zazen* amuses me. That would be true of most his friends, I'm afraid. You must remember Zen is not religion, as you in the West think of religion. It's a discipline leading to composure of mind, and in the arts work expressive of that composure. In my time we were led to believe it was more than that, always its arts were held to be significant. For some, war changed all that—what good's composure when threatened at every turn? Survival was what mattered.

STRYK: That's very Western!

SASAKI: So be it, but it's true, has been for years. I'm Zenist because I never lost hope, even in those dark days. I lived as one —have tried to all along. But my son, and his generation—that would be too much to expect from most. I'm afraid I'm disillusioning. I know your work in Zen, and you know mine, but I can only be frank in these matters. There was a time when Zen, its arts, was all-important to many. No longer true. One possible effect, and it's something I have certainly felt, is artists have looked elsewhere—to Picasso, Chagall, among others. I'd like to feel that isn't wholly bad.

STRYK: The change in your attitude, concerning Zen culture, came as the result of war. But you were in mid-career as artist at its start, your attitudes were by then surely well-established.

SASAKI: I fear I've overstressed the changing attitude. As you know I consider myself Zenist, in all matters. Perhaps what I'm trying to point out is the attitude of Zenists like myself was to some degree altered. Simply put, we became more international, less insular, without losing what Zen gave us.

STRYK: Was there an official view of Zen during the war?

SASAKI: No official view, no, and for good reason. The fortunes of Buddhism waned to some degree, because of its innate pacifism, while those of Shinto improved, yet Zen was after all the discipline behind *Bushido*, the Way of the warrior, and many soldierly virtues have been associated with it from the start. Thus Zen was in a highly ambiguous position at that time, something felt especially by the masters.

STRYK: Did many of your friends become anti-traditionalist, mistrusting the past, all those things which after all led Japan to war?

SASAKI: Do you mean artists?

STRYK: Artists, fellow Zenists.

SASAKI: Again a highly individual matter, depending on the degree of participation in war, something naturally overriding principles and theories. If one's son was a soldier, for example, those days were harrowing, if one's house was burnt down in a bombing . . . immediate things of that kind. I was more fortunate than most, my feelings about war are based on principles. But I could certainly sympathize, even then, with those in no position to consider questions of philosophy. And with them, right or wrong, I wanted Japan to survive intact—since by the middle of the war no intelligent person expected her to win.

STRYK: A painful subject—I hope you'll forgive me for bringing it up.

SASAKI: On the contrary—painful or not, war should be discussed by more than former politicians and generals. It's still something that needs cleansing from our system.

STRYK: What is your hope as artist?

SASAKI: At my age! That's a tough question, has always been—I've asked it of myself for years. Perhaps my hope has always been to give pleasure, make things which might be treasured by the discerning.

STRYK: It does matter who owns your work, who uses?

SASAKI: Deeply. Not that I have much choice! I always had to sell my work to live, at least to make some material difference to my life—as you know, I also teach. I don't suppose I would ever have refused a sale, yet whenever I've been able to control such matters I've tried. My art is delicate, perishable, must be handled with care. And as perfectionist, I've not produced that much. I believe my work is valued by those possessing it, and though I'm not as famous as the renowned men you spoke of, my work does cost a bit—twenty times as much as when I first began to shape my clay those fifty years ago! Yet it's my dream someone will see my work as more than just an object to place on a shelf, glance at occasionally, serve tea in on special occasions. The best I can do is fully expressive of my being—a poet like yourself would know what that means. Yes, that's my dream.

TEACHER OF AESTHETICS

Son of a Zen priest, Keisho Morikawa, thirty-eight, lives in Maiko, near Kobe, where he teaches aesthetics. He is a tea ceremony expert and a much-admired aesthetician with a broad knowledge of Western and Oriental art history, has written valued works in the field. Since childhood he has been intimate with Zen, and is never happier than when discussing the discipline and its related arts. I meet him at his gate, close to the railroad tracks, where he introduces me to his young wife, educated at the famous Nara College for Women and deeply attentive to her husband's work. Besides their two children, Mrs. Morikawa's parents live with them, and they all gather to greet me warmly as I enter the house and am shown into the guest room upstairs. Keisho Morikawa's father-in-law has been looking forward to our discussion, and asks permission to join us. He is a descendant of the great Zen painter Miyamoto Musashi, known to all students of Oriental art, and owns one of the master's most famous scrolls, a Daruma, often shown in books on Japanese painting. I very much hope to see it, but think better of asking, for strangely I have found over the years a great reluctance in possessors of such works to show them.

Sitting before the alcove, I watch Keisho Morikawa, slight and delicately featured, begin to prepare tea, which as an acknowledged master he does with grace and skill, though with movements surer, brisker than others I have seen. Soon he serves us tea in rare and beautiful Kiyomizuaki cups. Fully conscious of the honor, I express appreciation. As we drink he shows me, among other priceless pieces, a set of Ming cups, very precious, which I handle nervously, to their amusement.

When we have finished, the utensils wiped clean and replaced in their wooden containers, Keisho Morikawa asks whether I would care to see the Miyamoto Musashi scroll. I am overjoyed, and tell him so. Opening the container with great care, he gently removes the scroll and hangs it in the alcove by a bowl of flowers, specially arranged there by his wife for my visit. The small firmly-inked Daruma I recognize at once, having long admired it. Magnificent! I stare, wordless. Even my hosts, who know its every stroke, are affected by it. As Keisho Morikawa explains, it is the family's greatest treasure, and they unroll it only on very special occasions. His father-in-law adds it will be passed on to his grandson when he comes of age. Meanwhile the family enjoys, takes pride in its possession.

When Keisho Morikawa offers to show some of their other scrolls, I beg him to leave this masterpiece before us while we talk. Since they appreciate and understand my wish, my gesture of respect, Daruma watches us as we begin.

STRYK: A wonderful scroll. Is it customary for a family to pass such treasure on from one generation to another?

MORIKAWA: Well, first of all, there are few such treasures outside museums. As you know, our ancestor Miyamoto Musashi, who is also called Niten, lived from 1584–1645 and was a famous general and swordsman, serving the Miyamoto family. He was also an ardent Zenist, and perhaps the finest of the samurai artists—a most important historical figure. Naturally a work of such a man, held by his descendants, is thought priceless, and treated accordingly. Nevertheless sometimes such works are sold—many in the hard times following the war. Fortunately my wife's family would have chosen to starve rather than part with this scroll, and other treasured things. What it takes, I suppose, in each generation, is someone who values such works above whatever money they would bring.

STRYK: I realize that the scroll is infrequently displayed, but do you often find yourself tempted to look at it?

MORIKAWA: We often do, for pleasure, but rarely is it left hanging more than an hour or two. Occasionally someone, sometimes from afar, will ask permission to photograph it for an art book. As an art historian, I am always sympathetic—so long as I'm convinced of the book's seriousness and am assured that the quality of illustration is likely to be high. I feel that in a sense the scroll belongs to all those people, wherever they are, capable of appreciating it.

STRYK: Often those possessing great art works tend to be less generous, I've found. When living in Yamaguchi years ago, on asking to see Sesshu's great long scroll, I was told by a representative of the Mori family that it was unrolled once a year and too many had applied to view it that year. I care for Sesshu deeply, and was bitterly disappointed.

MORIKAWA: But Sesshu's long scroll is everywhere available in reproductions, in much reduced size of course, but fairly good as such things go. You must not blame the Mori family for trying to preserve what after all is one of the nation's greatest treasures.

STRYK: The reproductions I've seen, those sold at museums, so tiny, give no conception at all of the work's grandeur. No, I must admit to having been deeply hurt at the refusal, and with justice, I believe, since visiting dignitaries are never refused. But I was grateful to see recently Taigado scrolls owned by Mampukuji Temple at the Kyoto National Museum. Enough of my problems! How long have you been interested in the tea ceremony?

MORIKAWA: I've always been aware. After all, my father like other priests has a strong feeling for *chanoyu*. But it was in college that it became a passion. I was made leader of our tea ceremony club, overseeing weekly meetings, making sure our standards were kept high. We made full study of the art, reading the literature, visiting museums with fine bowls and utensils, going to famous tea houses, that sort of thing. We often visited, back and forth, with other clubs.

STRYK: I've been told the interest in tea is passing. Do you think most members of your old club remain involved?

MORIKAWA: Some are, we meet occasionally for ceremonies. What you've heard, alas, is unfortunately true—as with so many things.

STRYK: You teach aesthetics. Do you encourage students to take an interest?

MORIKAWA: Of course! I don't insist. One forced to it is hardly likely to benefit—I'm the first to admit that.

STRYK: How benefit?

MORIKAWA: In every way. It has had influence on my life, and my family's for years. Far more than ceremony is involved: study of tea scrolls, flower arrangement, architecture, gardening, pottery, utensils, dress, and, most important, cultivation of certain attitudes which reflect in conversation during ceremonies. A very complex art necessitating years of discipline and growing awareness.

STRYK: A number of my friends here, intellectuals, professors, seem to have little use for the tea ceremony, claiming that it's really for young ladies hankering for marriage and the life of gracious hostess. Unfair, I'm sure, but you must know such men. What do you tell them?

MORIKAWA: What do *you* say to those who have no use for poetry?

STRYK: It's true one is always up against insensitivity, particularly as teacher. There must be many in teaching who regard your field as impractical, useless, given the nature of contemporary life. Do you have male students?

MORIKAWA: A number, and they certainly are keen, as much and sometimes more than women, most of whom admittedly aren't likely to continue feeling interest once through school and married. Still their lives will have been affected for the good—of that I'm sure.

STRYK: How much time do you devote to Western aesthetics in the classroom?

MORIKAWA: A great deal, and of course inevitable contrasts are drawn between Western and Asian approaches. We read Aristotle's *Poetics*, Longinus' *On the Sublime*, and more modern studies.

STRYK: Are you affected by them?

MORIKAWA: Deeply. That's my calling. But most time is devoted to Asian aesthetics generally, Japanese specifically.

STRYK: With much time spent on Zen?

MORIKAWA: Zen's importance to all aspects of Japanese art makes that inevitable. And of course I am a Zenist.

STRYK: Can you give me an example from Zen painting, say, of the way you go about it?

MORIKAWA: A tall order! Let's see. All right, since you spoke of the recent Taigado exhibition in Kyoto, he will be our example. Though trained in Zen, he was really *Bunjin*, a literary painter of the Nanga (Southern Chinese School), learning something from, among others, I-Fu-Chu, the Chinese merchant painter who visited Nagasaki around 1720 and whose scrolls became so famous while Taigado was developing. Taigado, despite his brilliance, was something of a dilettante. His Zen studies, as well as his painting, helped him escape a world he thought ugly.

STRYK: That's no Zen attitude.

MORIKAWA: Precisely. When you compare his work with Miyamoto Musashi's, or any great Zen master's, that becomes clear. Take Ikkyu. For him painting was the expression of insight. His painting, in contrast to Taigado's, has *zenkan*, a very important principle of Zen aesthetics. *Zenkan* (*kan* means to watch), to put it simply, is the unity of watching, meditating. That's the quality in all masterpieces, Sesshu's, for example. There can be no Zen without it.

STRYK: Then would you value Ikkyu's work over Taigado's?

MORIKAWA: Far from it! I'm sure you too may find Taigado the greater painter. I'm simply trying to distinguish, with Zen in mind, to give you an idea how I conduct my classes. That's generally the way I take.

STRYK: I see. Though Ikkyu was, from the Zen point of view, the greater spirit—being after all one of the great masters—, you would place Taigado's art above his. I'm not so certain I would, greatly admiring Ikkyu's painting, yet I understand. Have you ever discussed this apparent contradiction with Zenists?

MORIKAWA: No, you must bear in mind that to a Zenist there's no eclecticism possible. He very naturally looks for things in art possessing *zenkan*, without being conscious of doing so—the purpose of art for him is to awaken.

STRYK: Reveal?

MORIKAWA: To express Zen spirit—only things accomplishing that are worthy to him. Really, there's no choice.

STRYK: Then he might have reservations about Taigado?

MORIKAWA: He very well might, feeling the work lacked *zenkan*. Not that he'd say so! It would be difficult to engage a master in such discussion, I can assure you.

STRYK: That's one of the difficulties I have with Zen

aesthetics. I feel I recognize *zenkan*, whether in poetry or painting, and admit there's less of it in Taigado than Ikkyu or Hakuin, yet Taigado and, say, Buson have something I believe equally revelatory. Perhaps I'm most concerned about the way art is approached by those who, automatically, dismiss works more elaborate or ornamental than pure Zen works. Could preconceptions regarding an ideal rule the eye, make it see more in some, less in others?

MORIKAWA: A problem of great magnitude, perhaps belonging as much to the realm of psychology as to aesthetics. When I said Taigado's work suggests he might have been trying to escape the real world, I had in mind his subjects, most somewhat ideal: perfect landscapes, rich branches of blossom. As painter he seems to have turned from less than perfect things, as if unworthy of his brush. Many revere him for that, reassured that certain things are finer than others—not wakened to truth, which is not always beauty, of the rest of life. The Zen painter, by contrast, never seems to be choosing the best possible subjects, because indeed for him there are no best among them. He treats humble and exalted alike, seeming to prefer the former.

STRYK: Thus exalting it?

MORIKAWA: Not consciously so, of course, but in a way, yes. For, as you know, no such distinctions exist: what's ugly? beautiful? high? low? Zenists always ask such questions, for good reason: only in delusion is the world divided up in such ways. That's the source of most unhappiness.

STRYK: How bleak a picture of what is after all normalcy.

MORIKAWA: To the Zenist, art has a very direct bearing on life—not meant for stacking in museums, haggling over at galleries. It either awakens, helping man rid himself of illusion, or does not.

STRYK: When it comes to such judgment, aren't there degrees? Though Sesshu is thought the greatest Zen painter, he may appeal equally to those indifferent to Zen—and there are others like him.

MORIKAWA: I can't concede that those who respond to Sesshu could possibly be indifferent to Zen. In order to appreciate him fully, one simply must value all those principles. There's no getting around that.

STRYK: To a greater or lesser degree, surely. One might value the economy and directness of Sesshu, on the one hand, the deli-

cacy and elegance of Korin on the other—that superb ornamentation
—, without reference to a given philosophy or aesthetic. Just widely
differing responses to the world. Must one give up one to have the
other? Would a Zenist consider love of Korin a betrayal of Sesshu?

MORIKAWA: Of course not! Yet he might with some
justice wonder by which of the two artists one is more fully addressed. Consider your own feelings about them. I'll speculate: by
one you might be pleased, even thrilled, by the other affected spiritually. You see, when it comes to art Zen insists on the necessity of definition, being generally somewhat suspicious of syncretism in all matters. Yes, one must define: either a work awakens to profound truth,
or it does not. There is art for the senses, art for the spirit, and there is
no true art without both. Every Sesshu painting examines the nature
of reality, the bones beneath the flesh, and in so doing involves one in
the process.

STRYK: Process?

MORIKAWA: Yes, the world of becoming. For to appreciate Sesshu one must penetrate surfaces, discover relationships only
suggested by his brush. It takes time to go below the surface.

STRYK: Whereas Korin, say, is nothing more than surface?

MORIKAWA: We must watch our language! You won't
get me to claim exquisite Korin, one of my favorites, is superficial.
Far from it.

STRYK: Yes, it is dangerous to use some words, but I
suppose the field of aesthetics has such pitfalls.

MORIKAWA: No more than others!

STRYK: Do you feel Zen aesthetics has been adequately
dealt with by writers—Okakura, Hasegawa, Suzuki?

MORIKAWA: Yes, and no. I believe that though they
understand the nature of Zen art, there's too much repetition: one
senses they learn as much from each other as from the works themselves. Perhaps they do not take sufficiently into account other possibilities, other approaches.

STRYK: The comparative, say?

MORIKAWA: Yes, mainly, for their work is generally
descriptive, and of course for Dr. Suzuki aesthetics is of important yet
nevertheless minor concern. Each of them, as an example of what I
mean, recognizes asymmetry to be essential to Zen art, but has there
ever been a highly developed art ruled by symmetry?

STRYK: Surely there has been, in the West.

MORIKAWA: When and where?

STRYK: Why, in Greco-Roman art, particularly architecture and sculpture. And Egyptian.

MORIKAWA: Yet, even so, there are subtle departures
from the symmetrical in the finest examples. In any case, I feel our
aestheticians overstate the case for asymmetry in Zen art—Korin, who
has no Zen in him, is surely not bound by ideals of symmetry.

STRYK: I see what you mean. I've discovered since turning seriously to Zen art something very curious. Perhaps you might
comment on it. Since learning to appreciate a scroll like yours, for
example, I find I'm less inclined to visit museums. This may in part
be due to the extraordinary quality of Zen art, the sense there's nothing to compare with it, but I've been wondering. Might it be teaching the profound lesson that nature offers all one needs—when
looked at in the right way, with *zenkan?* Is nature, in all its vividness
and thusness, beyond the reach of art, any art? It's as if my eyes have
been conditioned, particularly by *sumie,* to see a certain way, grasping significant forms more readily.

MORIKAWA: You speak like an awakened man!

STRYK: But I am not—far from it.

MORIKAWA: Well, as an aesthetician I can hardly be
expected to approve an attitude or disposition which would keep one
from museums! But I know just how you feel. Have you turned especially from modern art?

STRYK: No, certain artists still affect me deeply—the
eighteenth-century Venetian Guardi is a favorite. I began appreciating him since coming to artists like Sesshu. Perhaps it's the vitality—
not a figure in his many-peopled works is static. The effect is extraordinary, and is one chiefly of perspective, the eye being drawn to
every point of the canvas by gesture, very subtly orchestrated. Yet
nevertheless I feel as I've described, observing things out for a stroll
which strike me as impressive as the greatest works of art, including
Guardi's. The vividness of any passing face is beyond anything on
canvas.

MORIKAWA: That makes art, and people like me, dispensable! I suspect that it's a phase; you'll once again return to the
museum. In any case, art has taught you to see, Sesshu and Guardi
revealing what is vital in the world.

STRYK: Perhaps. Feeling as you do about art, and the
tea ceremony, do you sometimes feel isolated in a place like this? Have
you ever thought of moving?

MORIKAWA: All I need I have. No, I'm not tempted by big city life, even Kyoto—though admittedly I might feel different if I did not live close to the railway station. I teach in Kobe, as you know, and often visit other cities.

STRYK: When you have the chance, you must enjoy Kyoto.

MORIKAWA: Yes, because I go with hunger! That's something I once read in Paul Valery—a profound aesthetician, by the way. He said when you go to a museum you should go with hunger. Well, here the hunger builds, you see. Though there are things all around which satisfy, and there's always tea.

SCHOLAR

Professor Shoei Ando, fifty, teaches American literature at Okayama University. Among his many scholarly books is *Salinger and Zen*, a most intriguing title. I reach his house via the back streets of Okayama, not far from one of the most famous and beautiful gardens in Japan. His book-filled study takes on a glow from a lovely flower arrangement. He owns several fine pieces of Bizen ware, pottery famous in the region, and some excellent scrolls. With great charm he presents a scroll of his own calligraphy, specially mounted for me, with the characters "In nothingness, the inexhaustible." I am honored he has signed it with his first name, a gesture typical of this kindly man. I promise it will have a place of honor in my home.

Stockily built, warm, intense, and very witty, Shoei Ando has twice experienced *kensho*, thus is permitted to speak of these events. Also he has been given *inka* by his master, and is qualified to guide others. Many are his own students at the university with whom he meets informally, as befits a follower of Bankei-Eitaku, least formal of great masters of the past, who could say in all seriousness, "When you tire of sitting, walk in meditation." Shoei Ando is presently translating into English a large collection of Bankei's work, bound to be welcomed by the many who have felt strongly Bankei should be made accessible in English. He speaks of Bankei's "illuminated heart" and comments generously on my translation of the master, done with Professor Takashi Ikemoto, my old friend and colleague at Yamaguchi University. He shares my admiration for Bankei, valuing the way he could reach out to people of all natures.

Shoei Ando tells me how years ago Zen literally saved his life after the death of his first wife, when, suicidally morose, he came to it as a last resort. And now, a busy scholar and writer, he still finds energy to guide others toward awakening and the hope of a good life. The very words he chooses suggest a strongly moral man, who sees with the eyes of a Zenist. I wonder what he feels for Salinger, and ask.

STRYK: Salinger's famous silence has puzzled his admirers for years. To what do you attribute it?

ANDO: He has passed the first Zen barrier. His silence is nothing less than speechlessness before the second all-important barrier to realization. When overcome, nothing will stop him.

STRYK: Are you sure of that?

ANDO: He's a profound man, and it's not uncommon for such men to experience these things. When he's through the second barrier, he will write effortlessly, better than before, with greater depth and lucidity.

STRYK: I'm sure admirers hope so, but may lack your confidence, feeling it possible he's said all that he has to say, and as a serious artist will not repeat himself.

ANDO: As a student of his work and life, I know more will come, and it will astonish the world.

STRYK: Many writers have blocks, sometimes lasting a long time, particularly if they're as serious as Salinger. The best of his stories, "Franny" say, give the sense that what he can't abide is the useless, the talk about nothing, shams that make up a life. If he doesn't feel able to go beyond this statement, he won't write. Perhaps that's what you mean by barrier?

ANDO: Translated into literary and psychological language, perhaps, but it would be doing Salinger an injustice to reduce in such a way what is a veritable struggle for being. His best works clearly declare his philosophical commitments. It would be wrong to assume he has turned from his quest, and become a mere fictionist with a writing block. No, though I would hesitate to make such claims for others, with Salinger I do not hesitate. Who would deny his genius, the way he penetrates the very soul of contemporary man?

STRYK: You admire, I know, another great contemporary, Zen poet Shinkichi Takahashi. Is he an example of one who has gone through the second barrier?

ANDO: Yes, he is a fully enlightened Zenist—everything he writes bears that out.

STRYK: The fact that he's a lyric poet makes no difference?

ANDO: Why should it? Most poets find it impossible to write with such constant profundity. He's a Zen poet, first, because he's a true Zenist, one who has passed through the second barrier to self-realization—total, unmistakable.

STRYK: Salinger's silence is not confined to writing. He refuses to be interviewed, see anyone, is not interested in public concern with his career.

ANDO: Yes, in that he proves himself. Why should what others expect matter? Only he knows how far he's gone, how far there's still to go. He has no place for time, its chronologies.

STRYK: A remarkable attitude in our day. I know the importance of indifference to petty things, yet even among Zenists it must be quite rare.

ANDO: Not among true Zenists, and there can only be true Zenists—there is no such thing as half-Zenist. One is or one isn't, and if one is, one's attitudes reflect that absolute condition. It's unmistakable.

STRYK: You speak of the enlightened, surely. Most Zenists are hardly that.

ANDO: As you'll appreciate, this is difficult to discuss, but perhaps as one who tries to guide seekers on the way I must speak on the subject. *Kensho* is not realized by all. Those who experience it often wait for years, yet once one's foot is on the proper path, miraculously, one undergoes important change—quite detectable, I can assure you. Students never cease to be amazed as very real changes in attitude, viewpoint overtake them, usually soon after beginning their study. When I speak as I do of Salinger, I have in mind that in order to have gone so far he would have had to experience extraordinary insights, if not *kensho* itself. This his mature stories reveal. Thus I predict, once through the second barrier, he will glow even more brilliantly.

STRYK: Are there examples in Zen history of such development?

ANDO: Zen history is precisely the story of such becoming. There's Hakuin's *Yasenkana*, for example, or any of his writings in which he describes the way in which he rose from one *kensho* plateau to the next. Inspiring reading, I assure you. You have read much of Hakuin?

STRYK: Yes, and what impresses me about him is his moral basis of self-judgment. He found time and again something lacking in himself which *kensho* should have brought him—composure, that sort of thing. Each time he made such a discovery, he immediately went back to the mat for further rigorous training. Is that what you have in mind?

ANDO: Exactly. He knew that the composure, or whatever he desired, was there in him all the time, part of his original self. Some weakness had troubled, beclouded it, but he knew it was there. His writings are remarkable in the way they detail that heroic quest.

STRYK: And Salinger? He must know his creative strength is still within him?

ANDO: Else he'd be selling his precious gift of insight cheaply—to interviewers, gossip magazines.

STRYK: That's what you find in Salinger, then, the gift of insight? More acute than in others?

ANDO: He is a truly philosophical writer, the rarest of breeds—particularly among fiction writers. He has been, and will be again, a writer of wisdom literature.

STRYK: Wisdom literature? You speak of that as something rare. Is not all good literature essentially wisdom literature?

ANDO: Far from it. Most writing, even the finest, doesn't communicate this kind of wisdom. Few writers attempt it, few are sufficiently philosophical in their approach to things to make it possible. Very few indeed.

STRYK: Yet there are writers who, without reference to a given philosophy, create what might be called wisdom literature. T. S. Eliot's *Four Quartets*, for example—philosophical poetry if ever there was any, much of it, as you know, based on Asian insights.

ANDO: "The still point of the turning world." Yes, and remember that in his early years, the most formative intellectually, long before he turned serious Christian, Eliot was a profound student of Asian philosophy, even studying Sanskrit. That sequence of poems might indeed be a form of wisdom literature.

STRYK: What of others without any interest in philosophical thought, Western or Asian? Can they not be writers of wisdom literature?

ANDO: That's stretching things a bit, isn't it? There are limits.

STRYK: I have often wondered. It might be claimed any work with insight, whether story, poem, or philosophical in approach, can convey wisdom of the profoundest kind. I truly feel that. In any case, I'm curious about the restricting nature of such definitions. Is not all insight into reality a kind of wisdom, if only in a limited sense?

ANDO: There, the crux of the problem! Limited sense— I'm glad you added that, in your wisdom! The kind of literature we're discussing does not have limitation, dealing as it does with absolutes unrealized to those whose experiences are confined to the relative. That's the purpose, wouldn't you agree, of philosophy—to define, uphold the absolute? In his early poems, for example, Eliot does not write on the level of the *Four Quartets*—how could he have? It took a lifetime, as he says in one of those poems, of struggle with the inchoate, to come to realizations, whether Christian or generally philosophical, expressed so fully later. In such matters I'm inclined to insist on certain strict definitions.

STRYK: You've written on American Transcendental literature and are a student of Emerson and Thoreau. Do such writers deal with the absolute, according to the definitions you speak of?

ANDO: Pre-eminently—that's why they interest me. I think the Transcendental one of the most important phases of that literature. That's why I study, teach it. Zenists, as you know, value Whitman, Emerson, Thoreau, indeed, are amazed by their closeness to our own great writers, even the masters.

STRYK: I'm aware of that, and think I see connections, yet, frankly, have always been somewhat concerned by the tendency to look afar for similarities and parallels. Studying some of our Transcendentalists carefully, one is likely to become disenchanted. I've never been able to forgive Emerson, for example, for his ambivalence toward Whitman—the initial warm response, then the cold condescension. Hardly the kind of behavior one associates with an enlightened spirit. Thoreau is a case apart, at least in my judgment, very close in spirit to the masters, consistently, in all matters.

ANDO: Yes, one need not look for similarities and parallels. I share your distaste for such attempts at easy syncretism, yet when one finds, anywhere, an essential closeness, surely there's no harm in pointing it out—especially when teaching. It's often a great help.

STRYK: Students who work in Zen with you are probably interested in the arts, therefore somewhat exceptional. Do they read Zen literature extensively?

ANDO: Of course, but our discussions are hardly literary! They concern all major problems of life, the aspirations of those young people. If you were to overhear us, you'd be surprised, I think, to find how basic our concerns are. The usual problems of youth: family, friends. Indeed those who seek instruction are most sensitive to such things, often severely troubled.

STRYK: In the course of working with them you find them becoming more than students to you?

ANDO: Precious humans, rather, with the capacity to become awakened men and women. I stress the need for meditation, we have *zazen* sessions. To open up the mind they are given *koans*—and other things which would be used in guiding at a temple.

STRYK: What happens when one has a severe problem, say death in the family, that sort of thing?

ANDO: I try to imagine what Bankei would have done—nothing was too large or small for him to consider, which is why he was loved by the common people. If a student experiences great loss, as one did recently—it was his father—I try to console him, but also to make him understand, as I had to when my first wife died, that his responsibility is not only to live on but to awaken to reality of life and death, the birthlessness of spirit Bankei and other great masters insisted on. My student seemed genuinely helped by these discussions, and continues to be among the finest it is my privilege to guide.

STRYK: Like other masters, you "guide," not teach.

ANDO: Something of cardinal importance to Zen—we feel it impossible to do more than point the way. The only important discoveries are made by oneself.

STRYK: Do you actively proselytize at the university, in the community?

ANDO: Never! That's unthinkable, just as teaching Zen would be. Again I guide those who come to me, simple as that. It has never been Zen practice, throughout its long history, to lure people to its way. In that it differs from other Buddhist sects. What happens is that someone undergoing discipline informs his friends of his experience, its help in both large ways and small. If they are convinced, feel need themselves, they then approach a master. Almost all have come to me that way, and for such reasons.

STRYK: As teacher, do you approach works from the Zen view?

ANDO: How could I avoid doing so?

STRYK: Then is it difficult for you to be objective? I mean, though there are certain works, particularly nineteenth-century Transcendental works like Thoreau's, which lend themselves easily, naturally to such treatment, most works surely would not. Melville's for example.

ANDO: Approaching works in a Zen state of mind is not claiming there's Zen in them—far from it. I'm the first to admit such practice would be intellectually indefensible. Yet sometimes it's possible to discuss such matters most convincingly from a comparative point of view, as I'm sure you appreciate. The unknown related to the known—historically that's always been the method favored by teachers. Take modern philosophy: Sartre, for example, often writes of fellow philosophers who are not existentialists or phenomenologists, yet they are approached from the point of view of his philosophy.

STRYK: Do you sometimes make comparisons between Salinger and other contemporaries?

ANDO: Often. That's the best way of showing what Salinger's Zen, through fiction, is. I could not do otherwise.

STRYK: If I may pursue that, do you sometimes compare his writings with great Japanese works possessing Zen, Kawabata's say? Or when lecturing on poetry, Emerson with Basho?

ANDO: For me that's the natural way of going about things, though admittedly, with Emerson and Basho, there is very little similarity from a formal viewpoint.

STRYK: Little indeed! And Basho is a great poet, which few would claim for Emerson. Yet you feel, I take it, in spirit they are close?

ANDO: I am interested chiefly in the spiritual content of works I discuss. As a poet, you probably find that somewhat strange?

STRYK: In the sense that I find it impossible to separate form and content, yes. Basho enlightens directly, Emerson versifies enlightened thought. The difference is very great, which is why I could not myself use such a method of teaching. But I realize your approach may lead to greater appreciation and understanding.

ANDO: That's the hope!

STRYK: Are any of your associates at the university, other professors, equally affected by Zen?

ANDO: If you mean professors of literature and philosophy, yes—how could they help being, as Japanese? Even if not consciously, they could not help being touched to some degree by Zen thought. Our arts and philosophy are permeated by it. Even today, while there seems to be declining interest in traditional values, Zen culture is there to be reckoned with as a predominant force in life— true for nearly eight centuries.

STRYK: Always present then, in literature and life?

ANDO: Yes, always there, and all one like myself can do is point to it.

CALENDAR MAKER

Kazuo Takemoto, forty, having failed to become a priest, became a calendar maker, producing calendars illustrated with Zen scrolls and calligraphy well-known throughout Japan. He trained in Zen under the great master Shibayama-roshi, abbot of Nanzenji in Kyoto, who died in 1974. Undergoing strenuous discipline for six months, he then left the temple to begin his life's work, collecting for his superb calendars examples of *sumie* from living masters, one for each month of the year, and printing them with taste and delicacy. Still very much an active Zenist, he returns to Nanzenji for summer and winter *sesshins*, short periods in which disciples and laymen undergo strict training, practicing constant meditation in the most austere circumstances. He says summer *sesshins* are almost unbearable, but doesn't mind those held in winter.

Kazuo Takemoto speaks of Shibayama with warmth, describing him as tough disciplinarian when compared with his equally famous contemporary Mumon-roshi, known to be somewhat lax in spite of being, like Shibayama, a Rinzai master. The differences between these Kyoto masters is borne out by their writings, translated into many languages. Takemoto, once a successful film and television producer, awoke one day disgusted at the hollowness of his fast life and sought an interview with Shibayama. He remembers their meeting, his subsequent experience at Nanzenji, in great detail, is animated when describing them.

His office, simple, bare, has on the walls examples of his inspired calendars, the art thematically suited to the month. With little help, he is busily producing next year's, and excuses himself for the fact that, in order to make calendars of such quality, he must engage in other forms of printing. Each master supplying him with painting or calligraphy must be visited, many works examined, considerable time spent in selecting appropriate works, some of which have actually been made for him. Difficult as all that is, he is completely dedicated, gaining great insight through meeting such distinguished, gifted men.

He has learned two great lessons from Shibayama: devotion and selflessness. Following the master's counsel, he left the temple to try to find a way to spread the word of Zen as far as possible. He took counsel literally, and because he had profound feeling for art, and knew much through his earlier career of printing and publicity, he decided in an inspired moment how to reach out to people. Within six years, thousands all over the world (many of his calendars are ordered from abroad), have had their lives touched daily with his labor of love. Thus he fulfills himself while repaying a debt of gratitude to Shibayama and Zen. He has a most sincere, engaging manner.

STRYK: Besides distinguishing yourself as calendar maker, you are known as a *kendo* expert. How does your feeling for the sword meet with your interest in Zen?

TAKEMOTO: In *kendo* we learn the sword is used only against evil, in the opponent, his illusion. Early in *kendo* training the disciple is shown how curved ends of many swords form an *enso* (mystical circle), a thing of great importance.

STRYK: Fascinating. I'm familiar with the many paintings of the *enso*, the superb one by Hakuin's best pupil Torei, for example, but had no idea it had existence as a symbol outside art. Is its meaning in *kendo* similar, something like spiritual perfection?

TAKEMOTO: Precisely. As all involved in *kendo*, I have very complex feelings toward the sword. Are you interested, by the way, in the writer Mishima?

STRYK: Very much.

TAKEMOTO: Then perhaps you might know Mishima, the day before his ritual suicide, phoned Shibayama-roshi and begged the opportunity to discuss Zen and the sword. Evidently he was very troubled, and Shibayama told him he would be glad to meet next day. Well, he didn't show up. Shibayama was convinced—we all were when we heard what happened—that he could have swayed him from disaster, saved him.

STRYK: Amazing! Had they ever met?

TAKEMOTO: I'm not sure, but Mishima had high regard for the master's writings, knew his reputation as a wise man.

STRYK: Most incredible. Is it customary for non-Zenists like Mishima to seek help of masters in times of stress?

TAKEMOTO: I can't say how frequently that happens, but since Zen masters are revered by all, it wouldn't surprise me if it happens often. In their writings masters touch on the deepest emotions, attracting especially, I'd imagine, sensitive men like Mishima.

STRYK: Sensitive? Brilliant, perhaps, but I wonder how sensitive. I can't imagine a man whose actions were more opposed to the Zen spirit than Mishima's—self-indulgence, glorification of violence, that sort of thing. Though sadly nothing came of his last cry for help, it does great credit to Shibayama-roshi's memory that of all masters he alone was sought by that unfortunate man. Was it perhaps in part because of Shibayama's interest in swordsmanship?

TAKEMOTO: He had no interest in *kendo*, though he might have mentioned it in writing.

STRYK: Are you still involved in *kendo*, do you practice?

TAKEMOTO: Too little, I'm afraid. I'm busy these days trying to make a living selling calendars!

STRYK: Different from the old days, when your life, somewhat more worldly, was spent making films and TV specials? I know you've no regrets. Apart from summer and winter retreats, do you still do *zazen*?

TAKEMOTO: No, I can't imagine doing *zazen* on my own. Where would I? You see, to me a home is not a *zendo*.

STRYK: Yet there must be in your life, the way you see things, something that's a result of those long periods of meditation.

TAKEMOTO: Unquestionably, but how would one describe it—I'm no literary man! I feel my experience at Nanzenji transformed me, altogether. When I go for the retreats, it's as if I'm returning home, had never been away. I meet old friends, sometimes new people, including foreigners. In fact last summer an American sat with us. A very clever man! He brought some sort of incense with him —foul-smelling stuff—to keep off the mosquitoes. It seemed to work —fine for him, but bad for those near him—we were bitten all the more! An example, I suppose, of your compatriots' famous ingenuity!

STRYK: That's a great story. Shibayama-roshi visited America, as you know. Did he speak much of those trips?

TAKEMOTO: From time to time, and very warmly. He once said—I remember, for it made such an impression on us all— Zen is as much the world's as Japan's. I'm assisting at the moment in something which may be an outgrowth of his attitude, attempting to organize an exchange of Zen students with other countries. The planning is in an advanced stage—we had a conference a short time ago. All that comes from Shibayama-roshi. As his visits overseas and many writings show, he was strongly convinced that Zen was something which could benefit the world.

STRYK: Is that generally a Rinzai view?

TAKEMOTO: No, I wouldn't say so. I'm not sure to what degree, if at all, other sects reach out that way. The organization I mentioned is of the Nanzenji branch of Rinzai. I suppose, though, there are Soto and Obaku Zenists who feel this way.

STRYK: What do you think of other sects?

TAKEMOTO: I don't know much about Obaku—rarely discuss it—but Soto, well, I don't think much of it, I'm afraid. As you see, I'm a frank character! Shibayama-roshi occasionally spoke of distinctions among sects, but only when asked, as you are asking now —a very delicate subject. As you might expect, though, he was never critical of others. But, in going into distinctions, he made it fairly clear that through demanding more Rinzai would draw the very best from us.

STRYK: How did he make those distinctions, what did he say?

TAKEMOTO: Well, once he explained it this way: gold found in the earth, in order to become useful, valuable, must be processed. That's very much the Rinzai attitude. Soto Zenists, Shibayama-roshi felt, believe it is valuable as found.

STRYK: It is still gold.

TAKEMOTO: Yes, but in the master's view, and mine, that's far from good enough!

STRYK: Then, frankly, you've scant use for Soto Zen?

TAKEMOTO: How could I have, trained into Rinzai? It's not enough to sit without an effort. Nothing there, nothing happening—isn't likely to lead toward awakening, the experience we hope for.

STRYK: Have you had *kensho?*

TAKEMOTO: Not I, far from it. But that doesn't change my way of thinking, for I've worked alongside men who have, seen the results.

STRYK: Can you be sure?

TAKEMOTO: Absolutely—it cannot be faked by anyone.

STRYK: When you go back to Nanzenji for the seasonal retreats, is that your hope and quest?

TAKEMOTO: No longer, I'm afraid. It was my hope at one time—the greatest of my life.

STRYK: Then why keep returning, disciplining yourself for hours in heat and cold? If you no longer have such expectations, why?

TAKEMOTO: Perhaps I'm—what's the word—a masochist! As you've no doubt discovered, it's difficult examining a matter like *satori.* Fundamentally there's little, if anything, one can say. Masters, men like Shibayama-roshi, his successors at Nanzenji, discourage talk and speculation of that kind. If it comes, it comes when least expected.

STRYK: Well, let me put it this way: would you really go to those retreats without some hope?

TAKEMOTO: Admittedly there's hope! But one's ordinary self can hardly vision it will happen. When you consider the long road to such experience, all those aspects of life making it possible, or impossible, there's simply no real way of preparing. One can do too much, one probably does too little—each of us is different. There's the master, awakened, an exceptional human whose experience in turn has been testified to by a distinguished master, one whose life reveals him a man of *satori*—and there are disciples, not knowing where to go, always groping. The only sure thing is that the master is aware of our dilemma, and what he says or does is for our good.

STRYK: Please do not answer if this troubles you, but did you leave Nanzenji because you discovered you weren't cut out for the life, and were unlikely to qualify for the priesthood—unlikely to have *kensho?*

TAKEMOTO: Who knows why I left, why I sought

acceptance at the temple in the first place? I felt a powerful need when I began, a need for all Zen held before me—an equally powerful desire to try the lessons learnt from Zen, back in the world of affairs. As you see, I turned out a poor Zenist, in most ways a failure!

STRYK: That's too hard, surely, when through production and distribution of these beautiful calendars you're advancing the cause of Zen—exactly what Shibayama-roshi wanted for you. That seems far from failure to me.

TAKEMOTO: It's not all that selfless—I am making a living! But perhaps . . . we all have our aspirations, everyone, one way or another, fails to reach the highest of his goals. Perhaps that's how it's always been, even should be. We're all cut out for different roles, are lucky to learn in time. I know now I could never be a guide. I am a follower, a grateful one, who reveres men like Shibayama-roshi because life is enriched by them. That's enough for anyone, at least one with my limitations!

STRYK: Then you don't regret leaving Nanzenji so soon? Do you sometimes wonder whether with more time and effort you might have succeeded?

TAKEMOTO: At first, and for some time, I wondered, was bitterly disappointed in myself. I thought of all the difficulties I had there, particularly with *koans*. I suppose I'm somewhat simpleminded: they were too much for me. I was inclined to see them as little more than crazy stories, and was astonished that I'd imagined I could live in such a way. In any case I never came up with satisfactory interpretations—often during *dokusan* I'd laugh aloud!

STRYK: What did the master do?

TAKEMOTO: Well, he didn't join in the laughter!

STRYK: Were you told your interpretations of *koan*, and so on, were unsatisfactory, or did you feel it in yourself?

TAKEMOTO: Both! I was told all right—in no uncertain terms, I may add. You know Zen masters aren't shy about such things, especially Nanzenji masters, known for strictness.

STRYK: But in only six months, even if you had found interpretations of *koan*, is it not likely the master would have found other things to criticize? I thought it's always done, even with promising disciples, to keep them on guard?

TAKEMOTO: So I tried to feel, but no, that's not the way it was. I felt trapped, no way out, so tried to make use of reason or, remembering how I'd cope in my former life, became cagey. That made matters worse, I felt myself becoming neurotic—no exaggeration, I really felt that I was going mad. I'd calm down for awhile, begin absorbing temple life, then with another *dokusan* about to take place, I felt things come apart. Finally I had to face up honestly to problems. I talked with fellow disciples, and though some expressed grave doubts, none seemed to have problems as serious. For me, then, leaving the temple was not just the best, it was the only solution. Only then I talked with Shibayama-roshi about my future.

STRYK: And as a result you decided to produce Zen calendars?

TAKEMOTO: Oh no, that came later. As a result, I knew I had to do something in the world, be useful to others, to myself—and so to Zen. I wanted to repay the many things, in spite of pain, discipline had brought me. Suddenly I was inspired, and all kinds of ideas came.

STRYK: You were still at the temple?

TAKEMOTO: Yes—I felt I couldn't leave without a clear idea of what I'd do. The plan to produce Zen calendars came all at once, I knew I could carry it out. I really felt my life change!

STRYK: Did you know at the time you would never leave the discipline, returning for retreats and so on?

TAKEMOTO: That was Shibayama-roshi's suggestion. Frankly, at first I didn't feel I could—I'd made such a botch of things! Returning would only remind me of past failure. It was only when attending the first *sesshin*, the summer after formally leaving Nanzenji, that I knew it was the perfect answer. In fact, I found more that way than ever before. That was the biggest surprise of all! I was more relaxed, relieved to feel, I suppose, that not too much was expected of me. Suddenly things clarified, I was even able to handle *koans* with some success. It was exactly the right path, and I've not backtracked since.

WOOD CARVER

Son of a father whose father passed the legacy, the craft of wood-carving, to him, Hirohisa Kobayashi, carver of Buddhist sculpture and *Noh* masks, resides in Nara, a city where such legacies are commonplace. Nara, Japan's capital when Buddhism was introduced into the country, has always been the center of Buddhist art. Born there, Kobayashi has a small house dominated by his studio. The calligraphy over the entrance to his studio, vivid on a rough-hewn board, reads, "Every cut of the knife leads to Nirvana."

This most distinguished artist is also an accomplished *Noh* actor, and has practiced Zen discipline for many years. He carves on a large butcher's block when roughing out a work, then whittles with the object pressed between the knees, the traditional way of carvers in Japan. He is tall and spare with a thin, sensitive face, his hands firm, heavily-veined. He welcomes me together with his plump and smiling wife, who brings in tea, small cakes, and sliced *nashi* (Japanese pears). As we speak, she sits near on a cushion listening intently, proud as her husband tells about his work. Soon their son, home from school, is called to meet me. He too will be a carver of Buddhist sculpture.

As he speaks there is a child-like eagerness in Hirohisa Kobayashi's face. His work has been his life since a small boy, now he is passing the gift to his son, who at this stage, he confides, is not too enthusiastic. He says that at forty-seven he still learns with every undertaking, that he expects to be doing so forever. He works in the distinctive *Itobori* manner—quick, direct, close in spirit to *sumie*, for, like the painter, he cannot afford one false stroke. Itobori has long been associated with Zen.

The work I see is strong, especially the *Noh* play characters close to three feet in height. Other carvings, small, delicate things, some but six inches, are exquisite. These he shows wearing soft white gloves to protect the painted surface, and the painting is wonderful. He shows me pieces of a lord and lady, replicas of superb works finished recently for a friend of the provincial governor's daughter, who on seeing them wanted exact copies for herself. He seems a little troubled as he tells me this, and I plan to ask if this is something he often does. At his bench I see knives, brushes, paints, and work in progress. To my delight, he shows me a small, beautifully made image of a prince, and saying it is mine, places it in a fine wood box.

STRYK: When you spoke of producing replicas of those beautiful carvings for the friend of the governor's daughter, I sensed that was something you would rather not have done. Was I right?

KOBAYASHI: I'm afraid you were. It gave me quite a problem, but since it rarely happens I agreed to do it. Like all carvers, I work best when into something new, making replicas is somehow degrading—certainly it's boring! Yet it was a good commission; one must live.

STRYK: You are known best as an *Itobori* carver. When you do such work, it must go very fast?

KOBAYASHI: Not everything I do is in the *Itobori* manner—those companion pieces we discussed, for example. My *Itobori* works are usually *Noh* characters, the carving I most enjoy— then I can be myself, for such work is interpretive, the nature of one's character expressed in every knife-cut.

STRYK: Your *Noh* characters live for you? Like portraits of living people?

KOBAYASHI: Yes and no. Each of course has its mask, that's a constant. But it's possible, nevertheless, through gesture, stance, and other things, to suggest character.

STRYK: As at a particular moment of the play?

KOBAYASHI: For me, yes. It might be too much to imagine that others see a character at a particular moment. As most associate him with an action, I often portray a character in mid-dance —always the most dramatic point in *Noh.*

STRYK: The *Itobori* method is wonderfully suited to that work, yet the small, delicate things seem altogether different. One couldn't imagine greater contrast.

KOBAYASHI: Each piece, even each *Noh* piece, is approached differently, whatever the method. One thing is certain— they all give me trouble!

STRYK: In what way?

KOBAYASHI: Well, I work slowly, deliberately, thinking of the piece in hand both day and night. Occasionally a solution will come when I'm in bed. I get up to the challenge, work for hours— it's always been that way. Fortunately, my wife is understanding!

STRYK: Your works are very intricate, made of one piece of wood, including the fan and sword held in the hand. That must give great problems.

KOBAYASHI: At all times! Take the folds, creases in a dress: one of the formal problems of my art. It might be said one knows a carver by folds that fall in a kimono.

STRYK: You must have trained carefully in painting. Did that come naturally to you?

KOBAYASHI: Japanese carvers work at painting equally, for however fine the carving, if the painting doesn't match it in all ways, the piece will fail. The painting of a face, making the eyes just right for instance, takes years of training.

STRYK: Training and insight, surely? With all the training in the world, a carver could not make a head convincing unless he had some sort of insight into character. Are all your works commissioned, or do you carve things for yourself?

KOBAYASHI: For myself? Well, for exhibitions, which I have from time to time at galleries and museums. That's where my best work goes.

STRYK: Often?

KOBAYASHI: Not often enough! Because I have to feel the pieces are not only worthy but complement each other to some degree, particularly *Itobori* work, *Noh* figures, and the like. You see, an exhibition when carefully arranged gives a sense of progression.

STRYK: I assume you mean your development as artist?

KOBAYASHI: No, since for the most part I exhibit new work. I mean mood, or perhaps, intensity. I may show as many as thirty, forty pieces. Takes me a long time to plan, a nerve-racking yet exhilarating process.

STRYK: I was always under the impression that curators, gallery owners arranged exhibitions, with the artist's approval.

KOBAYASHI: I can't imagine that!

STRYK: You have won much fame. Is that the result chiefly of such exhibitions?

KOBAYASHI: I think so: they are written about, attracting attention to the work. There's another aspect which, though not interesting to speak of, is nevertheless important—my works are sold. And with commissions that provides livelihood.

STRYK: I know you are a carver of *Noh* masks, masks somewhat rigidly defined as to types—is there room for individuality?

KOBAYASHI: Well, a mask is fixed by tradition, the most famous type being *hana no komote* (Flower of the *Noh* Mask): there can be no obvious departure from the norm. Yet to a connoisseur, there are perceptible differences, fineness of detail, quality of lacquer, that sort of thing. Yes, I believe it possible to distinguish oneself in this difficult art—not that I think I've done so! Perhaps another twenty years!

STRYK: Does acting in *Noh* plays make a difference to your work with masks?

KOBAYASHI: Much, I should think. I might not have studied them so deeply had I not acted in *Noh*. For many years I've been a passionate devotee of the art. Living here in Nara how could I help but be? Besides, it's a family tradition.

STRYK: Are your masks used in performances?

KOBAYASHI: Yes—that's why I have none here to show you. Even the ones I use are kept at the local *Noh* hall. I supply masks from time to time for *Noh* groups, generally new companies. The older ones have their masks for generations and take great care to preserve them. There's a mystical feeling about a mask; all in *Noh* feel it strongly.

STRYK: Not a good prospect for a hungry carver!

KOBAYASHI: Well, I can't blame them for trying to preserve their masks. One can hardly be expected to carve such masks these days.

STRYK: A humble attitude—why not?

KOBAYASHI: Far from it. It's simply true. Why? Well, for one thing artists like myself can't afford sufficient time to their making. In the old days, say around a hundred years ago, a carver was paid handsomely, commissioned by a company to make masks. Could devote all his time, indefinitely, to the project. Thus the work was superb. Often he worked alongside a great company, with costume-makers, other craftsmen. A lost world, I'm afraid.

STRYK: True of Buddhist sculptors too, wasn't it? I mean sculptors and carvers worked for temples.

KOBAYASHI: Hundreds of years ago, when our great temples were created, carvers were engaged for years, not months. Time to make masterpieces such as the great gate, Kora Mon, at Nishi Hogangi Temple in Kyoto. I'm sure you know it?

STRYK: I do indeed—one of the most extraordinary feats of man.

KOBAYASHI: I've spent weeks studying details on that gate: powerful, complex, yet such great refinement. One of the few real wonders of the world, each line a Buddhist inspiration.

STRYK: Would you be happy carving such a project?

KOBAYASHI: Happy? Blessed! But of course I could not do it justice—no one living now could. We've lost whatever it takes, yet we go on and do the best we can.

STRYK: Are you intimidated by such works, made to feel small?

KOBAYASHI: As poet do you not have similar feelings about Shakespeare, Dante?

STRYK: Of course, but it's the poet's hope to express his own time, in his own way, and I imagined one in any art to feel the same.

KOBAYASHI: As Buddhist I can't feel such comfort. No, I would be too easy on myself, and my contemporaries, feeling we exist merely to express our time. I have often asked myself, since my emotions are so strong, so fully directed by Buddhism, why it isn't in my power to create a masterwork like Kora Mon. I simply do not have the energy, the vision. Sad but true . . . .

STRYK: But you might have had in those times—do you feel that?

KOBAYASHI: Perhaps I haven't made myself quite clear. I glory in works like Kora Mon, without envy or regret—the world would be an empty place without them. They were made lovingly for us, for all capable of being moved, enlightened by them. Yet for one like me, well, it's wonderful to be able to contribute, in this age, even small things to that tradition.

STRYK: Since *Itobori* carving is associated with Zen, and you are a Zenist, could you tell me a little of the way in which the discipline affects your life and work?

KOBAYASHI: Though true the *Itobori* method is associated in the minds of art historians with Zen, I'm not sure all those employing it are Zenists, even connect what they do with the philosophy. Things are never clear and simple as art historians and critics make them out to be. I suppose what they have in mind is the swiftness and directness of *Itobori* carving—it's true in such respects it resembles other arts of Zen, *sumie* certainly, but that's far as it goes.

STRYK: What of yourself?

KOBAYASHI: I've been a Zenist all my thinking life, as many with an interest in *Noh*. That's not difficult to explain: *Noh* developed along clear aesthetic principles derived from Zen thought, and, as you know, our earliest practitioners and writers, like Zeami, were profound Zenists. My family, my life and art have always been affected by it. You know, I've never been asked this before, and find it tough. I suppose the way might be to relate my work to one of the most cherished Zen ideals, though I don't think I've lived up to it: I mean in order to create anything, we must first create ourselves.

STRYK: Could you explain a little more?

KOBAYASHI: I'll try! In Zen there's strong belief man must be awakened to his true being, his original self—that takes great effort and long periods of meditation.

STRYK: Chiefly a Rinzai view, at least as you express it. Is that your sect?

KOBAYASHI: Yes, but I don't think the feeling is peculiar to Rinzai. In any case, all Zenists believe, as men and artists, nothing good is realized until the true self is attained. I know that sounds very mysterious, indeed is rarely talked about except by Zen masters and expounders on the subject, yet it's fully understood by Zenists.

STRYK: Is it perhaps a way of saying that before work can be strong and pure, the man must be?

KOBAYASHI: Yes, but it takes far more than qualities of character to make fine works, character in itself would be far from enough. Yet assuming the artist has the gift, training, and perserverance, those qualities will affect his work—which must be true everywhere.

STRYK: Westerners speak of style being the man, but not the style or man being of a special type. In Zen, since there's a certain way of dealing with reality, a particular kind of art results— it's unmistakable. Let's think of an example. Yes, in *Itobori* carving, as all true Zen art, there's avoidance of ornament, line being pure, uncluttered, that sort of thing.

KOBAYASHI: True, that much can be said, yet I'm troubled: one just can't talk about these things. They have to be absorbed over the years, a way of dealing with reality that may be as much Japanese as Zen. I don't know. It's true Zen's insistence on meditation gives its arts a special quality, distinct from other ways of working.

STRYK: Perhaps then we can say no more. Do you meditate regularly?

KOBAYASHI: Even that's hard to answer. If you mean formally, no. At one time I did, of course, under a master. Once in the habit one looks at things a certain way, even when no longer practicing *zazen*. And there are other aspects of discipline that stay with one, affect one's view of life. I'm sorry I can't be more specific. The one thing interesting me is carving—it absorbs everything else.

STRYK: When you were meditating under a master, did you have *kensho?*

KOBAYASHI: I truly don't know—that must sound odd. I mean, like all Zenists, I had sudden realizations which transformed my life. Have them still, realizations which might be *kensho.* A layman's type, perhaps.

STRYK: Layman's type?

KOBAYASHI: I must explain, though you understand I'm on shaky ground when talking of these things. Those entering temples who aspire to priesthood rarely have expectations of true *kensho* experiences. They're always saying that, and I believe them. It takes years, extraordinary application, something very few even at temples and monasteries can give. Like them, I can't claim to have had *kensho,* yet I wonder at the reluctance to consider certain unmistakable revelations in such light. Perhaps the difficulty is in the words we use to describe them and their effects.

STRYK: I often wonder at the reluctance myself. Were your insights always related to your art?

KOBAYASHI: Not directly, yet in some way. I suppose any realization of that kind is always translated into life-and-work terms. Has to be, if genuine. Anyway that's been my case for years.

STRYK: Perhaps that's why you are spoken of as Zen artist.

KOBAYASHI: I am? How interesting! Well, again that's probably because of *Itobori*. On that subject I've told you what I think. I wonder what a real Zen artist is? Isn't he first of all a Zenist who happens to be at the same time an artist?

STRYK: Like the poet Basho?

KOBAYASHI: Decidedly. His *haiku* are perfect examples of Zen, so it seems to me—I'm not really very learned in literary history. I do remember reading how he trained in Zen.

STRYK: Do you find yourself inspired by other arts? *Haiku* for example?

KOBAYASHI: Very much. Always I see connections between such arts and my own. Natural, perhaps. I like to feel my best carvings have the flow of pure *haiku*, and of course sumie. That may be wishful thinking!

STRYK: Have you ever written *haiku*, or practiced other arts?

KOBAYASHI: I once tried writing a *Noh* play, the only serious poetry I've attempted. When young, like many, I suppose, I wrote some *haiku*—meant for my wife chiefly. I never thought of them as poems to show. And there is *Noh* performance, which I've done for years—that's surely a Zen art.

STRYK: Has acting in *Noh* given as much pleasure as carving?

KOBAYASHI: In a sense, far more! But that's because, in spite of my love for it, *Noh* is not my life. Carving is not only my profession, it's my life's blood. What I feel for it is far more complex than words could suggest. I am as much enraged, you see, as inspired. Mainly though, I'm troubled at my inability to do the work I so want to do.

STRYK: Carve a Kora Mon?

KOBAYASHI: Yes, in a way. That which would extend and challenge more than that I normally do. Don't misunderstand, I'm not frustrated, most times I feel content with what I do. Yet always one aspires to finer, better things, faced with reality of one's small gifts and dwindling energies.

STRYK: But you're not old.

KOBAYASHI: Twenty years ago I had great energy, wildness of spirit—tried anything! If someone had ordered, "Carve a temple gate to rival Kora Mon," I would have plunged right in. It would not have turned out well, for, though I had the drive, I'd scant experience, the knowledge. An old story, I'm afraid. Today I may have the skill, but I also know my limitations. At times that saddens, makes the satisfaction you mention impossible.

STRYK: Yet all respect your work, and you have fame.

KOBAYASHI: Fame, respect. I'm grateful, to be sure, these make living the way I do possible. When I compare myself with others, I know I'm fortunate, but I must be honest with you, as with myself. I know what I can do, but it's accomplished at the expense of great effort and the hardly suppressed knowledge that it's not enough. My strengths are balanced against the limitations I've accepted; I've no self-satisfaction. Yet, each time my knife cuts into wood, I'm challenged—perhaps one can't ask for more.

STRYK: Your works give pleasure to so many—you are to be envied for the life you live.

KOBAYASHI: Perhaps that's the real answer to your question. A serious artist can never be content with all he does, but must at all times reach to others: in a profound sense must live for them.

OBAKU
ZEN MASTER

Mampukuji, main temple of the Obaku Sect, set on spacious tree-filled grounds, unique for its Chinese style—in form and color—is visited by those mindful of architecture and the arts. Every worthy book on Japanese temple art has illustrations of its structures and wood sculpture, among the most illustrious in existence. Gemyo Murasei-roshi, sixty, is abbot of Mampukuji, which has many sub-temples within its grounds, situated not far from Kyoto in Uji, a district famous for its tea fields. Founded by the Chinese master Ingen just over two hundred years ago, Mampukuji was the first Obaku temple and from the start considered foreign by Rinzai and Soto.

Knowing of my interest in Zen art, Murasei-roshi kindly takes me to the temple's Treasure House, where, among other true treasures, there are calligraphic scrolls by Ingen, impressive Bodhisattvas by great Kano School painters, remarkable sculptures in both metal and wood and, most moving to me, having always cared deeply for his work, a large collection of scrolls by Ike-no-Taiga, who approximately two hundred years ago trained in Zen here. The treasure house is carefully tended and a keeper is always present, assuring that no one touches this rare and fragile collection.

I have long known of Murasei-roshi as abbot, and editor of perhaps the most influential monthly dealing with, and entitled,

Zen. The magazine has a circulation of around three thousand throughout the world. The master is deeply informed on all aspects of the philosophy, the magazine not confined to Obaku Zen. I have many things to ask, but first he takes me round the temple grounds, and as we stroll explains, points out a structure, stops to admire a view of the surrounding countryside. He loves the temple he has served for forty years, is overjoyed to see how much I value all he shows me. He is extremely vital, laughing easily. As we leave one building for another, he is greeted warmly, with considerable respect, by priests and acolytes, even laymen wandering about the grounds—all stopping to bow before him.

Many companies send employees to train as laymen under him and his assistants for a week or two, the purpose being to gain confidence and self-composure. It always pleases him to see them: he welcomes their interest in Zen, which is bound to do much good. He is here to serve all men, from every walk of life. I am impressed by his patience and kindness, but since he will soon have to meet disciples for *dokusan*, his most important work, for which he must always prepare mentally, he suggests we return to Ryokuji-in, which also serves as Zen Culture Center for Youth. Reaching his large office, comfortable, hung with scrolls, photos, and testimonials, we are served tea by an assistant. After some easy conversation, he is ready to answer questions.

STRYK: You are aware that in the minds of most with interest in Zen, your sect is less considered. In the West, for example, though many know Rinzai and Soto, hardly anyone hears of Obaku. Does that trouble you?

MURASEI: Why should it? We are here to serve the ones who come to us, and many do. It is inevitable, considering our history, that we do not reach as many as the other sects. That never troubles us.

STRYK: Some think of Obaku as an "in-between" sect, perhaps having in mind your use of *koans* and, what's more unusual for a Zen sect, your chanting of Nembutsu (invocation of the Savior Bodhisattva Amida). Though traditional in many ways, you avoid the scriptures. Could you comment?

MURASEI: Well, that does appear to be our reputation, puzzling many, especially from afar. The reason for our strange way?

Perhaps we are trying to catch up—the others certainly had a head start on us! It is our purpose, a very well-defined one, I may add, to reach many, using all methods to make that possible. I suspect that is what's behind the somewhat purist criticism often levelled against us.

STRYK: Some feel your sect too syncretistic, offering everything to all, thus perhaps losing individuality.

MURASEI: The logic of that escapes me! In what sense lose individuality—there are surely many forms of individuality, even an amalgam has *that*. In any case, there you have the proof of their illusion: what, after all, is sect, what importance has it in the grand scheme of things? So-called differences are not as clear-cut, large as some might think—far from it. The greatest may be our use of the Nembutsu, which, by the way, we treasure. It helps establish a strong religious base—Zen, after all, is a religion, something which in their emphasis on disciplinary formalities others sometimes play down. If the chanting of Nembutsu makes us more popular in approach, less élitist, well, that's fine, the way it should be. We want to attract, and feel no shame about it!

STRYK: You do employ *koan*, of course, but as strictly as Rinzai?

MURASEI: That depends on masters—some are strict, some less so, in both sects. Certainly we believe in the importance of *koan* training, and we use the same *koans*, which after all are the possessions of no single sect.

STRYK: Rinzai masters take pride in their severity, in *koan* practice—are you personally thought severe?

MURASEI: The young here seem to think so! Yet I dislike the word severe—very misleading. Strict, yes. In fact, it is the greatest kindness to be strict in things designed to help. How easy to be lax, but it would defeat the purpose of the *koan*, which is meant precisely to keep a student on guard.

STRYK: Scriptures: do you avoid them as much as other sects?

MURASEI: I'm afraid I just don't know, never having made a comparative study. You must understand that, looked at from outside, sects might appear to differ as your questions suggest, but we are not—at least I am not—conscious of such matters. Far too busy! We don't recommend scriptural study, since students tend often to rely on learning, thinking it a substitute for what is all important— inner growth. A master, on the other hand, whatever he says about those dangers, is likely to know the scriptures well, find inspiration in them. I certainly do, read them constantly. What's more, I'm expected to.

STRYK: In part due to your being editor of *Zen?*

MURASEI: I don't think so, though many of our articles deal with scriptures. Consequently we have to know them well. No, I would be a student of scripture even if I were not editor of the magazine—which, by the way, is open to all sects, and read by all.

STRYK: When training, were you cautioned against them?

MURASEI: Not in so many words, far from it. They were simply not discussed much. It was made clear whatever truth the training would reveal was to be found in myself, not words, however exalted.

STRYK: How do you go about the problem with disciples, especially the studious ones?

MURASEI: By making them know the necessity of concentrating on personal development, suggesting they spend less time —in some cases, none—on reading. Meditation is everything, including and containing all that characterizes Zen. Like all sects, we emphasize work in the *zendo.*

STRYK: Do Obaku Zenists meditate precisely the same way as others?

MURASEI: Yes, but again depending on the masters. Some are traditional, more strict than others. As I've said, though I'm thought strict, I'm certainly not hard. We sit in lotus, and demand as much of ourselves as others. It is in the *zendo* rather than the library most important discoveries are made; hence, we encourage very serious meditation.

STRYK: As all masters you give *teisho* (lectures): do yours differ from those of others?

MURASEI: Of course—we don't parrot each other: unthinkable! In *teisho* a master distinguishes himself. I simply try to be myself, drawing from experience, the wisdom—if any!—I possess. My *teisho* are generally short, as most; their purpose to lead toward the awakened self.

STRYK: Do you give *teisho* on scriptures?

MURASEI: Not the whole of a scripture. Sometimes a sentence or two, a parable, rarely more. Mainly I lecture on ordinary things—the season, holidays, social ills, whatever interests me at the moment.

STRYK: As a lover of Zen arts, do you use Zen poems in your *teisho?*

MURASEI: From time to time—an enlightenment or death poem, a great *haiku.* When, that is, I think disciples may be familiar with the piece. Few of them are literary types, you see. I have to be cautious about introducing unfamiliar material.

STRYK: I'm surprised. Surely some respond to poetry.

MURASEI: A few, by no means all, and when I lecture it must be to all. Though there are some who have little to do with poetry, all are capable of appreciating insights of poetry, when pointed out.

STRYK: Do you prepare *teisho* carefully, using notes?

MURASEI: I don't use notes because it's best to be informal at such times, yet I think well on what I'm going to say, as you might expect.

STRYK: From what you say, I gather there are great differences among disciples. Are some more competent than others? I ask because in other sects such things are dwelt on: great masters like Hui-neng seemed so élitist, claiming in no uncertain terms their Zen was meant for the gifted. Do you consider such things?

MURASEI: I have great respect for the Sixth Patriarch, but what he said must be viewed in perspective. Zen was being formed in his time, indeed he was most instrumental in its rapid development in T'ang China. He must have felt a need to stress that Zen was meant only for those willing to make great personal sacrifice, the kind he himself had made. Thus, when he spoke of the less-gifted, he must have had in mind those incapable of gaining from Zen. He wanted to show the exceptional character of training, which is why he spoke of it being meant for the exceptional. When he is quoted in our time, such historical conditions are not borne in mind.

STRYK: Would Hui-neng have thought those who train with you exceptional?

MURASEI: What matters surely is that I think them so! I cannot claim Hui-neng would think them so, but I believe Ingen, the founder of our sect, would have been pleased with them.

STRYK: Do you choose carefully? Are some rejected?

MURASEI: Rejected? Those who come know great

demands will be made on them. That's enough to discourage all but the most earnest. Yes, they are chosen most carefully, for their own good.

STRYK: Do most stay on, complete their training?

MURASEI: If you mean for the priesthood, no, not all complete the training. Often things get in the way, personal things over which they have no control. Others find training too arduous, but we don't think of them as having failed, not at all. There are many things people do for which their training here prepares them better in one way or another.

STRYK: Could you explain?

MURASEI: Whatever one decides, he will have benefitted by serious training, whatever the duration. So long as the discipline has been carried on honestly, sincerely, whatever is done in the world will be to some degree affected—that's self-evident.

STRYK: Yet surely the point of training is to lead toward awakening, is it not?

MURASEI: Ideally, but few are awakened, even among those entering the priesthood.

STRYK: All masters say that, but historically isn't that the purpose of Zen life?

MURASEI: Awakening is easy—stimulating—to speak about. In the West dramatic *satori* experiences are always being discussed. We tend to be skeptical about that sort of thing—indeed consider it somewhat misleading, even dangerous. For one thing, it can be very discouraging to be told the chief purpose of Zen life is awakening—very few, after all, have such experience, and those who do are most reluctant to discuss it. They're hardly expected to, through fear, I suppose, of expressing improperly what is, all know, wordless. That is, if real, it is overpowering in effect. Very few have the gift to describe such a happening.

STRYK: Whether or not one was capable of expressing what happened, could you tell if it had?

MURASEI: I would like to think so. Occasionally I have observed dramatic progress which only sudden and great insight could have brought about. Yet such inward experience cannot be dealt with as, say, scientific discovery described in terms of formulae. One isn't suddenly possessed with the gift of tongue, however momentous the experience.

STRYK: Isn't that one of the major roles of poetry in Zen, expression of such insight?

MURASEI: When one is a natural poet, yes. How many are? For some it would not be possible to write convincingly of anything, however consummate the event. That's the advantage lettered men have always had, why we value so highly the achievements of great masters like Dogen, Hakuin, and Ingen.

STRYK: Leading to the intriguing thought that there might have been many whose Zen experience was as profound but who could not express what happened.

MURASEI: That's always been the way, I'm sure.

STRYK: Yet, as you've pointed out, the master is able to determine whether a disciple, whatever his gifts of expression, is awakened. There would be change in him, even great change?

MURASEI: To be sure, but such changes are rarely attributed to *satori*, even if the result of it. The disciples would not, for the most part, be disposed to talk about change in such terms. If asked about differences in behavior and attitude, he might simply say he has begun to glimpse the truth of certain things, or meditation has begun to enrich his insight—all quite normal, when you consider that's precisely the role of meditation.

STRYK: Once I might have thought such reticence to discuss *satori* due to sect, but having talked with Rinzai Zenists, I find all equally reluctant. I'm surprised: so much literature I've worked with stresses awakening.

MURASEI: Yes, but bear in mind it deals with experiences of extraordinary men, those who in Christianity might be deemed saints. You can't expect most of us to have equal experiences, or what is as much to the point, as we've observed, equal gifts of expression. In that sense, I suppose, the literature can be misleading as to what actually goes on in temples and monasteries—what always went on, even in the days of masters like Dogen and Ingen.

STRYK: For posterity it's obviously important that there are such men, in all cultures, but what has impressed me about Zen is that it has a number of *dō*, or Ways, among them *Kadō*, the way of poetry. Some of the other *dō*, *Judō*, for example, are of course non-literary, yet it is possible through following such a Way—as in *Judō* classes here at the Ryokuji-in—for one to gain as much of Zen as through any other Way. That's unique to Zen. I've thought of it as something like a wheel, the hub being the truth offered, each spoke like a *dō*. The spokes would have equal importance, all attached to the hub. Now it's that kind of thing I have in mind when asking how a disciple's progress can be judged.

MURASEI: I don't teach *Judō*, I'm afraid! You are right, of course—one Way is as important as the next—all lead to truth of Zen. But you must know we do not actively encourage the pursuit of a *dō*, feeling perhaps the most important Way is found in life as it is lived from day to day. There, too, you understand, one's progress in discipline is determinable—discovered in one's relationships, for example, and the manner one conducts oneself in everyday affairs, at the temple or in street. That may be the highest *dō* of all, the very center of your wheel.

STRYK: I can see why so many come to Mampukuji for training!

MURASEI: Yes, it is true we want our Zen to reach to all. Perhaps we are more active than other sects in seeking followers, starting with Ingen himself. By then Zen was established in Japan, had been for four hundred years, with two main sects. As you can imagine, there was resistance to the founding of another sect, and by a Chinese priest at that. Ingen actively sought help, support, and gave our sect the basis for more popular appeal. But not, I emphasize, to win converts. He felt Zen had become too aristocratic, that it needed to attract the common people. It had, after all, something profoundly important to offer to all, on all planes. That's always the ideal of Obaku, and today, more than others perhaps, we attempt to attract laymen, offering training in various pursuits. And more important, offering meditation courses to workers, businessmen, any interested. We even have an active school for the young—that kind of thing. In fact, in summer the temple becomes like a youth hostel!

STRYK: And some who visit might find the way to Obaku?

MURASEI: If not immediately, later. Many return in hope of having their lives enriched. We welcome them with open arms.

PRIEST

Katsufumi Hirano, Obaku Sect priest, a disciple of Gemyo Murasei-roshi of Mampukuji, serves as managing director of the periodical *Zen*. In his mid-twenties, this tall, finely-featured man is most serene and self-assured in spite of his many responsibilities. In addition to doing the major part of the work on *Zen*, under the guidance of chief editor Murasei-roshi, he is in charge of running the very active Zen Culture Center for Youth at Mampukuji's sub-temple, the Ryokuji-in. He has recently returned from Seattle, where he directed a two-week *sesshin* (meditation period) for some thirty Zenists associated with the University of Washington, which has always had strong ties with Asian culture.

He speaks warmly of his visit and the kindness shown him. The Zen group there had taken care of all expenses on their own, with no support from the university—an indication of their seriousness. He was deeply impressed by their willingness to do *zazen* for hours on end, in strict lotus, finding them astonishingly self-disciplined, with purity of vision and resolve to achieve something in Zen. He asks about Zen in America, whether there are many such groups, their organization, so on. Clearly he has been surprised by the ability and attitude of those he met.

His background is unusual. Having trained in Soto at the

great master Dogen's temple in Fukui, the Eiheiji (one I happen
to know very well, having always been affected by Dogen's life
and writings), where he made good progress, he left after some
years for Mampukuji to work under Murasei-roshi, because he
began to feel the famous "just-sitting" of Soto was inadequate to
his needs, and that through its meditation practice Soto could
not reach in the desired way enough people. Rinzai Zen, on the
other hand, was too severe and élitist for one of his temperament.

Thus Obaku, with its employment of Nembutsu (mystical
chanting), *koan* interpretation, careful avoidance of scripture in
early stages of training, was all he had been seeking. He became
an outstanding disciple and completed training for priesthood
under Murasei-roshi. He is deeply idealistic, which, more than
anything, qualifies him for his role at the Culture Center, inspiring through his life and teaching the young who regularly
come for *zazen* and often practice one or more of the Zen arts. I
greatly enjoy meeting this sensitive scholar.

STRYK: Were you surprised to find people you met in
America so seriously involved in Zen training?

HIRANO: Their invitation was the first surprise. I had
no way of knowing what I would find: I was astonished.

STRYK: Though capable of sitting for long periods, did
their *zazen* impress you in other ways?

HIRANO: It was true *zazen* in every respect, always full
lotus, alert. Indeed more pure, at least in the physical sense, than that
practiced by many here!

STRYK: Incredible. Where, how did they learn?

HIRANO: A number, after visiting Japan, began to
study Zen, reading everything, becoming familiar with Zen arts—not
difficult in a city like Seattle, where Asian art is so well represented
in museums, where there are courses in Asian civilization at the universities.

STRYK: Apart from *zazen*, were they practicing in other
ways?

HIRANO: Well, being for the most part teachers, students, they are very busy but serious lay Zenists. All in all, a worthy
group, which, if typical, speaks well for the practice in America.

STRYK: Are they especially drawn to Obaku—is that
why you were invited?

HIRANO: Their leader, a professor knowing Japan and the language well, is particularly interested in Obaku. Perhaps the work I do with young people at our Culture Center led them to me—they all knew of it.

STRYK: Does Obaku have a stronger missionary element than other sects?

HIRANO: We like to feel there's little proselytizing in Zen, whatever the sect, but it is true Obaku actively draws as many as possible. That's one reason for our Culture Center. We are known to welcome anyone genuinely wanting to gain from Zen.

STRYK: Perhaps your magazine is instrumental in drawing people here?

HIRANO: It well may be the most important publication, in a sense the only one, dealing exclusively with Zen. But missionary? Far from it. We publish articles on all aspects, most scholarly, dealing with scriptures, that sort of thing. And there are reviews by experts of current books.

STRYK: Were the Americans familiar with it?

HIRANO: One or two, but that was not my purpose there.

STRYK: What did you talk about?

HIRANO: I conducted *dokusan* regularly, there were *koans.*

STRYK: That surprises me, considering the shortness of your stay. How were the *koans* used?

HIRANO: You're justified in being surprised. The idea was to show how *koans* are employed, not too much was expected. Yet, for the most part, they were handled well under the circumstances: I had the feeling that a few might, with more time, have come up with striking interpretations. As you know, it takes months, even years, to work out satisfactory views.

STRYK: Was it possible for you to sense much difference in approach? Were interpretations more logical, more Western—all that implies?

HIRANO: Yes and no, yet I sensed behind their views the reading they had done in books of *koan* interpretation. Inevitable, I suppose, with all those popular publications purporting to give answers to classical *koans.* A strange species of literature! To be fair, though, many Japanese go to such sources for help, have always done so. In any case, I don't mean to suggest they read too many of that kind, but there was a sense that a dependency on such works had been created—I cautioned against it in the future. Most strongly, I might add.

STRYK: Presumably it is discouraged here?

HIRANO: Yes, but as I've said, there are many such books, and they are widely read, part of an old tradition in Zen—great masters, after all, wrote down interpretations in the hope of guiding disciples on the right approach to *koan*. The best disciples have always known, or soon discovered, that no help of importance is gained by it. You see, there are no right or wrong solutions, each person not only has but should have his own highly individual way, conditioned by his needs and aspirations. That's what the master expects of a disciple. Besides, *koans* are only part of training, with an important but at the same time limited purpose—to help the master gauge his disciple's progress. That is why he is often asked to work with the same *koan* for years, why his rendering of it will vary widely time to time.

STRYK: I see that *koans* are as important to Obaku as to Rinzai?

HIRANO: They are important to all, for in more limited yet significant ways they are also used in Soto.

STRYK: When you trained at the Soto temple were you given *koans*?

HIRANO: Of course.

STRYK: Why is it then that Soto is supposedly the sect of "just sitting"?

HIRANO: A most unfortunate, misleading notion, though it may be true Soto is literally based on the conception of gradual attainment. That goes back to Dogen, its founder. He thought it the most natural way of gaining insight, most human way —compared with Rinzai practice, which from the time of its founding in T'ang China was severe in approach.

STRYK: Based on Hui-neng's views, of course, as indicated in the *Platform Scripture*?

HIRANO: Yes, especially there: an élitist document, as you're well aware. Dogen knew it, must in spirit have rejected it. He was against all discrimination, in fact, saying there is only Zen itself. For him, all who hoped to gain from Zen were welcome to try—he had no use for Hui-neng's categories of superior and inferior, thinking them most dangerous.

STRYK: You have high regard for Soto, yet left to come here?

HIRANO: Hard to answer—I've been asked for years! Before I try, you should know it is not all that uncommon for disciples to move on while training. I came because of Murasei-roshi, because of what I knew of him, his life, his excellent magazine, which I'd read for years. In a sense, then, it was incidental that he was Obaku —that, too, I might add, is not uncommon among us. It's more the man we seek than sect, the master is everything to us. Frankly, had I not found it possible to work well under Murasei-roshi, I might have journeyed on, settled for a Rinzai master!

STRYK: Truly? In spite of the distaste you have for many Rinzai views?

HIRANO: Well, I might never have found a Rinzai master for my needs, but I speak in principle. No, I don't rule out the possibility. Sect is not important as some, especially from afar, make out. In that respect, Dogen was certainly right, all who follow seriously know it.

STRYK: Yet some, whose seriousness is beyond question, have strong views on sect, dismissing the rest in strong language.

HIRANO: It's not for me to doubt their seriousness, but most assuredly their wisdom! To a true enlightened man how can it be of consequence? The various sects, each in its special way, administer to the needs of different people.

STRYK: Then you yourself are Soto or Obaku, and could not be Rinzai?

HIRANO: In a sense, because I cannot accept, with my view of human nature, my weakness and strength, an insistence upon sudden method—of anything. If I could grasp all truth in such a way, still I would find myself sceptical regarding the claim that all should do so.

STRYK: At Eiheiji was there concern about such things? Did any others worry about being part of a sect so often criticized as Soto, for being among other things a refuge for the slow, the lazy?

HIRANO: Not at all! None troubled with such matters. You must remember some of those tangled up in sect disputes consider certain Rinzai Zenists—themselves most vocal critics of other sects—as being proud and vulgar. Some indeed think them literally mad in their pursuit of the unattainable.

STRYK: There perhaps is the crux of the problem. To non-Rinzai Zenists sudden enlightenment is unattainable, or at least there's doubt concerning its possibility.

HIRANO: Though I wouldn't care to be counted among them, I must confess to having doubts, or more explicitly, I doubt the importance of the issue. The main thing surely is discovery of true self. Sometimes for a Zenist it's simply a matter of geography: he may live in a Soto district, and it wouldn't occur to him to seek guidance outside, his understanding of Zen is conditioned by Soto views and practices. That's very common. In any case, in Soto, in Obaku, the discovery of true self is thought to require a great deal of time and careful discipline, persistent, graduated, with clear, day-by-day evidence that development is taking place.

STRYK: So, sudden awakening is impossible?

HIRANO: We would not claim that! After all, the history of Zen is full of such experiences, the most significant recorded. Yet it's impossible to base a system of training on such probabilities—simple as that. As you know, Rinzai Zenists often experience what is called the Great Doubt, many literally going mad early in training. How can that be seen as ideal discipline, how can it be marked the best way to the fruits of Zen?

STRYK: There are no cases of the Great Doubt in Soto or Obaku?

HIRANO: None to my knowledge, though when one is working on *koans* there are necessarily moments of anxiety, periods of depression. There is not, however, the same kind of pressure—of that I can assure you.

STRYK: Most troubling. I think the difficulty arises from the belief that for anything important to be attained great effort is required. One has to go beyond one's normal self, however much the pain. Perhaps that's why to Westerners the Rinzai view seems plausible.

HIRANO: Great effort, of course, but surely not great pain, great doubt, which if not controlled can lead to disaster. In Soto, in Obaku, equal effort is expected, but there are simply no illusions, of the kind one finds in Rinzai, regarding possibilities of everything happening at once, just like that, utter finality! After all, judgment is based on observation, slow, scrupulous. I am not aware Rinzai produces supermen! It too has variety of types, some progress very slowly, if at all. It is them I worry about. Considering the ideals of their sect, they are in the greatest danger.

STRYK: You think such people would be better off with Soto or Obaku masters, expecting less, guiding with more patience?

HIRANO: Unquestionably. But it's not simple as all that. Sometimes a disciple of a Rinzai master finds himself trapped in a system, unable to escape with self-respect. He may persist, there may be a successful outcome, or there may not. It's all too risky. Why shouldn't the pursuit of Zen be normal, healthy, even joyous? Why should an intelligent, sensitive person with ambition to achieve greatness of spirit be made aware constantly of his shortcomings?

STRYK: Have you ever thought Zen a form of therapy?

HIRANO: Indeed not! Zen is religion, not psychoanalysis. As an editor I am faced constantly with that kind of problem: often I get articles from those who think of Zen as such, and in rejecting them feel it my duty to give honest reasons. You can imagine! What I'm telling you I tell to others all the time. Our magazine tries to uphold the religious and philosophical character of Zen, defend its nature from those who would make something altogether different of it—a form of therapy, for example.

STRYK: And yet there's the pragmatic element. In your Culture Center you surely encourage that. I mean you train those who want to be better at jobs, better athletes, that sort of thing.

HIRANO: A different matter. We don't expect such people to pursue beyond what they seek in such ways—of course, there is always the hope some will, a very strong hope. We exist only to serve the community, a feature of Obaku we are proud of. When it comes to training those who hope for priesthood, on the other hand, we hardly emphasize the pragmatic. If anything, we discourage that approach.

STRYK: Do you think the day will come when the three sects will merge? Do you look forward to it?

HIRANO: Realistically, I don't think it will happen. We all know Dogen was right when he said there is only Zen, yet different sects seem to be meant for different human types. Not such a bad thing. I know, have always known, I am not a Rinzai type. Have never aspired to be, would certainly feel out of my element in that community. Yet as Zenist I know Rinzai Zenists are my brothers, we share the deepest communion in the essence of Zen. Our similarities, when we are seen alongside others, are far greater than our differences—something none would dispute. And even supposed rivalries between us do some good, keeping us alert to strengths and shortcomings.

STRYK: The sense of competition?

HIRANO: Hardly! Yet our differences do represent the wisdom of experience and history—are very real.

STRYK: Are you a man of *satori*?

HIRANO: No.

STRYK: Do you aspire to be?

HIRANO: I cannot understand your question. If, as I think, you mean when you speak of a man of *satori* one whose development is based on revelation of a single momentous insight—and I think you do mean that—then I am emphatically no such man. But I may be wrong about you. Perhaps you have in mind someone who over the years has many insights, most coming very naturally, as if blossoming from within, few most sudden, yet, by virtue of being so, no more impressive than the others, well, then perhaps I can claim to be such a person. Obaku tends to be cautious about such matters; we fear they are overemphasized, particularly by writers on Zen— everywhere and at all times.

STRYK: It must be wonderful for disciples to work in such an atmosphere. Yet is what you offer very different from the education offered by a university?

HIRANO: Altogether different! Just as those who speak of the primacy of awakening, we have something special in mind training ourselves and others, something far above those humanistic qualities one associates with academic life. Our quest is for authentic spirit—none could claim otherwise.

STRYK: It's no wonder you attract so many!

HIRANO: Not more than others, if anything, fewer. As you know we are the smallest of the three, no doubt always will be. What may be true, however, is that we attract a certain type, certainly there is more lay participation, as at our Center. For good reason. In our Center, for example, we offer something which, however unique, is meant for all. The source of our growing strength.

STRYK: Obviously you are reaching out, judging from activities at the Culture Center, the numbers involved. Looking around, I wonder how many are attracted by the place itself, its extraordinary beauty, the serenity of its surroundings.

HIRANO: An important thing, though by no means most important. To some less than to others.

STRYK: Yet to some, Mampukuji must be a paradise compared with their own world. Is that altogether good?

HIRANO: I know why you ask *that* question! I can assure you our very purpose is to make such people see that their own
world, wherever, whatever it happens to be, can also be paradise—
seen with awakened eyes.

STRYK: It's interesting, Murasei-roshi felt that when I
asked him about living here. Felt each place offered its own beauty, its
own possibility of serenity. Yet that must be the hardest lesson of all.

HIRANO: It is indeed, such realization offers the profoundest proof of attainment. Unless one feels its truth, one is
doomed forever to frustration.

STRYK: Do you feel privileged in having lived both at
the Eiheiji, surely another of the most beautiful temples in Japan,
and now here?

HIRANO: How could I not feel so, but not so much because of the physical element, for I have never been anywhere I could
not find some beauty. Above all, I am grateful for outstanding masters, would have found any place satisfying, working with them. I
was asked a similar question in Washington by those fearing that
when it became necessary to leave their beautiful mountainous surroundings they would be at a loss. Our discussions on the matter
meant very much to them.

STRYK: What of your life now: considering your many
duties, are you able to give the best within you?

HIRANO: I wonder what is best of oneself! I try, I'm
very fortunate to be at an Obaku temple, precisely because it does ask
so much of me. Our magazine, for example, though hard work, is very
satisfying, having important things to teach. Sometimes we may seem
wrong, somewhat partial, but we do reach those who find it challenging, stimulating—that's good to know. Then the Culture Center,
which may be the most enlivening part of my work—the wonder of
working with those who aspire, especially the young.

STRYK: You are a happy man, and you deserve to be.
That in itself must mean so much to those who come here.

HIRANO: For the Zenist happiness is the feeling of integrality, of life and work. In that sense I am happy. Yet day to day, I
have moments of doubt, difficult decisions, problems to solve. Whatever serenity my life has, I can assure you, is hard won!

HAIKU POET

Noburo Fujiwara, whose handsome face belies his fifty years, is a prominent member of the Ten-Ro School of *haiku*, most traditional and successful of many such schools throughout Japan. He informs me, as if confessing a youthful sin, that he once belonged to the So-Un School, practicing free-verse to the point of ignoring the seventeen-syllable limitation, to which he now refers, embarrassedly, as the "one-line-poem" school. Members of the Ten-Ro question whether what is produced by So-Un is *haiku* at all. He feels and expresses himself strongly, leaving the impression that *haiku* is very important to his life.

Ten-Ro has approximately two thousand members in Japan, possessing a creed, *Shasei* (on-the-spot composition, tracing all subjects to their origins). A loyal member of the school, he is active in its behalf, devoting most spare time to it. There are a number of special activities, and members sometimes meet in groups of fifteen to twenty at a designated place, often an old Zen temple, where they write up to one hundred *haiku* a day, perhaps only one of which, Fujiwara hastens to explain, may be perfected after a year or so's work. Like other members, he selects possibly ten poems for the school's annual anthology, the publication of which is the high point of the year. Since only thirty or so poets have work printed, he is quite proud of being represented yearly.

He has often written sequences of fifty to a hundred *haiku* on given themes, on love, a season, creating thereby a long poem. It is such writing which most interests him, on which he works the hardest. We are walking in the garden of the Hagi-no-Tera Zen Temple in Sone, a suburb of Osaka, a temple famous for its autumn flowers and large memorial stones inscribed with *haiku* exalting flowers by writers famed as Shiki, one of Fujiwara's favorites. A remarkably beautiful place, it is literally dedicated to poetry. Fujiwara often visits for inspiration and to practice discipline. He has meditated years under the priest's guidance, along with other local members of Ten-Ro. It is, he says, their spiritual home.

Fujiwara feels indebted to his *haiku* teachers, especially one who is able to do the seemingly impossible—live on his writing and teaching of *haiku*. Fujiwara explains that his master also writes for newspapers and periodicals on art and aesthetics, does some editorial work and often judges *haiku* contests. I am astonished to learn this teacher must sometimes read more than a thousand *haiku* a day, few of them good. Fujiwara's devotion to his teacher is interesting, and I begin by asking about it.

STRYK: Do you ever find yourself disagreeing with your teacher's judgment?

FUJIWARA: Hardly ever—he is a master *haiku* artist. I am always grateful for his criticism.

STRYK: Do you meet with him to discuss your poems?

FUJIWARA: Rarely—he is so busy. I send poems I feel I've worked on to the best of my ability, and he returns them with suggestions and corrections.

STRYK: He serves you as a kind of editor?

FUJIWARA: Much more than that—a teacher in the full sense. He comments not only on details, but relates to what he knows of my life and aspirations.

STRYK: Is he a Zenist?

FUJIWARA: Profoundly. *Haiku*, we like to feel, is the greatest of the Zen arts. As you know, Basho, our greatest *haiku* writer, was a Zenist. All important *haiku* artists have been.

STRYK: Did your interest in Zen come before or after your work in *haiku*?

FUJIWARA: I was interested early, it was my family's

sect. But I didn't understand too much, certainly wasn't aware of anything special: a branch of Buddhism, that's all. Only when I became involved in arts at the university did I discover, with surprise, how Zen had been always profoundly important to their development. Then I began my studies in earnest, started meditating.

STRYK: Did other members of your family meditate?

FUJIWARA: I don't think so, at least they never mentioned it. Most Zenists are only nominally so, hardly conscious of its significance to the arts. They know of course priests meditate, or do in training, and they themselves are urged to tranquilize their spirit through the practice, but few engage in what is true discipline. I hope that doesn't disenchant you!

STRYK: Did your formative years in Zen lead you to *haiku*?

FUJIWARA: I doubt those early years had much importance, except that the beauty of our temples must have had some sort of influence. Hagi-no-Tera is not altogether typical, being in a sense dedicated to the spirit of art, particularly *haiku*, as you see on the memorial stones here in the garden, but it has the kind of beauty I mean. Most Zen temples have fine gardens, often rock gardens, some have great paintings—*sumie*, for the most part—, all that's bound to make an impact, stir artistic sensibility.

STRYK: How were you first affected by *haiku*?

FUJIWARA: Like all children, I learnt about them in school, was strongly drawn to them, especially Basho's. We were encouraged from time to time to write our own, as a form of writing exercise leading to the cultivation of good style. The practical element was emphasized, the rules held all-important—the spirit of the poems only occasionally looked into.

STRYK: When you first felt the need to express yourself, did you begin with *haiku*?

FUJIWARA: *Haiku* and *waka*, but I felt constrained by difficult formal demands, perhaps intimidated by models constantly held up before an aspirant. I then wrote in freer forms—often the way with youth in our time. I suppose in Basho's age things were different: poets wrote formally, or not at all—nothing else was poetry.

STRYK: Do you not feel that way?

FUJIWARA: Now, yes, but not at first. Indeed, it took a long time to see into the reasons for the strictness of form—the seventeen syllables, seasonal references, tonal unities, so on. Such things, I was to discover, were meant to liberate, not confine. For many that discovery is made.

STRYK: When you speak of freer forms, do you mean freer *haiku* forms, specifically the free verse of the So-Un School, to which at one time you belonged?

FUJIWARA: No, much freer than that. I mean what you know as free verse in the West—indeed ours was much influenced by Western forms. We even had a group of poets calling themselves after T. S. Eliot's famous poem, the Waste Land poets. It's interesting you ask that, for what happened was that I began with modern free verse of that kind, then moved toward the So-Un style *haiku*, which, as you know, does not even apply the seventeen-syllables rule. After years of experimentation, I became more formal in my style. Indeed, having become a member of Ten-Ro is the best indication, since it is one of the most traditional of *haiku* schools.

STRYK: How long did the transformation take?

FUJIWARA: Perhaps ten years, but once part of it, I knew I had found my place.

STRYK: What interests me mostly is that, as development, yours is the reverse of what usually happens in the West, where many young poets begin formally, using rhyme, say, and gradually become freer. That's the usual route.

FUJIWARA: Well, I do not speak for others, of course, but of how it worked for me.

STRYK: Your school's credo of *shasei* (on-the-spot composition) fascinates, but at the same time, puzzles me. I think I know what the term signifies, but doesn't all writing start that way?

FUJIWARA: With *haiku* poets, no. What our teachers tell us, regarding *shasei*, which like all credo may be more ideal than practice, is every place is full of poetry. All one has to do is go find the poems. That's why we can write one hundred poems in a day about a place we visit. We select an interesting and beautiful place and, on the spot, compose *its* poetry.

STRYK: But you said earlier that few if any such poems are good. Perhaps only one, after months of selecting, polishing, may turn out good enough to print.

FUJIWARA: Quite true, though at the time we feel all are good, at least might be worked on. The main thing is we really open our eyes, whether or not good poems come—and so discover a spirit there. We're made aware, through active seeking, of the presence of poetry all around us; we begin, slowly to be sure, to see our personal world in the same spirit. I assure you the practice is based on fundamentals which lead to great discoveries.

STRYK: Do your long sequences of *haiku* come when you visit such a place?

FUJIWARA: No, my sequences are generally on more abstract themes, written over long periods of time—the way any poet might work.

STRYK: Do you often work on such a sequence and does it give more satisfaction working on an extended piece?

FUJIWARA: I like working that way, but should add there's nothing in *haiku* tradition to encourage it. Few sequences are thought effective—by *haiku's* exacting standards: the individual poem counts. The danger with a sequence is that a really fine piece coming somewhere in the middle, say, may be spoilt by lesser things surrounding it, losing effectiveness. Thus a sequence is a true challenge.

STRYK: What is a typical theme?

FUJIWARA: The seasons, as you might expect, and familiar places. I think there are more "Spring" sequences than any other. That leads to a kind of problem for the poet hoping to be original.

STRYK: Yet you keep at it?

FUJIWARA: Yes, but cautiously, without claim to any outstanding sequence yet. Most I've broken up, salvaging effective things.

STRYK: I still wonder at the practice of a group meeting at an appointed place and time to write scores of *haiku*. Though you've explained well why it's done, it must be very daunting to go off with expectations of doing so much. I can't imagine anything similar happening elsewhere, even by other *haiku* groups. What if one just isn't feeling up to it?

FUJIWARA: Simple—one can write about that too! Who knows, that may lead to something very special. I'm afraid, mad as it sounds to you, the practice is of cardinal importance to us. Our teachers long explain the reasons for it, adequately answering objections, which often they attribute to natural lack of confidence in beginners, failing powers in the more experienced. Always they set examples for us, never fail themselves in writing many *haiku* at such times.

STRYK: Always good?

FUJIWARA: Of course! They are the masters—have the gift, all that it takes. You're skeptical! I cannot say that everything they write meets their own standards, but they believe so strongly in *shasei*, practice it so fully, that whatever they produce is interesting. We follow; some do well, others not so, but all believe it can be done and work accordingly.

STRYK: What goes on at such gatherings besides writing?

FUJIWARA: We talk, look at the sights, have tea ceremonies, dine together. Yet, with all that, we're really on our own, our purpose never forgotten. We constantly make notes, observe. Then at night, we write.

STRYK: Do your teachers show you their work?

FUJIWARA: Only published work!

STRYK: Is that fair? I mean, wouldn't it be instructive to see the way *they* improve poems? You seem astonished—why?

FUJIWARA: They are *our* teachers! It isn't up to us to find fault with *their* works.

STRYK: Do you hope to become a teacher one day?

FUJIWARA: I'm not good enough. To become so, one must produce fine poems, collect them in books which are highly esteemed.

STRYK: Is publishing so difficult?

FUJIWARA: Books, extremely. Though one can have them printed privately, which most do. There's hope a publisher will ask to do one's book, a slim hope. Many write without hope of such publication, satisfied to see their poems in anthologies produced by their respective schools. That's the best way for us.

STRYK: Why do you write *haiku*?

FUJIWARA: Because I love *haiku*, and because I am Japanese: it expresses the spirit of our people. It makes one feel part of something essential to the culture of our nation. There are many personal reasons, I suppose, but none that I could adequately express— except in poems!

STRYK: Have you favorites among old *haiku* poets?

FUJIWARA: Basho, Buson, Shiki—so many. Basho is my favorite, greatest poet of our nation.

STRYK: What of Issa?

FUJIWARA: I'm afraid he's a bit too light for my taste.

Makes me laugh at times, but perhaps that's not enough. No, I must confess a blind spot for Issa.

STRYK: Do you value any contemporaries as highly—your teacher, for example?

FUJIWARA: I prefer contemporaries! They write of things I live, using our language. Yes, my teacher is among the finest of them.

STRYK Surely language hasn't changed that much in two hundred years or so. Shiki lived into our century.

FUJIWARA: What I have in mind is that a good writer ignores no aspect of contemporary life.

STRYK: Machines, automobiles, highrises, such things?

FUJIWARA: Why not, among many? They make our world, whether we like it or not. In Ten-Ro, with our *shasei* credo, we examine everything, nothing is too low or high for us. Traditional in method, we are very modern in spirit.

STRYK: Then the work of Basho is archaic in language?

FUJIWARA: It's not that so much—the themes are not as interesting. It excites me to see how far one can take *haiku* into reality—very challenging to write of things never before associated with the art.

STRYK: How many feel as you do on that subject?

FUJIWARA: In my judgment, all good writers! The others are for the most part poor imitators of Basho and Buson, using their language, images, and I suspect they know it. Disgraceful, yet they can't help it.

STRYK: Why are they encouraged to continue?

FUJIWARA: Not exactly encouraged. Still it's true many *haiku* societies are made up of such people—inevitably. Take Ten-Ro, among two thousand or so, can one say a handful are true poets? But the rest support the school, purchase the magazine, attend meetings. We couldn't exist without them.

STRYK: Are teachers honest then about their work?

FUJIWARA: I'm not sure—mine certainly is. Judging from our annual anthology, I'd estimate fifty members write well, those who get poems included year by year. Standards are very high, I can assure you. The anthology is always warmly received by the press, some poets gaining national attention in that way.

STRYK: As university lecturer can you devote much time to writing?

FUJIWARA: It's the center of my life, has been for years. All my spare time and energy go into it, along with the activities of Ten-Ro. I write my teacher constantly, send poems, revise, revise, revise! It's full-time work!

STRYK: I know you often translate English poems, some rather long ones, into *haiku*. How do you manage that?

FUJIWARA: The *haiku* I produce that way is a response rather than translation. My poems form a sequence, like stanzas in a long poem. What I produce, then, is a sequence of images based on the original. A common practice among us—anything and everything, we feel, can be made into *haiku*. We're after essences, you see, nothing more nor less.

STRYK: Incredible. The aesthetic has broad application, it would seem. Are you able to read poems of non-*haiku* writers, contemporaries, with appreciation?

FUJIWARA: Few, I'm afraid. As you can imagine, I find their work for the most part dreadfully prolix.

STRYK: What of Shinkichi Takahashi, the Zen poet?

FUJIWARA: An exception, a genius. Even apart from his short poems, he's never prolix. As a true Zenist, he couldn't be. I read once he also thinks Basho the greatest Japanese poet. Yes, his work has been thought extraordinary for years, even when it is most difficult.

STRYK: Are some *haiku* difficult to understand?

FUJIWARA: I don't think there has ever been an obscure *haiku*. The form won't permit it. That's one of the reasons they are so admired. There are pieces very highly concentrated—that's the ideal—but never beyond understanding of intelligence and awakened sensibility.

STRYK When *renga* cycles (sequences of related *haiku* by two or more poets taking turns) were popular, that wasn't always the case, was it?

FUJIWARA: The finest *renga*, say of the Basho circle of poets, are not at all obscure—Basho wouldn't have permitted it. They are fine because the connections are lucid. In *renga* of lesser poets, of course, that doesn't hold true.

STRYK: And *haiku* sequences?

FUJIWARA: There again, in a good sequence there is clarity, of development, of juxtaposition. No, obscurity is not a problem, even when the poems deal with highly abstract themes. It would go against the very nature of the art.

STRYK: Perhaps that's one of the most incredible features of Japanese art in general—its directness, clarity. Have you an idea of the reason for that?

FUJIWARA: Well, I suspect it has much to do with our attempt to discover essences. About which Zen teaches us more than anything else. Take a *sumie* work: purely the essence of a scene, details absorbed, harmonized. In *haiku* it's the same—a weeding out of all that would clutter, muddy, confuse, leading to great incisiveness, clear purpose. What we are looking for, guided by Zen, is revelation, and our masters always reveal truths to us. Small as it is, the *haiku* is a repository of great wisdom, has been now for centuries.

STRYK: How difficult it must be to achieve that! Even the freedom to try to do so, when you are set so firmly into a school, a master over you. Have you ever found yourself doubting the wisdom of such association?

FUJIWARA: I've never doubted. Tradition shows how many achieved greatness working in such a way. Only when one has learnt all there is to know about an art is freedom possible—always assuming the spirit is there.

STRYK: But frankly I still wonder how working this way one can find those personal insights leading to important achievement. Isn't there the risk that however good the work, it could never be as good as the master's—I mean, the fear that it could never be, whether or not true.

FUJIWARA: Your question calls for a personal answer. I too shall be frank. It may be true I am limiting myself in some ways, but when I consider how much I gain from criticism, how important the encouragement, I can't feel anything but gratitude. I don't feel I'm competing with my teacher, or anyone else. There's always the sense among us that it may be possible for anyone of us to write a masterpiece. For that we strive—and should one of us achieve this, what one might see from outside as submission would have been more than worthwhile. I'm quite sure my teacher felt that way himself, his teacher before him.

STRYK: I know that attitude is common among Japanese artists, in all media, but it's difficult for most to understand. What of the feeling that influence can be as harmful as useful? That in order to achieve work of importance one must become in a full sense oneself, a difficult thing indeed. I think that's the source of power in a poet like Takahashi. From an early age he was an individual, had to rebel against society—there was a price to pay, a harsh one.

FUJIWARA: But Takahashi is a genius! Most of us live ordinary lives, even though in a sense we have to rebel in order to become artists. In that respect we're no different from poets anywhere. When you consider the high regard we have for tradition, you must feel there's small scope for adventure in our lives and art, but many of us feel the old *haiku* so far from satisfying that we try to introduce the most unpromising elements of contemporary life into our works. That, I can assure you, represents to many something very close to revolt, and they are horrified by *haiku* dealing with things of our time. So we are thought far from conventional.

STRYK: One thing is clear—*haiku* is deep in you.

FUJIWARA: Yes, everything to me. Though it's doubtful I'll achieve great reputation, the fact I am able to print my work, such as it is, increasingly, that it's appreciated, means much to me. I can't tell you how much! What would I be otherwise? A teacher of linguistics, an academic, not creator, though that's how I earn my livelihood. My life may be richer than those of many of my fellow teachers. I have something important to live for. There are many things a man can do with his life. For me there's no question what it is.

STRYK: For you, then, in the Zen sense, *haiku* is the way to truth?

FUJIWARA: Yes, as it can be for anyone, wherever he happens to live.

CONTEMPORARY POET

As in all arts, there are many poets involved in Zen discipline, its spirit has always appealed to Japanese artists. Shinkichi Takahashi, seventy-five, is considered the greatest Zen poet of our day. Many years a legend, he is a man of *satori*, deeply trained in Zen, his enlightenment testified to by Shizan-roshi, one of the most distinguished masters of the modern period. Represented in all major anthologies of Japanese poetry, his work is read not only by poetry lovers but by those with knowledge of the philosophy. As his friend and translator, I have impatiently waited the chance to ask that which I know many of his admirers would like answered.

Takahashi, his wife, and daughter live in a quiet, narrow street in the Nakano Ward of Tokyo. The very steep staircase of his modest house leads up to his tiny study, stacked with books and box on cardboard box of manuscript. There is a photo of his Zen master on the wall, placed beside the *inka* presented by the master, the traditional "Moon and the Water" testament (*Inka:* the awakening of a disciple formally testified to by his Zen master). Pasted on the cardboard boxes are illustrations of paintings cut from magazines, some Western, for he is also a well-known art critic and has produced in recent years a series of art books with introductions and commentaries. There are numerous collections of poetry on the bookshelves, some in foreign languages, including English, which he reads and writes but does not speak.

It is late August and extremely hot, so Takahashi pulls down his light *yukata* to the waist, turns on the fan. He is short, sturdy, extremely strong and vibrant for a seventy-five-year-old, though almost toothless. His delicate, fine head is tilted back, alert, though he is very much at ease, speaking thoughtfully with a poet's care for language. He pauses, often illustrating responses with a passage from his books, among them a study of the great Chinese Zen master Rinzai.

Having long known him to be one of the world's great poets, I have much to ask, hardly know where to begin. Sensing this, he suggests some lunch first, and his wife brings a large tray of luncheon meats, some beer and *sake*, which he knows I like. The *sake*, very best, is from Hiroshima. So we eat and drink, chatting. His daughter, shy and charming, half hides a camera behind her back, finally gathering courage to ask permission to photograph her father and his "English voice." The poet sits back formally, and I move to his side, greatly affected by the family's deep pride and devotion to him.

STRYK: My friend, you have long been thought one of the most revolutionary poets in Japan. Were you surprised when your *Collected Poems* received the coveted Prize for Art from the Ministry of Education last year?

TAKAHASHI: Such awards always surprise, but fundamentally they are of little importance. I doubt whether those awarding it know anything of my poetry—except that there is interest in it. Largely due to your translations, I might add! Your book, as you know, has been much discussed in the press over here, always of course for the wrong reasons. Everyone is impressed when one of our artists is taken notice of overseas, his work published by a famous company, reviewed and so on. That must seem reason enough to give a prize. Please understand, I'm not ungrateful, but I've serious doubts they saw my poems on the page. If through you they hadn't been published in London and New York, they would have been ignored. Anyhow, if the judges were to read the poems, could understand, I wonder whether they would be so anxious to award the prize to another like myself in the future.

STRYK: Yet you've been known for many years to all who care for poetry.

TAKAHASHI: That in itself means little. Mainly I'm notorious because of my involvement in Zen, my writing in that field.

STRYK: Are you suggesting whatever fame has come your way is not due to the quality of your poetry?

TAKAHASHI: Only that there are few capable of judging—if any!

STRYK: But why is that?

TAKAHASHI: Well, as my translator, you should know!

STRYK: For all that, many, especially in the West, respond forcefully to it.

TAKAHASHI: Ah, responding is somewhat different from understanding. One can respond to images, for example, without a notion what they add up to, their reason, the kind of world they build. That's not news to you.

STRYK: Do you mean only fellow Zenists are capable of reading your work seriously?

TAKAHASHI: There are Zenists and Zenists. Most would indeed be incapable.

STRYK: Is that your belief, or the result of experience perhaps with critics or readers?

TAKAHASHI: The latter. I haven't read, heard anything, apart from work like yours and Takashi Ikemoto's in your volume of translations, which convinces me I have been understood, for only one prepared to see the world as I do could possibly get my meaning. Perhaps I should be translated into Japanese itself! You know, I'm getting on, have been scribbling poems now for fifty years. . . .

STRYK: Do you write only for those few capable of appreciating?

TAKAHASHI: Of course not, I write for the world—not that it shakes it much.

STRYK: What would it take, spiritual revolution, to bring about the insight to perceive what you do?

TAKAHASHI: Nothing short of it.

STRYK: Is that likely to happen in our lifetime?

TAKAHASHI: Yours perhaps—what's left of mine, hardly.

STRYK: Are you embittered?

TAKAHASHI: Not at all. Why should the perception of

any reality, including so small and personal a one as that, embitter one? Life, muddled as it is, goes on—we make the most of it.

STRYK: Are there Zen poets living whose work you admire?

TAKAHASHI: I admire all who write, just for writing! But hardly anything I read makes sense. To put that another way, hardly any strikes me as being worth the trouble.

STRYK: As a Rinzai Zenist is your work appreciated chiefly by members of the sect?

TAKAHASHI: I've no idea. Shouldn't think it would appeal to Soto or Obaku—but then are they really Zenists at all?

STRYK: Isn't that severe?

TAKAHASHI: Isn't life? All they do is offer something worthless, making Zen a pleasant activity for people with time on their hands. As you well know, it isn't that at all. As humans, I cherish them along with all others, as Zenists, bah!

STRYK: Are there Zen artists you respect—painters like Munakata, composers like Takamitsu?

TAKAHASHI: Munakata, though Buddhist, is not Zen-ist—I can understand why you may think he is, his work often is close to Sengai in spirit. Not close enough for my taste, though. He's a respectable artist, that's all. Takamitsu the composer seems authentic to me, but having no professional interest in music, I can't go beyond that. I suppose you are still trying to discover whether there are living Zen poets I respect? As I said, the best way I can put it is that I respect them for writing what is thought poetry by most people—at least they try.

STRYK: But you don't think it poetry?

TAKAHASHI: It is, for them!

STRYK: Have your views on poetry always been tough?

TAKAHASHI: Perhaps I've mellowed just a bit—you should have known me twenty years ago!

STRYK: Well before then you were a dadaist poet, first in Japan. A lonely role?

TAKAHASHI: Exhilarating! Thought I'd made a great discovery—so exciting it might revolutionize not only art but life here in Japan. I was young, my optimism was unjustified.

STRYK: Was there hostility to your work?

TAKAHASHI: It would have been poor dadaism if there hadn't been! Isn't it the purpose of such movements to arouse hostility—through questioning society's sacred values? Our society at that—you can imagine!

STRYK: Yet you abandoned it for Zen.

TAKAHASHI: Dadaism was meant to be abandoned, it served its purpose. I had to get to more important things, like saving my life.

STRYK: Your life?

TAKAHASHI: Nothing less—for that I turned to Zen. I had no life, had to find whether one was possible. If so, whether it was worth keeping.

STRYK: About that time you often got in trouble with the police, for anti-social conduct?

TAKAHASHI: Yes, I was lost, didn't care for anything or anyone. My troubles were small suicides.

STRYK: Then you found Zen?

TAKAHASHI: Lucky for me, and it was right.

STRYK: Most Zenists go to a particular master. Did what you had heard of Shizan-roshi make him special in your eyes?

TAKAHASHI: I was told he was a disciplinarian not likely to be impressed with my literary talents and ambition. It was fortunate I went to him. I might have given up with someone else—so very easily.

STRYK: When you began training, did you have any idea what it would come to mean?

TAKAHASHI: Shizan-roshi would not have bothered with me if he felt I wasn't serious. I had the usual problems, even suffering the Great Doubt fully (The Great Doubt comes—and is severely felt—by Zen practitioners when they are totally unsettled by the very real struggle to attain awakening, usually early in their training), but persevered because I felt increasing need for what I imagined Zen could offer.

STRYK: Did other poets you knew also take it up?

TAKAHASHI: Many were interested—after all, we are Japanese—yet few, if any, persisted as I did. Possibly they lacked the inner need.

STRYK: For what?

TAKAHASHI: You know me better than most: need for the certainties it expresses.

STRYK: You feel your poems offer answers to questions posed by Zen.

TAKAHASHI: All good poetry offers answers to questions, though only the poet knows what the questions are.

STRYK: Intriguing. Could you explain?

TAKAHASHI: The poet's world is a puzzle, full of wonders, full of questions. His poems attempt to come to terms—if serious, that is.

STRYK: As a philosophical poet, what you say would bear that out, but surely not all poems are of that kind.

TAKAHASHI: I think they are, though some offer simple, some highly complex answers—which is good, leading to varieties of response. The questions are similarly deep and troubling. Am I a philosophical poet? I've never thought myself that: just a Zenist who happens to write. As you know, I spend much more time on prose. In fact in recent years I've written four, five poems a year, whereas my output on Zen increases.

STRYK: So these days your answers to those questions are offered in conventional form?

TAKAHASHI: Let's say a form more easily understood.

STRYK: Is that in itself important?

TAKAHASHI: Why else would I be writing explications, commentaries? Nothing is *more* important.

STRYK: Is that the result of feeling that your poems have not been rightly understood?

TAKAHASHI: You make it sound as if I've suffered a defeat of some kind! I never expected my poems to be popular. Could such a vision of life ever be? No, I write books on Zen in the same spirit in which I make poems, to reveal truths—only the terms, points of reference are different.

STRYK: If, as they say, art imposes order on chaos, surely you have offered precisely that for many years, in the form of insight, to the world as you've known it.

TAKAHASHI: By the response to my ordered world, it would appear as chaotic as world without order! Though some might have such ambition, there are other ways of looking at it: the poet might attempt to discover significance in flux, showing that what is normally ignored, taken for granted, is dynamically part of the *becoming* world. As you know, my poems deal for most part with the subjective world, giving it objectivity, bringing a little light into darkness. Perhaps that's the same thing as imposing order, I'm not sure. When I was writing poems, almost daily, what fascinated me was the possibility of anything, everything being made poetry. Though I was hardly conscious of having an aesthetic program. All I wanted, truthfully, was for the poems to express world's vibrancy.

STRYK: As revealed by Zen?

TAKAHASHI: Created by awareness. You see, I don't think world reveals itself, it is we who reveal ourselves through proper relationship to it—when awakened. Truth is, all is there to be awakened to.

STRYK: Was there a great shift in your work after you experienced *kensho*?

TAKAHASHI: As if I'd been shot to another planet— one I've lived on ever since.

STRYK: That's amazing.

TAKAHASHI: Would it have been *kensho* otherwise?

STRYK: I've never been less than astonished at such transformations. Hakuin's, for example. Yet few contemporaries speak of them—indeed many are reluctant to admit even the possibility, for most, of *kensho*.

TAKAHASHI: For most, yes, but not to admit it happens is, for a Zenist, sinful.

STRYK: Sinful?

TAKAHASHI: Nothing less—casting doubt on the most revered goal of Zen, alongside which all is as nothing. What is Zen without *satori* as its goal, life opened up by it? Clear and simple as that!

STRYK: Even among Rinzai Zenists, that's an unusual view, altogether inspiring. I must confess to being disillusioned by the many apologies and disclaimers—as if there's fear, embarrassment. Meeting such people has been, to say the least, a puzzling experience. Not that I doubt their integrity.

TAKAHASHI: It's clear you've encountered the wrong people. I can't believe awakened men would fear discussing the center of their lives.

STRYK: But they are Zenists, masters among them.

TAKAHASHI: Nominal Zenists, perhaps, not what I'd call true Zenists.

STRYK: There must be very few!

TAKAHASHI: Indeed. What did you expect? Not knowing of your work in Zen, they see you as a Westerner with curiosity. Perhaps that's why they are reluctant to speak. Don't be fooled by that: they all take for granted there's something to strive for, that they'll be transformed by it. Why meditate, discipline oneself, undergo austerities? Only in hope they realize their ambition.

STRYK: Could it be as poet you have the gift, words to express insight? Is that possibly the difference?

TAKAHASHI: Ha! Now you force my hand—how would I know? Men make such disclaimers, yet Zen history is rich in detail of *kensho* experience, indeed it's made up of such accounts, meant to inspire us. In every walk of life, in most pursuits, how few there are who succeed. Poet yourself, you know that's true. How many real poets are there, among thousands who would be? Either insight and power's there, or isn't. Same holds true for Zen. Only few can transmit insight.

STRYK: Transmit—is that necessary?

TAKAHASHI: Most necessary. Isn't that what poetry does, transmit? In Zen it matters more than anything. Why do we honor Hui-neng and Rinzai? Because they transmitted rare gifts of enlightenment. As poet I too have that responsibility.

STRYK: Even more so writing on Zen?

TAKAHASHI: How more so? Can one tell whether one's poems transmit whatever wisdom one has gained? Perhaps with works on Zen one can make sure of sharing in that way.

STRYK: So what, and to what degree, you communicate matters very much?

TAKAHASHI: You know the old saying, "After *satori*, teach." We learn that at the start of training, and hold it very dear. I feel responsibility to communicate what I know—on different levels, to be sure, the highest being poetry.

STRYK: Isn't there conflict when a poet writes philosophy? Language used differently? Are you actually satisfied, as poet, when writing books on Zen?

TAKAHASHI: No conflict, none at all. Nāgārjuna— you've a chapter on him in *World of the Buddha*—spoke of two kinds of truth, for that matter so did Buddha: absolute and relative. The poet deals with absolute truth, offering witness to it directly, experientially—the philosopher relative truth, using strategies of all kinds to assure understanding. Zen masters are aware of that distinction, deal with absolute truth during *dokusan*, when disciples stand before them individually, dealing with relative truth when disciples gather to hear a *teisho*. Then they discourse on the meaning of things, perhaps a passage from the scriptures. You see, they make allowances for many and real differences among disciples—in training, in insight, in the depth of their learning.

    STRYK: So when you write poems, you really are writing for the few?

    TAKAHASHI: I don't know, can't afford to care. When I write poems, no allowances can be made. Thought of a poem's difficultness never troubles me, since I never consciously make poems difficult.

    STRYK: Your symbolism appears to casual readers very complex—for example, use of sparrow as protagonist in poem after poem. How strange that must strike some readers.

> *The Position of the Sparrow*
>
> The sparrow has cut the day in half:
> Afternoons—yesterday's, the day after tomorrow's—
> Layer the white wall.
> Those of last year, and next year's too,
> Are dyed into the wall—see them?—
> And should the wall come down,
> Why, those afternoons will remain,
> Glimmering, just as they are, through time.
> (That was a colorless realm where,
> Nevertheless, most any color could well up.)
>
> Just as the swan becomes a crow,
> So everything improves—everything:
> No evil *can* persist, and as to things,
> Why, nothing is unchangeable.
> The squirrel, for instance, is on the tray,
> Buffalos lumber through African brush,
> The snail wends along the wall,
> Leaving a silver trail.
> The sparrow's bill grips a pomegranate seed:
> Just anything can resemble a lens, or a squirrel.
>
> Because the whole is part, there's not a whole,
> Anywhere, that is not part.
> And all those happenings a billion years ago,
> Are happening now, all around us: time.
> Indeed this morning the sparrow hopped about
> In that nebulous whirlpool
> A million light years hence.

And since the morning is void,
Anything can be. Since mornings
A billion years from now are nothingness,
We can behold them.
The sparrow stirs,
The universe moves slightly.

TAKAHASHI: But I don't use the sparrow as protagonist in my little lyrical dramas. I write of him admittedly quite often, because I believe in his wisdom. I trust him, believe he has answers to our problems, perhaps—I don't know. The truest way of putting it is I love watching, meditating on his life. If people think in writing of the sparrow I write of them, well, that's their privilege. I've no such motive. What strikes them unusual is the result, maybe, of few other writers having noticed creatures that I love. Like most things, they are taken for granted, ignored, despised along with other creatures, pigeons, dogs, cats—other "protagonists" of mine.

STRYK: In a review of *Afterimages* appearing in the American periodical *Hudson Review* some years ago, the writer said that Westerners, when they wish to enter nature, the world of creatures, have to descend into it, whereas you are always there, emerging occasionally with a poem like a seal rising from the depths of the sea. That struck me as a very true image.

TAKAHASHI: Interesting, I suppose. One's always a bit puzzled by criticism of one's work, inevitably, because it's assumed one is conscious of things one hardly ever thinks about.

STRYK: You've written fiction—stories, parables, and there's your novel, *Dada*. With such prose, do you feel you are treating reality, truth, in an absolute or relative sense? Is it more like poetry or closer to your expositions of Zen?

TAKAHASHI: There's nothing close to poetry. Fiction is possibly farther from it than prose exposition—when writing poems I'm a different person from the one who writes those things, including fiction.

STRYK: You said you're often puzzled by judgments of your poetry. Is that true when Zenists write on it?

TAKAHASHI: I must be cautious here. You've written on my work. In your case, what convinces me that you know what I'm after are your translations. I can read them in English, and find them remarkable. I see I'm embarrassing you, but really, nothing anyone can write about my work could possibly have the significance of those translations. Criticism I've seen (and I am interested in what's thought of my work) strikes me for the most part as overly defensive— as if when a writer admires my work, he feels obliged to justify himself for tastes so strange. Often they write ingeniously because of that.

STRYK: Yet you find yourself wishing critics were not so defensive? Feeling they've nothing to be defensive about?

TAKAHASHI: I find myself wishing they would make clear my poems are the expression of my Zen—not less, not more. Why should I apologize for that? I am doing what Zen artists have always tried to do—change those who stand before my work.

STRYK: That's an extraordinary ambition.

TAKAHASHI: So? It is the only sane one. Else why bother, why give oneself the trouble? I say through my work that it is possible for man to be freer than he finds himself, awaken to things he has hardly noticed around him.

STRYK: Art carries responsibility, then—a moral task?

TAKAHASHI: More simply what I try to do is share my sense of the world's wonder, possibilities of living freely, magically— the Zen way, after all. What is written in its name has that kind of responsibility, its poetry is surely its most perfect expression.

STRYK: An American poet, reviewing *Afterimages* in *American Poetry Review*, expressed exactly that about your poems. Could it be that your work is better understood in the West?

TAKAHASHI: I don't think so. There perhaps its strangeness makes for the same kind of attraction as Japanese films. I don't wish to give the impression that I doubt their understanding, especially to you, but I am a bit suspicious. What I ask myself is how one, not a Zenist, could get much, if anything, out of my words.

STRYK: Zenist is but a *word*. I believe there are those with natural feelings for the world resembling that of Zenists. Without ever having heard of Zen, they respond strongly to your poems, even as they do to Basho's *haiku*. I know it to be true among young students hardly sophisticated in literature and philosophy—they are deeply affected by your poems.

TAKAHASHI: No doubt by their strangeness! How wonderful to know my poems are read by the young—that pleases more than I can say. I'd like to hope they benefit by reading and discussing them, but I've grave doubts about their being able to absorb them on the highest level. How could they?

STRYK: You're much concerned, then, about that?

TAKAHASHI: Were I a painter, I wouldn't want my reds taken for blues, even though the perceiver finds what he thought was blue delightful. A poem is meant to express a definite state of mind, a highly particularized world—nothing approximate can do.

STRYK: Who can confirm whether a poem is properly understood?

TAKAHASHI: The poet alone—those who think otherwise delude themselves.

STRYK: Once, when writing dadaist poems, you may have been influenced by foreign poets. Have you been since?

TAKAHASHI: I wasn't really influenced even then. I've never been influenced by others, though I should qualify: there are many great ones I've admired—Basho above all, greatest of our poets. Very few moderns, however. That's something I'm neither proud nor ashamed of. I've gone my own way, the Zen way, important influences on my life and art have been Zen masters.

STRYK: Are you aware of having influenced others?

TAKAHASHI: Not at all, I can't imagine it. A man develops over years his special way: eyes see differently, senses mesh differently. One becomes his own man, preserving vitality the best way he can—his own. Only thus will he be taken seriously, only then has he the right to take himself and all he does seriously. No, great artists are never influenced beyond their earliest years.

STRYK: You seem convinced your following in the West is the result of strangeness, but I would say you underestimate the seriousness of those responding to you anywhere. In some poems, "Burning Oneself to Death," for example, which you wrote on hearing of self-immolation of a Buddhist monk in Viet Nam, protesting war, you gave a perspective totally fresh to any eyes. You write as an insider, knowing, feeling things few outsiders can imagine. Now, you may regard that as a quality of strangeness, but it's a most important quality and much appreciated by your Western readers.

TAKAHASHI: Well, that's a special kind of poem. I have in mind those based on *koan*, feeling certain they are read as forms of Japanese surrealism. It's that which troubles me, but as you say, it's as true here. Nothing could be further from my intention than surrealism. My best readers, wherever they are, know it.

STRYK: Reviewers of your work here do not give the impression that your work is all that difficult.

TAKAHASHI: You've only seen a select handful,

chosen by Professor Ikemoto to illustrate points made about my work. They're hardly typical, I'm afraid. By most my work's dismissed as merely odd—true ever since I began publishing.

STRYK: That's why you've become indifferent to your public?

TAKAHASHI: I am not indifferent on the human level, not at all. I simply do not respect their capacity to absorb my work in any meaningful way.

STRYK: Yet you're surely the most productive poet in Japan!

TAKAHASHI: Nothing to do with my public! I've been productive because for years I've arranged my life to make work possible. For more than twenty years, I've been helped in that by my dear wife, in recent years, my daughter. We're a close family; they care, respect all that I do, give all assistance possible.

STRYK: Do you still meditate?

TAKAHASHI: I always meditate, not necessarily in lotus—if that's what you have in mind. For years now, as you know, I've seen the world with eyes reborn, result of meditation. That lies behind the quality in my work you've described as mysterious. Surely it's the source of any originality I may have.

STRYK: Hui-neng said one should not look at, but *as* things. That's something you do more fully than anyone else.

TAKAHASHI: Well, as my translator you may be somewhat partial, but I appreciate your saying that. Hui-neng was right, as one of the greatest Zen masters he had to be right—about everything.

ENCOUNTERS WITH LUCIEN STRYK

Part III

THE RANGE OF ZEN

(Interviews by Anthony Piccione)

Cherries

Because I sit eating cherries
which I did not pick
a girl goes bad under

the elevator tracks, will
never be whole again.
Because I want the full bag,

grasping, twenty-five children
cry for food. Gorging,
I've none to offer. I want

to care, I mean to, but not
yet, a dozen cherries
rattling at the bottom of my bag.

One by one I lift them to
my mouth, slowly break
their skin—twelve nations

bleed. Because I love, because
I need cherries, I
cannot help them. My happiness,

bought cheap, must last forever.

The Word

How inadequate words are
to all we know and feel—

Love Justice Honor Truth—
each emptier than the other.

If there were one word, not
spun of cloud but struck

from stone, a sudden cry,
brief, mighty, to show us as

we really are, small, cruel,
it would to our amazement

gather, merge into a final
tongue, echoing years—

the silence that would follow
prepare us for the world.

I   **ANTHONY PICCIONE:**   Today's guest comes to us eminently known in several directions. Perhaps we know him best for his own poetry, for his translations of Japanese and Chinese Buddhist and Zen Buddhist poetry, and for his scholarship. Soon to be released will be his *Collected Poems* and *Of Love and Barley, haiku* poems of Basho, and the long awaited *Triumph of the Sparrow*, Zen poems of Shinkichi Takahashi. Welcome to the Brockport Writers Forum, Lucien.

LUCIEN STRYK: Thank you, Tony.

PICCIONE: As you began with the two poems, there's a sense of your full circle. I say this in these terms: that you've returned to those things that bother us most as ordinary human beings. And, you return informed with the knowledge of Zen Buddhism. Could you tell us perhaps how, especially, "Cherries" relates to this knowledge, and then move on to "The Word."

STRYK: Well, I think when one begins a discipline like Zen, one is very much aware of the need to create within oneself a condition of calm, tranquility. And in order to do so, there is a certain amount of detachment required. In fact, the Zen term "nonattachment" is one that is constantly heard at that stage. There are numerous Buddhist *sutras* and Buddhist anecdotes which *turn* on the need to acquire the condition of nonattachment. Now at the very early stage of one's work in the discipline, it's *that* which must be cultivated. But after one has attained something or one has disciplined oneself for a long period, one is made aware of the need to, as Zenists put it, return to the world. The period of preparation, and the Zenists understand this, makes it all the more possible to return to the world successfully, compassionately, full of what in Buddhism is called *karuna*, or compassion. Now, this might not have come about without the earlier period of isolated discipline. Sometimes, of course, this is a monastic experience. And a poem like "Cherries"—and perhaps "The Word"—would reflect an attempt at returning, fully aware of the need to involve oneself in that reality.

PICCIONE: And I think in the West we have a preconception about nonattachment, perhaps that being the hardest attainment for people such as we are. And yet, I don't think we are aware of the return, that full human return, with compassion. How does one undo the nonattachment which we can begin to attain as novices? How does one avoid that nonattachment *and* feel compassion upon such a return?

STRYK: Of course, first of all in the early stages one does not attempt to avoid it. One understands a need, indeed, to realize nonattachment, and it's only after some attainment has been made, some realization has been earned, that the return to the world is *called* for, is expected of one. I'm going to read a poem by Shinkichi Takahashi which gives a very full sense of the way in which an enlightened man returns, and as you know, Tony, Takahashi is thought to be one of Zen's most fully enlightened beings. The way in which such a man returns to the world is expressed in the poem called "Burning Oneself to Death," which was written after Takahashi saw, on television as it happens, the self-immolation of a fellow Buddhist. This was a protest against the Vietnam War. Now, I once asked Takahashi about this poem, and I thought at the time of asking him that this represented superbly well the movement from the wall—that is, the Zenist facing the wall, back turned on reality—to the world itself: a return to the world, a facing from the wall into the harshest aspect of the world's reality. And he concurred that this would be a good example of that. And, with your permission, I'd like to read that poem.

> *Burning Oneself to Death*
> *by Shinkichi Takahashi*
>
> That was the best moment of the monk's life.
> Firm on a pile of firewood
> With nothing more to say, hear, see,
> Smoke wrapped him, his folded hands blazed.
>
> There was nothing more to do, the end
> Of everything. He remembered, as a cool breeze
> Streamed through him, that one is always
> In the same place, and that there is no time.
>
> Suddenly a whirling mushroom cloud rose
> Before his singed eyes, and he was a mass
> Of flame. Globes, one after another, rolled out,
> The delighted sparrows flew round like fire balls.

So if I may expand briefly on this since it's such an important issue, and relate what I say to the poems "Cherries" and "The Word." Initially, at the beginning of discipline there might be—and this incidentally, is symbolically most interesting—there might be a great attraction to, shall we say, sitting under the cherry tree. The great ease that that would suggest, and in terms that would be fully understandable to Japanese Zenists, the symbolic importance of that, is that the cherry represents all that is most refined, most beautiful in Japanese culture. But then comes a realization that as one does that, as one sits under the cherry tree, or even more, as one eats its fruit, the act is relatable, must be relatable, to other beings. There are people who pick the fruit and there are people who may suffer as a result of one's indulging oneself in such a way. Thus, the enlightenment achieved under the tree through discipline, through the simple pleasure of being there, is suddenly colored by these concerns, by compassion, by *karuna*. In the case of the other poem ("The Word"), words which perhaps at one time were acceptable—and in the case of the Zenist, this might be in early discipline, or actually at any time in his life prior to Zen realization—words which might have been quite acceptable, full of meaning, such as "justice," "honor," or "love," are suddenly called into question because suddenly the Zenist has been made aware of their illusory quality: that in fact, in terms that the world should understand, there is no justice. There is no honor. Now, the fact that he *says* so, and is waiting for the one word that will make all the difference, suggests that he is on the quest, that it's important for him to reach that point of understanding, that it *is* possible to transform the world, and maybe the right word will do it. The right action will do it.

PICCIONE: If I could suggest that "The Word" cautions us to begin at the beginning again, to recognize our own failure as a culture, and begin again. . . .

STRYK: Exactly.

PICCIONE: And then "Cherries" calls up to me part of the guilt we often feel. I have a particular guilt for loving a long shower and I cannot help thinking of a sidewalk of Calcutta, and so I turn the water off. "Guilt" wouldn't be a word associated with Zen Buddhism, and yet, there is a consciousness of others out there.

STRYK: There is a consciousness, not guilt. The assumption is that in order to act properly one must strip oneself of guilt and everything else of that kind. One can act most effectively when not enfeebled by, weakened by, perhaps emasculated by, concerns of that kind. I think we have to be very strong to be compassionate. We have to be very wise to act properly in the world and in feeling stupid or guilty we are not likely to act properly. So this leads to a kind of paradox. In order to feel the kind of compassion that is held up as one of the great ideals of Zen, one has to feel something of what we have to call "guilt," or difficulty with problems. But in order to act upon those impulses, one has to be beyond, *beyond* those effects. One has to go beyond those effects which such feelings might have on one. One must be strong. One must be firm. In order to do proper things in the world, one cannot allow oneself to be weakened, do you see. And that's a very important aspect of Zen.

PICCIONE: I wonder if you could address not just the poetry of, say, the poem "Cherries," but I have the sense in reading that poem that there is repesented the history of philosophical questing and the history of its failing. And it suggests at once that there is no real distinction between "I" and everyone else, and yet in my act of eating cherries someone else is deprived of cherries. This can't be a debilitating awareness. This is simply a conscious awareness that there is no distinction. Is that how you intended that?

STRYK: Yes. That's absolutely so. And I think that it's very important to remember that the Zenist is always measuring himself in such ways. He's eating cherries and he begins feeling these things. Part of the discipline of Zen is this eternal self-measurement, self-gauging that goes on. I have a poem which very well indicates the realization that the Zenist is made conscious of in the very earliest stages of his discipline. Perhaps I could talk a bit about it and read it.

The poem is called "Willows," and it concerns the discipline of what in Zen is called *zenkan*, and translated freely that means "Zen seeing" or "Zen observation." It's something which is suggested by a disciple's master early in their relationship. That is, the master suggests to the disciple that in order to avoid the kind of mind-drifting mentalizing which always leads to problems, it is necessary to focus the mind or fix the mind. And this is a very difficult thing to do, so the first disciplinary act, perhaps, might be to focus upon objects. If you can, for example, place an object before you—it can be a bowl of water—without immediately taking off from that bowl of water and thinking of numerous other things, perhaps metaphorizing or relating that bowl of water to rain, a pond, a tear, whatever it is that would come with the thought of water. If, in other words, you do not see the bowl of water as a kind of Rorschach test, but simply, clearly, and at all times as *just what it is*, a bowl of water, then you're progressing properly in Zen. The fact is that very few people are able to do that.

PICCIONE: So *seeing* as opposed to *imagining*?

STRYK: Seeing as opposed to imagining. Now, "imagining" is a term that might properly be introduced here, but it's not altogether the term we want because when we use the term "imagining" we think of something rather favorable. It is good to be imagining. But I think I would prefer mind-wandering, because that's what the Zen master is concerned about. It's different to let your mind wander, you see. That's different from imagining creatively. Now, in any case, when I was last in Japan, actually this was in 1975, quite a while ago, and was about to begin my work on *The Penguin Book of Zen Poetry*, and *Encounter with Zen*, and then the most recent of all, the book that's coming out in the fall, the book of Basho translations, when I was involved in these things I had a chance to see Taigan Takayama again. He's the master under whom I began disciplining myself on one of my first trips to Japan, and in the course of our conversation, he asked me how I was doing. Well, when a Zen master asks you that, it means only one thing: how is your Zen progressing? Where are you in Zen? That's what he means. He doesn't mean, how is your job? Or anything like that. And I had to say, as always when I'm with him, I must always be very forthright with him, I had to say that it was constantly slipping, that my awareness of it had constantly to be examined, and that I found myself often drifting. And he said, "Well, do you still practice *zenkan*?" I emphasize "still" because he began our discipline, our disciplinary discussions began with his suggesting that I meditate on objects: a stick, a bowl of water, a lump of earth, what have you. And in fact, some of the poems which have meant most to me, for example the poem "Awakening," were based on that kind of close observation. Anyhow, he asked whether I was still practicing *zenkan*, Zen seeing, and I said, "Not as much." And he said, "Have you ever tried doing this while walking about?" He then said, "Perhaps the formal focusing on objects is something you've tired of or no longer find useful. Why not think of it as you walk about, looking at things, anything?" And he asked, "As you're a poet and are very much alive in nature, why not a stand of trees?" It could have been anything. He could have said "fireplugs" or "garbage cans." It wouldn't have mattered, and I understood that, and he understood that I did.

PICCIONE: I'd like to ask you something in terms of students who will be viewing this as well. Walking about, I take it, would be one method of perhaps inducing the thinking mind into letting go for a while?

STRYK: Exactly, letting go for a while so that you're not looking down at, say, a stick or lump of clay but just letting go, letting go for a while.

PICCIONE: I see. Then there are many ways to this seeing.

STRYK: Many ways to this seeing. In any case, there is near where I live a stand of willows, and very consciously I went there a number of times and attempted to practice *zenkan*, one willow after another. "Willows" is the poem that came of that experience. (Here Stryk reads "Willows.")

Willows
(For Taigan Takayama, Zen master)

I was walking where the willows
ring the pond, meaning to reflect
on each, as never before, all
twenty-seven, examine twig by twig,

leaf by pointed leaf, those delicate
tents of greens and browns. I'd

tried before, but always wound up
at my leafless bole of spine, dead
ego stick, with its ambitions,
bothers, indignations. Times
I'd reach the fifth tree before
faltering, once the seventeenth.

Then, startled by grinding teeth,
sharp nails in the palm, turn back,
try again. Hoping this time to
focus on each bough, twig, leaf,
cast out all doubts that brought
me to the willows. This time

it would be different, could see
leaves shower from the farthest
tree, crown my head, bless my eyes,
when I awakened to the fact—
mind drifting to the trees ahead.
I was at fault again, stumbling to

the flap of duck, goose, a limping
footstep on the path behind,
sun-flash on the pond. Such excuse,
easy to find, whether by willows
or bristling stations of a life.
Once more, I'm off. This time

all's still. Alone, no one to blame
distractions on but self. Turn in
my tracks, back to the starting point.
Clench, unclench my hands, breathe in,
move off telling the leaves like
rosary-beads, willow to willow. Mind

clear, eye seeing all, and nothing.
By the fifth, leaves open to me,
touch my face. My gaze, in wonderment,
brushes the water. By the seventh,
know I've failed. Weeks now, I've been
practicing on my bushes, over, over again.

PICCIONE: There are so many ways of learning from
this poem, I think, and I think especially once again of our students.
I think of you and many poets in this country who teach as well as

write, and part of the teaching impossibility may be the teaching of creative writing. I sat here for a while feeling utterly serious before this body of knowledge, and I was wondering about teaching the way of beginning to write. As we spoke of Zen mind, of Zen seeing, that might well be the beginning point of teaching poetry as well as the end point of the process, certainly somewhere beyond considerations of surface and so on. How do you approach this, the difficulty of teaching poetry and the way of poetry?

STRYK: For some time now, perhaps this is my good fortune, students have been aware of my other interests, that is, other than the making of my own poems, the interest in Asian thought. They might know a book like my *World of the Buddha*, the introduction to Buddhist literature. They might know some of my translations and are very much aware of this special, not only interest, but life choice of mine. Consequently, when I recommend as I always do, though I don't use the term *zenkan*, that they practice something like close observation, they're not surprised. I tell them to go out and look at something very fully without worrying about the thought process which might accompany this looking, but simply looking and noting down very, very fully what they're observing. And then I suggest that if this were pursued properly it might be possible for them to come up with very fresh imaginings, very fresh perceptions, and that in fact they might very well surprise themselves. Most people, young poets, coming into a writing course, do not perceive freshly. They give us essentially what they have read. Their images are usually composites of received things, received from other poets, often. Now, in order to make impressive poetry, another kind of looking has to go on. I'm the first to admit that it need not be Zen, of course. In fact, it rarely is. We have numerous good poets who have never taken an interest in Zen, and yet, they are able to achieve these miracles.

PICCIONE: And we sense this great eagerness for Zen Buddhism and other Eastern ways of looking at things. We seem to be ready for this. We may even have been doing part of it without knowing so.

STRYK: Of course. The point—I might have added this to what I just said—is that if they haven't needed it, these other poets, I have. And others have. Obviously someone like Gary Snyder without question has been largely affected as a poet, largely formed as a poet by such interests, but there need not be that many formally. Others come to it very naturally, and they're blessed for being able to come onto it very naturally. My own development has been in large measure the result of this kind of probing and this discipline, but it is by no means the only way of proceeding. Anyhow, back to your question. Yes, in my case there is the suggestion to young writers that before anything else they begin looking at things as never before, with their own eyes very carefully, very fully.

PICCIONE: So you begin in vision and work toward vision.

STRYK: Toward greater vision, yes, an all-encompassing vision, but you begin with the humble vision, the look at that flower, that stone, that whatever. That problem even. It can also be a conceptual thing, but it has to be looked at. But it should begin with the object.

II*

Lucien Stryk reads:

*Crumbs***

Along one of the villa's hundred
paths, I reach the spot where
bamboo dips into the half-moon pond.

Under the relics of the castle walls,
shaded by redwoods, sycamores, I
toss lunch-crumbs to pucker-mouthed

goldfish, flash-orange fins translucent
as the spiderweb traced on the
bamboo fringe brushing the water,

where two mallards glide out from
the grotto, move as one, as one
feed lazily. Tempted to stir their

sweet monogamy, hurl my offerings
far, this way and that. Calmly they
steer from one side to the other.

---

* This is edited from a transcript of a videotape, "With Lucien Stryk," in the Brockport Writers Forum Video Tape Interview Series, coedited by Anthony Piccione and Stan Rubin.
** *Bells of Lombardy*, Northern Illinois University Press, 1986.

Feast done, satisfied, they turn tail,
drift back to their secret place.
I forge on uphill, from the lofty

point view the maze of paths carved
out by men Duke Alessandro salvaged
in the 1815 famine. Like bees

they tunneled through the cliff,
cut winding shelves from stone,
grateful for a Duke who cared enough

to swap his fortune for a starving
horde—a daily bowl of cornmeal
mush, crumbs between life and death.

STAN RUBIN: Thank you and welcome to the Writers
Forum. Our guest today, Lucien Stryk is a very well known Zen Buddhist translator, teacher, essayist, lecturer, and poet. Author of over
thirty books, his *Collected Poems 1953–1983* was published by Swallow
Press. His most recent book, *Cage of Fireflies*, translations of modern
Japanese *haiku* appeared in 1993. Three books are forthcoming in
1995. Among Mr. Stryk's numerous awards and honors are fellowships
from the Ford Foundation, the National Endowment for the Arts, and
the Rockefeller Foundation. He's held full grant lectureships in Iran,
and the Fulbright Travel Research Grant to Japan, among others. He
was named the Illinois Author of the Year in 1992, and in 1993 received
an honorary degree from Northern Illinois University, where he
taught, for over thirty years, courses in creative writing and Asian
literature. He is currently an emeritus professor at Northern Illinois
University. This is his fourth appearance at the Writers Forum. Lucien,
welcome back.
　　STRYK: Thank you very much.
　　RUBIN: Also talking with us, Anthony Piccione, professor of English at SUNY Brockport, poet, author of three books of
poetry, including *For the Kingdom*, forthcoming from Boa Editions.
Since we're all old friends, this is an informal discussion today. I'd like
to begin by going back to the poem you just read, Lucien. It seems to
connect very nicely to your well-known poem "Cherries," which you
read here a decade ago.
　　STRYK: Yes, I think it does, principally because what
moved me to write the poem was the sense of what was at that time,
what must have been seen at that time, an extraordinary gesture on

the part of Duke Alessandro, in the famine of 1815 in Lombardy, Italy. He actually made it possible for his townspeople to live by bringing them onto his estate and having them do what actually turned out to be very important work, in improving the estate, but the motivation was to keep them alive. And that, I think, is very impressive. Now in the poem "Cherries" there are, I suppose, impulses, which are very much like those that the Duke must have felt when he decided to "swap his fortune," as I say in the poem, for the food for his townspeople, and there were many needs in order to survive a famine that was laying waste to the region, so perhaps that is a connection. I am not sure if there are others, technically or whatever, but thematically, certainly.

RUBIN: In "Cherries" the poet has to come back to the world, really.

STRYK: That's right, exactly. I think that's what we find here, a Duke who could have avoided all such contacts and horded his wealth, but *felt*, and, given the nature of those times, it was an extremely bold act, one that would have been seen as deeply compassionate.

PICCIONE: In another connection, as we go through the process of "Crumbs," natural beauty, grand, human gestures, the reality is still really tight to the chest as you play it out: the goldfish satisfied for a moment, the mallards. So we have the intimation that no matter what is done, right at the edge is a very precarious exchange of energy, and I'm most interested in how you end this poem. After the great gesture of the Duke, "swap[ping] his fortune for a starving horde," there is now a "starving horde" who will get by, and barely, between life and death. And so I wonder if we could talk about the greater view of things, how really close to the edge this place is: fish, mallards, and people.

STRYK: That's what moved me so much, that it had to be a very decisive gesture, an act which actually committed him and his fortune to an extraordinary moment in the history of that place. It's very possible that, had he not done that, the town would have been devastated. Other towns were. And that's what moved me so much, and explains, perhaps, the urgency of those final lines.

PICCIONE: I wonder if I could have you speak a little bit about the way the mallard and goldfish eating is connected here.

STRYK: The wandering up there, the tossing of the lunch crumbs, of course become very important to the poem, and the connection: I'm there doing that, warmly, casually, even playfully. Remember in the poem I say, "where two mallards glide out from / the grotto, move as one, as one / feed lazily. Tempted to stir their / sweet monogamy, hurl my offerings / far, this way and that." Now, the Duke was not tempted to stir the monogamy of the mallards or anything comparable. He was urgently aware of the need to provide food, very, very simple food for his townspeople, but still there is, perhaps, an ironic connection.

PICCIONE: And just to take this one more step, we remember that also in "Cherries" we are reminded of how closely bound we are to cause and effect, that whatever we do affects others, and it's not an abstract thought.

STRYK: No, it has to be borne in the mind, it has to be accepted, and of course there was a call for action, a denial, self-denial. Why should *I* eat all those cherries?

PICCIONE: Self-consciousness: this is either Zen or not Zen. But it seems to be one of the realities.

STRYK: Yes, the spirit of compassion that obviously has roots in Buddhism. As I've said in relation to "Cherries" whenever asked about that poem, the spirit of *karuna*, or compassion, is involved. Of course if one allows that spirit to enter, almost everything one does, sees, writes about, to some degree reflects that spirit.

RUBIN: I'm interested about how this got your attention, that is, this incident.

STRYK: I was reading about the history of the place. I was at Bellagio, actually a guest of the Rockefeller Foundation, to complete my *Collected Poems*, and I found that kind of historical anecdote so moving in the light of what I was seeing there. This glorious villa and a town which was prospering from, among many other things, the active tourist trade, and here was a gentleman who might have done what most of the others surely did: close their eyes and not worry at all about the peasants, the workers, the town. But he actually swapped his fortune. Now that's a historical truth. He gave up all those things, he sold things. He made it possible simply by providing a daily bowl of cornmeal mush. This is an extraordinary act. I mean these sorts of things are too rare to get into history, the perhaps isolated act of a very remarkable individual. And I think for poetry, it's enough to know that, and to want to write about it.

PICCIONE: And we notice that whenever anything goes right, even momentarily in the world, that something profoundly human has occurred.

STRYK: And that's what we look for. I think poets must always be aware of such things happening. So many other things they can't touch, can't do anything about, but I think not only are they tempted to honor such actions whenever they have occurred, hundreds of years ago, or now, but feel in a sense obliged to, at least the kind of poet that I am most interested in. The poets who move me the most are aware of such things. They're not playing games; they're involved in the toughest actions, the toughest parts of life, which are so often forgotten or ignored by most people. That's the role of the poet, I think. You know, I wouldn't go so far as Shelley went in calling the poet an unacknowledged legislator, but I do think that a poet at his best takes on such responsibilities, social responsibilities, that is, by honoring such men, by pointing to such achievements and so on.

PICCIONE: As witness. If we take this a bit further, we know of your long and serious discipline in Zen, but one wouldn't have to go east or west for this.

STRYK: Of course not, of course not. It just so happens that perhaps through predispositions some people gravitate in such directions. I feel that in my case, my involvement in Zen thought and working on books like *World of the Buddha: An Introduction to Buddhist Literature*, learning these things rather decisively affected my view of reality. There's no question in my mind that that happened. I'm not so sure, in other words, that without that kind of involvement I would have written poems like "Cherries" and "Crumbs." I'm not claiming that this is something that we all need in order to become more compassionate, more humanly involved, but in my case I was so profoundly affected by the work I was doing as translator, or commentator on the great Buddhist works, whatever, that the effect was more than gradual, it was right there, it happened rapidly. I began to sense that my life was being profoundly changed, my views were being profoundly changed.

PICCIONE: At the base of this, we would assume that what is required for the rightness would be at least the state of being wide awake.

STRYK: Exactly, and keeping wide awake. You see, that's the difference between the kind of occasional insights that most people experience leading off into the best possible action in the world, and a discipline like Zen which continues to affect one through becoming part of one's normal life.

PICCIONE: So can we say that if there are any rules in Zen discipline that being wide awake would be among the first?

STRYK: Absolutely, wide awake. You know, that's easier said than accomplished, and it's not really a matter of watching the news on television and commiserating, that's not it. It's a matter of knowing that one is in a sense responsible for the things happening. Unless one is committed to change them in whatever way one can, one is not doing anything of importance. Now as a poet, a poet can bring about changes. A poet can. If, for example, the poem "Cherries" has affected people, then I have done what I set out to do: not to make them see it as a good poem, that's only part of it, but make them feel that it is possible for someone to feel so deeply concerned about the plight of the poor that he feels self-disgust at what he thinks is a selfish action.

RUBIN: It's been ten years since you were here last. Quite evidently and surprisingly, you are working the way you have worked; the connection between the Zen discipline and your own work in the world is there, tight. I wonder, in the last ten years, has the work of the spirit, as you see it, gotten more difficult? Are there more, or fewer, obstacles? How has your sense of your work gone in this last decade?

STRYK: I think that there has been a rather steady progression; I am not aware of any deflections along the path. I guess my publishing history bears that out. The next two books are related to Zen thought and translation, Zen poetry, essays on Zen and so on, and Buddhism, but I am presently preparing a new book of poems for publication in 1995, and some of those poems do exactly the kinds of things that "Crumbs" does and "Cherries" does. They're a very important part of *Where We Are: Selected Poems and Zen Translations*, the book I'm into now. I even have a poem about Bosnia. I'm affected by what's happening there; that's part of it.

PICCIONE: At no time does one take oneself to task in Zen in order to write poetry. One takes oneself to task in order to live rightly, you are reminding us.

STRYK: Exactly, and the poetry comes of that, of living rightly. If one lives rightly, if one moves through the world properly, the poems come of themselves and they will carry that spirit. There's no intention any longer. It's just part of you. I mean I can't see things in any other way.

PICCIONE: You spoke in *The Penguin Book of Zen Poetry* that "Enlightenment, the point of meditation," brought about a transformation of the spirit. Writers of such poems did not think of themselves as poets, but wrote that which only a poem could express. Takahashi, you wrote, can "sense the homogeneity of all things," and you say of him, "He clashes his idea of timelessness against the temporality of all phenomena, to cause a fissure through which he lets us see personally, convincingly, the reality of limitless space." Now if I get these things together, then they are talking about a condition of reality which is here and now, and which we are required to see clearly.

STRYK: Yes, I think that is absolutely true. The main thing is to bring into oneself the possibilities of such responses to reality. Now in order to do that, certain steps are necessary. Once they are taken, once there is that kind of fulfillment, then everything comes of itself. When I speak of the Zen masters I translate in such books as *The Penguin Book of Zen Poetry* as not being poets, not thinking of themselves as poets, I am complimenting them, I mean to, and I'm saying that there is something beyond the making of the poems that interests them, that compells them to write. As I go on in that quote, you might remember, these poems are altogether startling, you see.

PICCIONE: Yes. I wanted to get the word "witness" right; we're witnessing. You know the eternal debate between those who say that we invent reality because we are human, and those who say we discover reality because it is there. That sort of thing comes into poetry.

STRYK: There is a wonderful sense of that in Zen discipline, as I discovered in Japan, and that's where my Zen experience is centered. I discovered that no, there was no special attention paid to the "art" of what was being done, even the painting, actually, curiously enough. In the case of the great Zen painters, they painted these things in order to share with others their sense of discovery, their sense of this oneness that you mentioned, and the sharing aspect of it all in the Zen community is very powerful. Take, for example, the way in which the *death* poems by the Zen practitioners are meditated upon. These become documents. The *awakening* poems have the same, the most extraordinary kind of expression, and are wonderfully made, no artificiality, no showing off. This is something I often say, you know, when I'm talking about Zen poetry, that coming to grips with an extraordinary sense of what the world must be in order for us to live properly in it, to discover what we must become in order to see the world as it must be seen.

PICCIONE: And then what we must become as a result of seeing the world.

STRYK: Yes, the hope of integrality.

PICCIONE: It's not an idea in any book, ever.

STRYK: And the poems, the great Zen poems, that I've translated for so many years, do all that. In extraordinary ways. In Takahashi, of course, especially.

RUBIN: I want to ask you this, Lucien, given what was just said in the last several minutes. What are your feelings about creative-writing programs which, of course, are set up to emphasize craft and to convey a certain attitude of a poet as a maker that may, in fact, be independent of the qualities that you are advocating?

STRYK: Yes, it becomes a problem. What I think is sometimes accepted by some young writers is that if the craft is achieved, if enough is learned about making a poem, then the great things will come. I think that going along with the evident, the obvious need to learn something about the art of making poems, there has to be another kind of growth, a more important growth, and that is, of course, of the spirit. We can't expect a young person going to such a workshop to write impressive poetry unless while learning craft something else is happening. I don't mean to suggest that it has to be anything like Zen discipline, but something that takes the young writer beyond himself or herself, something which guides the young writer towards important discoveries about reality and the need to express those discoveries. Now very few people feel that. I think that while it may be too much to claim that a poet is born, not made, it is certainly true that although to a limited degree all poets have to be both born and made, they also have to learn, have the capacity, the spiritual capacity, to move beyond the word, to bring something to the work which only the rarest insight can afford.

RUBIN: It would almost stand to reason that, in simple mathematical terms, the many creative-writing programs and the many students in them would not produce very many of these illuminated poets.

STRYK: That's right, and let me hazard something. I would guess that the same proportion of good poets to poor is found in our time as was found four hundred years ago and maybe a thousand. We have to remember in Shakespeare's play *Julius Caesar* the poet Cinna was surrounded by the mob and his life threatened for having written bad verses. There are always Cinnas, but around the same number, proportionally, in any time, whether workshops or not, whether high concentration on the making or not, will emerge as important poets. How many Montales has Italy produced? How many Zbigniew Herberts has Poland, and so on? I'm not going to mention Americans for obvious reasons, but among our contemporaries we know that certain people are doing it, a great many are not; though they are perceived quite interestingly as good writers, they are not doing what we are talking about. They are not giving us the kind of vision that helps us live, and that's that.

PICCIONE: In the play there was an "informed" mob.

STRYK: An informed mob, that's interesting. You are suggesting that we have something similar to that. Takahashi has a poem which I think very well expresses the kind of thing we have been talking about:

> *Wind Among the Pines**
>
> The wind blows hard among the pines
> Toward the beginning
> Of an endless past.
> Listen: you've heard everything.

PICCIONE: I'm glad to have that in this discussion because the most concern that I have for any student is that we're here, we use books, we review books, and yet none of what is capable of being seen is quite in books, so there's that paradox.

STRYK: And that returns us to what I spoke of as the kind of preparation for—we'll have to refer to it as a spiritual preparation—for the task of making important poetry. Now it isn't enough to say to such a student "go out and read philosophy, go out and read history." It's not enough. There has to be a very powerful sense of what happened and how people were affected. An interest in Duke Alessandro, for example. We know the history of that; we know there was in Lombardy a famine in 1815. What the poet has to find is whether anything was done about it, and who did it, and why. Do you see? That is the way the poet evolves, not through an amassing of dates and names and all that sort of thing. It isn't enough to say to the poet, "Okay, you have to have a rounded education, you can't merely do

---

* *Afterimages*, Shinkichi Takahashi, translation by Lucien Stryk, Swallow Press, 1970.

workshops and become a poet." No, you have to feel powerfully enough. That's what we're really talking about.

PICCIONE: Something even more incredible to add to that is that down underneath the words of "Crumbs" is the profundity of a vision that sees a bare, meager exchange, the crumb in the world always being passed. And for anyone to see that, one would have to go read philosophy in the woods for a while, or something. So it's not an idea, which is why I am drawn to that poem.

RUBIN: I have another question there to pose to both of you gentlemen and poets. "What do you attempt to teach in your own classes, for if a student should go outside of books and to the real world, what is the function of the classroom?"

STRYK: Well, what we could do, Stan, with that in mind is in a sense to evolve something from our last conversation. Tony published our inteview in *loblolly*, and in the very last part of it was a discussion of that sort. We were talking about how to teach. What do we tell young writers? And you might remember my suggestion was this: to make them understand that for the most part, the images that they were bringing to poems had been received from others, a very natural absorption of things from other writers. In order to write important poetry one has to begin looking at things very, very carefully, and that is why I suggested, as in Zen discipline, for example, the focusing on objects. Not forgetting what others have said, but to make an image, an arresting image, one that will become an important part of a poem, one has to use one's eyes, and there is a way one can achieve that: through very close unobstructed observation. I remember that in our last conversation we had ended with the reading of "Willows."

PICCIONE: It sounds so simple, and some students would conclude that you imply "don't read," but you suggest that you must get down away from the forehead of reading, so that you can see; not that you *can't* see, but you can't while you're thinking.

STRYK: And this returns to what we were saying a few moments ago about going into the woods, not to read philosophy, but to make it, to find it. Now how do you do that by that close observation? And this includes not only, of course, objects but a development from that to a consideration of many, many other things, concepts, historical events, news, whatever. We want our poets to be responsive to whatever is happening, and we want them, if they're to write good poems, to understand that in order to express what is happening, far and beyond learning, there has to be powerful emotion. Can that be taught? We were talking a little earlier about the poet being born, not made. Well, to a degree, the poet is made. In order to write good poems one has to learn a great deal about language, one has to learn a great deal about structure, one has to approach poetry in such a manner. But in order to write important poetry one has to bring along very powerful feelings, a sense that what is happening in the world means something, and that one has something to say about it.

RUBIN: It shouldn't just be an assignment for next week. Let me ask you something about your own working methods. I have a couple of questions. What role does revision play in your work?

STRYK: It's an amazing thing, and a timely one, that you asked me. I have just been through something rather interesting I can tell you about. I generally work a very long time on poems. I was tempted to send some things out, and unwisely did before they were actually ready. One, for example, went to *Partisan Review*. It wasn't ready, but it was accepted. I felt very unhappy about that poem, so I bore down on a body of poems and that was one of the ones that I changed drastically. Fortunately I got it there in time and it's being printed in the current issue. That was the first time in my experience as a writer that such a thing happened. I would have disgraced myself had that earlier version been printed. So on revisions, well, who was it said, "There's no writing, there's only re-writing"? It's true. I mean, the poet especially must be aware of that, and must learn the importance of patience. I've taken years over certain poems, and only recently, since a few people have asked to see things, I succumbed to the temptations of print. How very wrong that was!

RUBIN: This leads to my next question, if I might. What is it like to balance the translation work that you continue to do, and your own work? Do these things go quite nicely for you or are they separate endeavors?

STRYK: They're not separate. They never have been.

RUBIN: Does a poem of your own arise while you're in the act of translating?

STRYK: That's right. In an essay that perhaps you've seen, "Making Poems," I speak of these things going hand in hand. In fact, never have I felt that I was translating with the left hand. The work is serious, and I've never thought that it was secondary. I never felt that.

RUBIN: If I might change the topic for a moment, about the last ten years, I wonder now that you have not been teaching regularly, do you find more or less receptivity toward Zen and all it embodies in the places you travel and so on?

STRYK: Yes. It's an interesting thing, Stan. My first book on Zen came out in 1965. It's been a sort of continuous stream of books, translations, and so on related to Zen thought, Buddhism. At that time, and you know well of course, in the late sixties and early seventies the interest was essentially faddish, not always, certainly not in all cases, but everyone knew a little bit about Zen. It was a dilettantish endeavor in many cases. These days there is great interest, but it is invariably more serious. And that's what I feel when I go out to give programs: the questions I'm asked, the things said about my work, and translation, are of a more serious kind, with no tinge of the "new age," none of that any longer. It's true that in many cases at that time there was a "Beat" connection. I never thought there was anything wrong with it, but sometimes it got in the way of true understanding, a cultish affair. But now people have a very good sense of my work. When people speak of my books, I feel they've really read them, not just skimmed them.

PICCIONE: Sometimes you're placed in the position of talking about what cannot be talked about. It's a very hard place to be.

STRYK: This is what we've been doing. We've been talking about things, it's possible to talk about things, and I think it's possible to convey to students that kind of gravity. If one approaches such things, one has to understand that people have given their lives to them. In the case of Zen Buddhism, for fifteen hundred years people have written these poems, giving the best of themselves. I think, not confining our discussion to Zen, this is true for all poetry. We honor poets with or without spirit connection or religious interests, for the quality of their work, for the amount of life that they put into their poems, for the range of their interests and emotions. The poets I love do it all, the soft and the hard; it's all there.

PICCIONE: I'll remind you, too, in the last visit we had you read "The Word." If we get down to, if we could clear language away, which has been so squandered and misused, and come down to one word, the "silence that followed would prepare us." How are we doing at this winnowing, anyway?

STRYK: Getting better. We're winnowing, through the kind of work that is being done at this moment. We're talking about things which, as you realize, I hope will interest students especially. They're the ones we want to reach because obviously they are our future. What they do in poetry makes all the difference. Either our poetry lives or dies. It has at moments been close to death, and it has been resuscitated. Strong figures have come onto the scene and said, "Oh no. We have to do something new." And it's to those people we have to take these messages.

  RUBIN: Lucien and Tony, it's been all too quick, because it's near the end, it's my unfortunate duty to inform you. I think the two of you had talked earlier about Lucien bringing a close to this discussion, which I know is a discussion-in-process, with a poem from the *Collected Poems*.

  PICCIONE: Yes, and to pursue what we were just talking about, I began to sense that not only is there one world to be seen by anyone, but that Jung and depth psychology was another avenue towards this. I hope you will say a few words about seeing clearly as the result of individuating the self, or connecting the lower and upper consciousnesses clearly. Could you speak to that?

  STRYK: Let me tell you a little about that, and then relate it through the reading of the poem. I think there is an awareness, a very powerful awareness, of being directed. Call it what you will, there is something that directs us. I think there are two ways we can deal with that. We can bow to it, succumb to it, be its slave, or recognize that it nourishes us. There are moments when we are troubled. Are we allowing ourselves to be directed slavishly by this *whatever*, call it soul, call it spirit, call it the deepest human need?

  PICCIONE: When you say "it," is there an "other" of self?

  STRYK: I think it's an awareness of that *whatever* living within us. That's what I tried to do in this piece. (Stryk ends by reading):

*Soul**

Often evoked, exalted,
the soul might crouch
for years between

---

* Stryk, Lucien, *Collected Poems*, Swallow Press, Ohio University Press, 1984.

breastbone, esophagus,
conscience in a cage,
buzzing the ears,

pulling firm strings
behind eyes, patching up
heart-sores with cloudy

visions. My soul just
sits here, out of
action, arms wrapped

around stiffening knees,
sour looks on its
once friendly face.

I resent its power,
the scorn for all I write—
wrung from dreams it

feeds me, now and then.

ENLIGHTENMENT: HOW CAN WE BE SURE?

(Interview by Kent Johnson)

KENT JOHNSON: Your work in the past two decades as translator and scholar has been instrumental in bringing Zen literature to the English-speaking world. Your translations of the poems of Shinkichi Takahashi are among the work that has caused the most impact. Sadly, you received a call from Japan a few months ago* informing you of his death. I was wondering if you'd be so kind as to reflect today on what his work and friendship have meant to you, both personally and as a poet.

LUCIEN STRYK: The friendship has meant everything, and I have felt strongly for many years now that he was one of the great poets of the world. This obviously made my sense of him very special. I felt always, in his company, that I was privileged in being with a very great spirit. This led, I suppose, to my taking the greatest possible care with his poetry. The desire at all times was to give the English-speaking reader as full a sense as possible of this man's genius.

So because of the high regard I had for his character and his poetry, the friendship was very special; I would say, in fact, that the feeling was more familiar than such relationships tend to be. It certainly

---

* Takahashi died on June 4, 1987. This interview was conducted in September of that year.

wasn't a literary relationship. I have a very great feeling for his life, not only as a poet, but as a husband and father of two daughters. I also had a very strong sense of his position in the literary community of Japan. He, of course, benefited, as all would, from his special gift, and was recognized for it. But at the same time he was thought by many as something of an oddball, an outsider—his was a very special kind of position. The feeling, I'll tell you, was very exceptional, and I've never known anyone like him. He set the standard for me. I take it we're going to be talking about the nature of Zen poetry, or of matters along those lines, and perhaps I might say at this time that when I think of Zen poetry written by anyone, wherever in the world, it's always measured against what he accomplished. And this is something that I have become conscious of, if anything, more acutely in recent years, when I have been asked rather often to comment on the work of Zenists—some of the moderns who write what is sometimes termed "Zen poetry." There's always the feeling that he accomplished the very rare feat of expressing his Zen spirit fully through poetry. And this, I think, is very rarely achieved, in Japan or elsewhere. Now when we talk of the older Zen poetry, the sort that I included in books such as *Zen Poetry* and *The Crane's Bill*, well there, of course, we have great masters and the pure expression of profound insight.

Takahashi's verse is filled with the depth of those older poems. He was of an extraordinary character, as might be expected of an enlightened man, given formal testimonial of his achievement by Shi-zan Ashikaga, one of the great modern masters. He is, in my judgment, unsurpassed as a poet of our day. What his person, his friendship, have meant to me, is very difficult indeed to put into words.

JOHNSON: Judging from comments of his, Takahashi also thought quite a bit of you.

STRYK: A very remarkable thing, for I had no idea why! What I think he felt was that I made a very great effort to understand him and to render his poetry as it should be in English. Takahashi read English, as you might know, so we worked closely with him through the drafting process. When I say "we," I am speaking, of course, of the late Takashi Ikemoto, my friend and collaborator on so many projects. A very interesting, often complex process. . . . Takahashi gave permission in many cases for things in the original to be left out, simply because they did not work well in English. One of the best examples is in the poem "Burning Oneself to Death," one of the best known and most admired of his poems. There was material—about a stanza—that

I felt was too discursive. Not in Japanese, perhaps, but no amount of trying could bring it over adequately into English. Hence he agreed, after discussion, that it would be all right to cut that out. This actually happened in a number of cases, and Ikemoto mentions this in his brief account of our translation practice in *Zen Poetry*. So in many cases you have pieces that are greatly compacted, but always with his stamp of approval. The creative element hence became enthralling, because, you see, I was given virtually a free hand in working with the material.

What Takahashi saw as my major qualification was my involvement in Zen thought. It certainly wasn't linguistic, because that work I couldn't have done on my own; I had to work very closely with Ikemoto and Takahashi. There was a sense of exuberance working on texts that were far more than poetry—they were documents, spiritual documents of the most important kind. And when *Afterimages*, the first collection, came out, there were responses that suggested the poems could indeed affect lives in a very profound way.

JOHNSON: I remember Jim Harrison's essay in the *American Poetry Review*.

STRYK: Yes, his was especially moving—and as you may know, Zen is of deep importance to him. The work on the Takahashi poems has always been of that kind, a spiritual exercise, more than just the making of literary translations. Anyhow, these are some of the things I have felt for him.

JOHNSON: I was aware that there were a few poems that were "compressed," where things were left out. But it seems some might object, on the basis that the original text was being manipulated.

STRYK: I think that when the translator is privileged to work with the poet, it's not so much a matter of literalness, because, you see, the poet has made a judgment regarding the nature of what is being done. Takahashi's approval in some instances of deleting material came out of his understanding of the difficulties of bringing certain things into another language. The question of literalness is a central one in translation, of course, but I think in the case of our work with Takahashi, we were seeking always to transmit—as "literally" as possible—the spiritual energy of the poem.

JOHNSON: Could one say that the more highly charged the "spiritual energy" of a text—such as one tends to find in Zen poetry —the more open to interpretive possibility the translator should be?

STRYK: Exactly what I have to do as translator of Takahashi is to rise to the challenge; rise with passion and tact when that is called for. I've never thought of a translator as someone who should be an apologist, always worried, hat in hand, about the degree of faithfulness to the original. But as someone who when working intensely can spark those magical moments, when in fact he is the equal of the person he is translating—he must be that equal in order to render those poems properly. This is particularly true of Zen literature: an energy level as great as the poet's, a like degree of linguistic inventiveness, simply has to be there, there cannot be a gulf between such things. Otherwise there is only the husk.

    JOHNSON: When was your last meeting with Takahashi?

    STRYK: Two summers ago. It was when I was in Japan putting together *Triumph of the Sparrow* and also beginning an Issa volume.

    JOHNSON: Did he give you new poems at that time?

    STRYK: No, he was too ill to be thinking of new poetry. When I was with him that last time, he couldn't even stand. You might remember my mentioning that he postponed a visit to the hospital to spend time with me. That touched me very deeply. But he had said the important Zen poems were behind him, and in his last years he was occupied mainly with prose, though far from prolifically. Actually, the poems I've translated were selected from a large group—they represent only that part of his work that I felt capable of dealing with. Other translators, perhaps, will attempt those other poems someday.

    So many of the poems still overwhelm me when I think of them: poems such as "Position of the Sparrow"—I have rarely found any work of poetry which is as compact and full of the deepest philosophical insight and velocity. It's amazing to me how much he was able to get into those verses.

    JOHNSON: Clearly, then, the work with Takahashi has influenced your own poetry.

    STRYK: I think profoundly. But I must qualify immediately. I don't mean I have hope of ever matching his greatness—far from it!

    I think the best things I have done—and some of the poems in my new collection are perhaps among them—may have a trace of his velocity and the impact that comes of the arresting image. In others I'd like to feel I've won through to moments of stillness, though one must not counterpose stillness to energy—and often in Takahashi's work there is an amazing interdependence of the two . . . but it's very difficult to characterize one's own work. You are familiar, I'm sure, with Stephen Berg's book *Singular Voices*. I'm represented there by my poem "Awakening," and I discuss it at some length. I think that poem shows to what degree there has been from time to time in my work an attempt at that kind of compactness and rigor.

JOHNSON: Were you aware of Takahashi when you wrote "Zen: The Rocks of Sesshu"?

STRYK: I was, though less completely. The thing about that poem to me is that it was, almost by design, an attempt to deal clearly and overtly with Zen principles. Later poems, such as "Awakening," are not ostensibly about Zen, but more personal, maybe take things beyond that stage into areas of further clarity and suggestiveness. Which doesn't mean, incidentally, that I would dismiss the earlier poem. I would think of it as one of my lucky moments in poetry. But it so happens that at the time I wrote that I was clearly involved in trying to grapple with and straighten out my attitudes toward Zen at a relatively early stage of my practice. Now I feel that poems written about my immediate world, sitting out in my backyard, here in DeKalb, capture the spirit more fully than anything. There are poems in the last section of my *Collected Poems*, like "Where We Are," which I feel are as deeply grounded in Zen as the earlier, might one say, more "doctrinaire," pieces.

JOHNSON: Or "Willows," which is clearly about your practice, yet somehow also a ceremony of place.

STRYK: Yes, "Willows," and what makes that an important poem for me is that it represents a serious effort to come to terms with problems of discipline, when one lives away from the Zen community for long periods of time. That is, "Where am I?" and "What am I doing?," and "Is it still possible for me to feel that way?" and testing, pushing those questions to their limits. I found, in doing so, what I hope is a productive metaphor.

JOHNSON: You used the term "a lucky moment" a few minutes ago to describe writing the "Rocks of Sesshu," and that seems a curious way of referring to a poem that took you two years to compose.

STRYK: Well, there are "moments" and there are moments! You see, this poem led me to other things, opened up paths I had never suspected, and I speak of this in my essay "Making Poems." Incidentally, I had a very special experience recently in Japan, the time I saw Takahashi for the last time. I visited the Joeiji Temple where "Zen: The Rocks of Sesshu" was written and made—and I hesitate to use the term, but it certainly felt like it at the time—a spiritual return to the very house in which the poem was done. It was not occupied at the time and I was able to go to the very window and look in where that was experienced, when I stayed up all night, literally, beginning to think in the early afternoon and working until six the next morning, restructuring and reworking and getting a sense of what I might do with the *haiku*-like patterning that was emerging so insistently.

I had a powerful sense, looking into that empty room, that I had begun there something that was central to my life. I say "lucky," for in a sense the poem was sparked by my having said something shallow about the rock garden to Tenzan Yasuda, who did not hesitate to dress me down and to challenge me to look at it with fresh eyes. "Willows," I think, was another such moment. It is a poem that deals frankly with the difficulties of practice, and it seems to have struck a chord in others to whom Zen is important: a friend wrote me recently that he's at the "seventh willow"!

As long as we are talking about poems, let me show you this one, which is very recently finished. May I read it to you? (Stryk reads "Translating Zen Poems.")

> *Translating Zen Poems*
> *(I. M. Takashi Ikemoto)*
>
> The sliding doors open in
> the house hugging the mountain-
> side where my children sled
>
> in sandpapered orange-crates,
> downswoop into our garden under
> snow-glazed cypress, walnut,
>
> fig, persimmon trees, mowing
> dried stalks of tall eulalia
> grass along the way. Inside,
>
> we sit crosslegged, flushed
> with hibachi embers, before
> the plum-black Sado vase,
>
> under your gift, the Taiga
> scroll plum-blossoming out of
> season. Over green tea and sweet
>
> bean cake, I watch you shuffling
> pages where I've englished
> sparrows, temple gardens, fish,

time, universe—waiting
your word.

Now, thumbing through

years of those poems, I see you,
old friend, in flickering
light of sunset over snow-roofs

of this midwest town, recall
a moment under a mountain, when we
knew a master's words need never die.

JOHNSON: That's very fine. The image of the vase . . .

STRYK: It is written in memory of Takashi Ikemoto, of course. This poem was another return to a room—to the one in Yamaguchi where we sat together and worked. The memories of those days are very intense. It is from a new collection, *Of Pen and Ink and Paper Scraps*, which will be published in 1989, and I'd like to feel that it exhibits the kind of thing we've been talking of—where such spirit takes over the work when I'm lucky. Anyhow, I was very fortunate, of course, in having Ikemoto as a friend and collaborator. He was very patient with me, and there was a perfect balance in that he was a very careful scholar, with a deep appreciation of poetry. He knew that I would have to take certain liberties, but never too many, and often he would pull on the reins!

So it was a marvelous thing; we shared in the spirit of the enterprise and in all practical ways. It was a trusting and, really, a loving relationship—a rare thing. All of it a wonderful sense of our doing something important, not only to us, but to others.

JOHNSON: This comes back to Takahashi. In his youth Takahashi was influenced by Dada, and his first book is, in fact, titled *Poems of Dadaist Shinkichi*. I'm curious about the possible relationship between his intellectual and emotional involvement with Dada and his later Zen, particularly in regard to his poetry. It seems one could find analogies between the alogical dissociations in Takahashi's Zen imagery and those informing much Dada poetry and art. Are these similarities superficial, or is Dada and its iconoclastic spirit perhaps informed, at a deeper level, by intimations of Zen awareness?

STRYK: I think in Takahashi's case the *predisposition* was clearly there, the movement away from all things conventional. For Takahashi the literature of 1920s Japan, certainly its poetry, was empty of spirit. And one day he was galvanized by an article on Dadaism which seemed to him absolutely what he was looking for. Well, Takahashi became the central figure of Japanese Dada, publishing a manifesto, his poems, even a novel entitled *Dada*.

He was quite confrontational during this time and was often in trouble with the police. You may remember the story, as I have told it, that he was in prison when his book of Dada poems was published. When he was handed a copy through the bars of his cell, he went into a rage and tore it up. You see, attractive as the feeling was, and as spirited as the work was that came from it, Takahashi realized that he wasn't doing anything for his life. It was that simple.

In Japan it's been a long tradition that when an artist needs help he goes not to an analyst, but to a Zen master. There's a remarkable story, mentioned in my interview with a calendar-maker in Japan, in which Yukio Mishima sought out Shibayama-Roshi just before his ritual suicide and then canceled the appointment at the last minute. Who knows what might have happened had they met. Mishima was not a Zenist, but clearly there are instances of a Zen-like sensitivity in his work—no artist in Japan, really, can avoid being affected by Zen culture. And one might well find glimmerings of a Zen awareness in those Dada pieces of Takahashi, but—and this must be emphasized—not in any essential way. Perhaps it is useful to speak of the comparison on the level of the individual's psyche: clearly, the state of spiritual completeness and harmony associated with Zen is quite different from the nihilism so often exhibited by those involved with Dada.

Now Takahashi wanted some advice and guidance, and he went to the right man. He went to a man who was a distinguished Zen master, who would not be impressed by his poetry, but would see him as one who might use his poetry as an integral part of a spiritual quest, in handling *koans*, for example, as in the case of the poem "Collapse."

When he became a Zenist, naturally the poetry he wrote would reflect the kind of freedom Dadaism called for. But it was suddenly anchored in a very special world, with definite principles and clear aspirations, with concerns of a very special sort; the sort, of course, that Dada would never have. Dada had no concerns.

So he brought to his Zen inquiries that same freedom. And one might say he was prepared, as poet, for the kind of freedom that the Zen pursuit requires. But if you look at his poems with their wildness of imagery in mind, you find that when examined properly, they make the most absolute sense in Zen terms. There's nothing "Dadaist" about his Zen poems. One thinks, for example, of "Burning Oneself to

Death," a poem of profound spiritual and, I might say, political message. Of course, there is also much precedence in Zen literature for the kind of strange vision expressed by Takahashi—in the work of Keso, Zekkai, Hakuin—and many others.

JOHNSON: I'd like to return to the dynamics of form and content in Zen art, but since you mentioned the political implications of one of his poems, I'll pick that up and ask you about Zen's relevance to social issues today. In the Introduction to *Afterimages*, Takashi Ikemoto writes of Takahashi: "He had read Marx and Lenin and set out to discover whether Marxism or Zen had the ultimate truth." What seems implied here in the counterposition is that Marxism—and even perhaps the idea of any activist stance towards social reality—decisively lost out to Zen. Could you speak on your views concerning the relationship of Zen art and culture to the social and political issues of today?

STRYK: Takahashi discusses his early attraction to Marxism in an essay called "Komu," an autobiographical essay, where he speaks of his youth and of the philosophical issues that preoccupied the young during that time. He was born in 1901, and Marxism was in its heyday—in Japan as elsewhere—during the twenties and thirties. So there was a climate of political excitement sweeping up the young intellectuals of the day, and Takahashi came to feel that too many were allowing themselves to be too easily swept up. It is in this sense that his option for Buddhism may be seen as a statement, as the taking of a stand. It was not so much a rejection of the nature of Marxism, as it was an assertion of the essential value of spiritual life. Very difficult point to make, and I'm not sure I'm making it well. But Takahashi was not then and never was "apolitical" or "reactionary."

You see, he could not compromise; the undertaking of Zen study is all-consuming. One cannot have, in Zen, two masters: one that guides and challenges the disciple to revolutionize his or her spirit, and another political or ideological one. But the full commitment to spiritual practice by no means precludes an involvement with social concerns. There is no solipsism in Zen. To the contrary, Zen practice may be seen as a ripening of the subject for a more profound and effective engagement with the world. In fact, this is the disciple's vow, to act compassionately for others. I have never encountered a Zenist who was anything less than hopeful about social progress, and indeed, the Zenists I've known were all strongly progressive in their views.

What is important to recognize is that in the Buddhist worldview, there can be no meaningful social change without an equally radical transformation of spirit. The coupling of these two tasks is, really, an expression of the Zenist's quest to break though the subject/object distinctions that govern our daily consciousness.

JOHNSON: You mentioned that training is importantly a preparation to "act compassionately for others." Can "compassion" encompass activist positions that assume ideologically oppositional stances to the social order? One thinks of Gary Snyder, for instance.

STRYK: Absolutely, and Snyder of course is our most eloquent spokesperson—and example in practice—for that joining of compassionate attitude and full commitment. Hard to measure the extent of his contribution—how the writing, life and political vision are so interwoven . . . an exemplary person, I feel. And of course, we have countless examples of Buddhist monks in Asia who have been visible participants in many movements and causes: against nuclear weapons, for human rights and democracy in various nations, against the war in Southeast Asia. One mustn't deny that there has been, at times, a quietist impulse. Snyder himself has spoken critically of this; certainly Zen has not had throughout its history a hegemonic stance in terms of social action. But, clearly we know that there is no fundamental conflict between Zen spirit and enlightened action. I would say that Buddhism has had, and *must* have, a meaningful role to play in movements for peace and especially in defense of the planet's environment. There is no question that the current disregard for the planet's ecology is a profoundly *spiritual* problem.

I had an interesting experience a number of years back. Let me tell you about it, as it may strike home with the things we are talking about. During the sixties, Alan Watts befriended me. He admired, and was kind enough to say so, the early book of mine, *World of the Buddha.* It was around the time of the '68 election. Watts was invited to give a talk to Purdue University, and he suggested that I be invited to be on the panel, which also included Van Meter Ames and a Japanese Zen master. I myself had the highest regard for Watts's book *The Way of Zen* (Random House, 1965) and found him to be a most generous person. Anyhow, Watts was the keynote speaker and he was very persuasive, because he was a very brilliant man and a thoroughly engaging orator.

There was a huge crowd and the election was very much in the air. McCarthy had spoken at Purdue the day before. During the discussion period someone directed a question at me, asking if my statement that "Zen would guide one's life in all ways" meant also that it would guide one's decisions in an election year. And I said that of course it would, and that it would tell you necessarily for whom to vote, and that if it didn't, questions might be raised about Zen's relevance to modern society. Now Watts did not receive this practical association too kindly, and I found him looking over at me with an expression of—should I say—marked skepticism! But I believed then and I believe even more today that, yes, Buddhism does guide one in making choices in *all* areas of life.

JOHNSON: Watts, then, viewed political involvement as interfering with spiritual life?

STRYK: He might have explained it that way. But again, if you read carefully the books he was doing in those days, Zen for him was a very personal quest, and if one had personal problems and hangups, this was a way of getting rid of them. I don't mean to sound critical here. He was a very brilliant man and his writings—especially *The Way of Zen*—will continue to affect lives for a long time to come. But I think there was a sense on his part that one could go too far in bringing Buddhism into the practical arenas; and certainly that concern was legitimate during the spontaneous atmosphere of the sixties. But for me Zen has a vital role to play in the moral and social issues of the day. The people I most respected in Japan—Takahashi and Takayama—expressed this clearly as well.

JOHNSON: And yet you recently spoke of Takahashi's personal option for Zen *over* a practical involvement with the issues of his day. Could you clarify?

STRYK: It's important that we make a distinction here between the period of formal discipleship, and what may follow a completion of study. One must also distinguish between the responsibilities of the disciple and the lay person with a Zen practice.

You know of the idea of "nonattachment" in Zen. I think that the nonattached state is not only desirable, but absolutely necessary. If one is going to make progress in discipleship, one cannot hope to work properly under the guidance of a master while at the same time attending political rallies and getting excited about things outside the Zen community. In *World of the Buddha*, I have a chapter based on a special *sutra* in Buddhism that is shocking because it suggests that a disciple should not only be apart from, but be virtually disdainful of all life outside the Zen community. The purpose—and I say as much in my commentary—is to lead to the kind of nonattachment that would make progress in a community possible.

Now this is meant, of course, to be abandoned. And the length of time will vary, from disciple to disciple. That attitude reflected in the *sutra* is meant to be supplanted by a healthy, positive attitude of commitment to all living things. But in the process of training there can be no divided allegiance. To an outsider, the intense, nonattached spirit of training in the early stages may seem indifferent, cold, lacking in compassion. And that can be a problem, I think, for many.

The assumption, you see, behind the principle of practicing nonattachment, is—and this may seem a paradox—that action is better performed when one is free of those concerns and concepts that will lead to a kind of unsteadiness; so that if one's hands are free to act without being misdirected by a confused, agonized mind, the action will be all the more perfect. There will be no impulsiveness that might lead to harmful action.

JOHNSON: Such as violence?

STRYK: Zen is uncompromisingly nonviolent.

JOHNSON: In relation to this theme of Zen and social commitment, could you comment on one of your better-known poems, "Cherries"? (Here Stryk reads "Cherries"; see p. 305.)

STRYK: Yes, the poem is an attempt to deal with the suffering of others, not in a self-righteous way, but in the sense of recognizing my own complicity in their suffering. As we luxuriate in our privileges, others suffer; it is not enough to just recognize suffering and injustice. Many of us do indeed "care," and proclaim our opinions, but our lives are so often falsely lived: we go on, taking our pleasures for granted, not thinking that the root of the fruits we enjoy is so often the pain of others. I believe this very strongly, and I think that one might relate that poem to Buddhist *karuna*, or compassion. I can see it being read very much in that context.

I think we have to examine ourselves constantly. You know this more than most, perhaps, because of your work in Nicaragua; that experience must have helped you more clearly perceive these connections.

JOHNSON: The poem works for me as a kind of "ethical *koan*," if such a thing is possible—a challenge to reevaluate the relationship of one's personal life to one's stated values. It seems that without such self-reflection on deeper motivations and desires, political values will become rigid and self-righteous. You're right that working in Central America opened my eyes to a number of things. It was a rich experience. But frankly, what's interesting to me is how easily upon my return I was pulled back again into the kinds of complicities you deal with in the poem!

STRYK: I would say that to truly transform one's life— that's the task of Zen. And to be aware of that complicity, to feel that there is something infinitely richer, is a first, difficult step.

JOHNSON: On a different theme, but which might bring us back in suggestive ways to some of the questions we've been discussing: Are you familiar with Language poetry?

STRYK: I'm familiar with the term and I've read some samples of the writing, yes.

JOHNSON: Well, as you might know, the Language poets have had a prominent role in the growing interest toward the relationship between politics and poetry here in the U.S. The political "content" of their work is not didactically posed, but rather implicit in the ways the writing itself unsettles conventional constructions of "meaning." I was wondering if you might find any points of convergence between this writing and that of Takahashi, in the sense that he also is involved, insistently, in defamiliarizing conventional ways of seeing and thinking. I've brought along a few poems from Michael Palmer, whose work I admire, and I thought we might use these as a point of reference. Is it possible to see in the ways that both these poets disrupt expected narrative frames, an affinity in attitude toward the relationship of language and world? That conceptual structures are not reflections of reality, but illusions? (Stryk reads "Dearest Reader," "The Night Sky," "Poem in Two Parts," and "The Painted Cup" from Palmer's *First Figure*.)

STRYK: I think the great problem with finding a similarity between such poems as these by Michael Palmer and those of Takahashi is that Takahashi would leave such formal kinds of concerns behind in attacking what Zenists would see as the important issues. I think theme dominates his most important poems, hence you have pieces such as "Position of the Sparrow," "Burning Oneself to Death," "Disclosure," so many others. These poems advance, of course, in very startling, seemingly fragmentary ways, but never lose sight of their central theme. I think the poems I've just read by Palmer would appear to be a denial of theme and reference. I think the poems are impressive on the intellectual level, and I might find, were I to read more, that there are other stimulations, attractions, interesting nuances, but not of the kind I could relate to the Zen poems I most value.

JOHNSON: I was wondering if there might be points of contact in the attitude toward the "self." The Language writers are working to an important extent out of post-structuralist theory, and there is an implicit but consistent critique in the work of traditional conceptions of the unitary "I." Clearly, there would seem to be some analogy here to Zen's attitude towards normative perceptions of self. In a related way, it would seem both Palmer and Takahashi might share some affinity in their epistemological stances towards the "outer world." That is, a strong sense that the narrative continuities we take for granted are not natural, but imposed.

STRYK: An interesting question, but I would maintain that there is a significant difference. One cannot reduce the intuition of "non-self" to a linguistic or formal matter. And if one adopts the view that language is all-pervasive—impenetrable, these poets might say—then one can easily get caught up in the repetitious exercise of the "imitative fallacy," where "non-self" is mimicked through all sorts of disjunctions and fragments. Takahashi's poems go far beyond being mere critiques of standard ways of perceiving life; they are that, you see, but they are also profoundly assertive of realms beyond the linguistic. They are, we might say, studies of the "non-self," of the oneness of *sunyata* and *tathata* (respectively, the Buddhist concepts of "emptiness" and "suchness").

Now I must say that these remarks are given in a cautious spirit, as I do not know the work of the Language writers all that well. I am saying this all rather instinctively, based on the examples you have just shared with me. Certainly I would be interested in learning more about the views of these poets.

JOHNSON: But couldn't that avoidance of "theme" you were talking about in Language writing be valuable in that it might help re-direct our attention toward the fact of *language itself*, forcing us to pay more heed to the ways in which meanings are constituted? That is, help make us more self-reflexive about the "themes" that structure our assumptions about the world?

STRYK: It may contribute. But what I would suggest is that fine poems of whatever persuasion or school do that. The fine poem by a Hart Crane, Dylan Thomas, or Wallace Stevens would exhibit all that finesse with language that would ask for the greatest kind of focus on words, the greatest concentration on the manner in which these words mean. I would think that the ideas that inform Language poetry are implicit in many important poems that *also* communicate with—are grounded in—the world outside language.

There are too many urgencies of life, demanding issues which make us constantly aware of our humanity and challenge our spirit. I suppose some would regard my views as conventional, but how can we forget about these things, or counterpose them to the interests of linguistic experimentation? That we must be aware of language, always look at it afresh, why, yes, this is at the heart of the poetic enterprise. But formalism can be taken too far, I think, and method become a substitute for the poet's responsibility to communicate in ways that can make a meaningful difference.

JOHNSON: Your comments are interesting and raise, I think, further questions. Again, it *is* possible, I think, to find significant affinities between deconstructionist critiques of language and the Buddhist views toward self and conceptual thought. Nagarjuna's writings, for example, which are essential to the Zen doctrine of nothingness, posit that the space between the object and its sign is unbridgeable. Wouldn't the questioning of the assumptions we make *within* language—an exploration of those linguistic gaps—be a legitimate undertaking from the Zen point of view? In fact, you yourself, in discussing the poems of Takahashi in the Introduction to *Zen Poetry*, quote Pingalaka to illustrate the Mahayana doctrine of interpenetration:

> If the cloth had its own fixed, unchangeable self-essence, it could not be made from the thread . . . the cloth comes from the thread and the thread from the flax. . . . It is just like the . . . burning and the burned. They are brought together under certain conditions, and thus there takes place a phenomenon called burning . . . each has no reality of its own. For when one is absent the other is put out of existence. It is so with all things in this world, they are all empty, without self, without absolute existence. They are like the will-o'-the-wisp.

There are strong suggestions here, it seems to me, of what deconstructionist criticism would term the endless "deferral" of meaning in language.

STRYK: Let me tell you that Pingalaka's comments are very much the Buddhist view. But as you can see, in order to express it, Pingalaka had to give us very clear images. I think that Language poems might somewhat suggest the *feeling* of non-self, but as with the danger of the "imitative fallacy," they could at the same time be expressing innumerable other things. Pingalaka, like Takahashi and all Buddhists who write of such things, gives us clear, assertive expression. When Takahashi is writing about denying self, or speaking of the disgust he feels with self, that is the *theme*. I don't know quite how to put my complaint, but it's just that the poems—and I take it that these are typical, even distinguished among the Language group—do very little for me, they don't direct my imagination. I would think that they tend to be less effective than surreal poems, which they might, at least superficially, resemble. But in the case of surreal poems, with their force and boldness, there is an assertiveness I think can be engaging. What I suppose I am asking is this: if Language poetry is meant to make us more aware of the ultimate ingredient—the word itself—what makes it so very different from a random selection of words taken from the dictionary, when examined very carefully. What is there about the poem itself apart from what I suppose might be seen as tonal unity— the words seem to be tonally chosen—what is there about these words which calls for greater focusing and greater examination than perhaps would the random choice of words from any source? You see, what is so compelling about those words? Why not turn to five pages of the dictionary?

JOHNSON: Well, this actually brings up another question I had, which is the relationship between Zen and chance. There are American artists and writers—John Cage and Jackson MacLow come immediately to mind as artists deeply influenced by Buddhism—who would argue a deep value in chance operations. And actually, a technique employed by some Langauge writers has been to go to the "dictionary," relying partly on the force of randomness.

STRYK: Yes, well I'm very much aware of Cage's ideas; I'm very much interested in them. MacLow I know less of, but I'm aware that his name is being increasingly recognized. In the case of the random element in Cage—and here, of course, we are dealing in sound—and I see the parallel and it's a very real one: why not just open your ear to the window, rather than playing Beethoven's Fifth for the five hundredth time . . . the ear becomes accustomed to the pattern so that it no longer listens with the kind of attention sound deserves. Why not choose from the air, and delight in the pattern—it could be infinitely more exciting than one of those old warhorses thrown at us! There *are* wonderful possibilities in the sounds that come at us spontaneously from the wind, the sound of the cars, the sound of glass against glass, what have you. That I respect very much.

But language is very different, I feel. It doesn't so much come at us as that we go for it. In other words, the randomness is of a very different kind. Who knows if when we look at that page of the dictionary, the randomness is always pure? It seems to me that there are many other factors, pressurings if you will, that direct us, nudge us toward a choice. Of course, this is because words and our relationships to them are always bound up with meaning and the complexities of their signification.

Sound is different. The cry of a creature, and the wind's murmur, let us say, rise out of a pure realm, one that doesn't have its source— as language does—in reflective and conceptual thought.

Again, a personal experience, and one that I speak of in my interview with an aesthetician in Japan, when we are talking about museum-going, and I say that there have been periods in my life when I had a sense that the movement toward the museum, the walking there, is more visually exciting than anything that happens in the museum. *If* I look as I should look, if I *look* at that face moving toward me on the street—*look* at it, couldn't that experience be more vital than what any painting could give me? The leaf, as I stop to look at it on the branch, or on the pavement, and what Morikawa says to me is, "Well, you can hardly expect me to agree with *that*, I'm an aesthetician!" But, you see, what I'm saying at that moment is very much what Cage is saying: whenever you look at something as it should be looked at, your learned concepts of what is "mundane" and what is "art" begin to collapse.

JOHNSON: Yes, well then to go back to my question about the possible affinities between Dada and Zen, couldn't Duchamp's "found objects," for example, be regarded as an expression of—or at least a desire for—"pure seeing" and pre-reflective awareness?

STRYK: Hardly. The Dadaists were, I think, searching for oddness, very deliberately.

JOHNSON: This leads me to a question I had on the relationship between form and content in Zen literature and art. One finds a distinct difference in representation between, for instance, a Ryokan and a Takahashi. Or between the meditative quiet of the T'ang poets who were very close to Buddhism, like Wang Wei, Tu Fu, or Li Po on the one hand, and the almost surrealist tone of your translations that appear in *The Crane's Bill* and *Zen Poetry*. It seems one could draw similar distinctions between a Sesshu, whose most famous paintings seemed infused with a delicate stillness, suggesting at the same time a connection to traditional perspective, and the explosive boldness of a Sengai or Hakuin, whose works have a clear thrust toward abstraction, where the figure's representation is most tenuous. What of the relationship between Zen spirit and form? Are these different styles inscribed in different experiences, or perhaps different levels of enlightenment, or is there a single source?

STRYK: Surely a single source. Now we have to make allowances for very great differences in temperament. We also have to make allowances for the fact that some Zenists, masters included, have been strongly predisposed to the making of powerful poems. Others have been predisposed to responding in ways that might be seen as more delicate. But one must in no way assume that these differences reflect a greater or lesser spiritual experience. I think that when you examine some of the Zen death poems you must have in mind, you will find differences in temperament—some poems, as with Nansen, express a profound stillness; others, such as Dogen's, speak of shattering the very universe. Yes, one must make allowances for those differences in temperament that will result in differences in expression.

I think that Takahashi, for instance, would have been seen as a genius even had he not gone into Zen. He was, in a sense, the Japanese Rimbaud. But I don't think he would have become as great a human being or as great a poet. Those flashes which distinguish his poetry would still have been there in the formal sense, but of course, we would not have had the powerful resonances that came of his struggle with *koans*, with those giant issues set before all Zenists: the nature of time, the nature of space, those remarkable insights which derive from his pursuit.

The question is a very interesting one, and I'm sure silently asked by many who are drawn to the Zen arts. Why such great differences in expression between people who are part of the same tradition? But I don't think it would be proper to assume that the poem's *form* or its tone is necessarily an indication of the depth of the Zen experience.

JOHNSON: To what extent might those differences in temperament and expression take place in a single individual involved with Zen and still reflect an integral spiritual experience?

STRYK: The feelings of the Zenist will differ according to all sorts of circumstances, but the spiritual feeling of the poems will bear a consistency. I think that each time there is the inclination toward poetic expression, whatever forces would be generated by that *will*, will come to the surface. In other words, when the poem is triggered, when it is called for, all those predispositions which lead to the poem are funneled toward a determined end.

JOHNSON: I ask, partly, because I find that in your own work there is a diversity; in the "Rocks of Sesshu," for example, where there is a terseness and compression, a chiseled quality, which seems to differ markedly from some of your newer work in *Bells of Lombardy*, which is clearly more traditional, in a lyrical sense, than your better known "Zen" poems.

STRYK: This is a very good question, and I want very much to explain what I think happened. You may remember, from some of the things I have written, the term "man of no title." The Zenist abhors being pigeonholed. When I began *Bells of Lombardy*, I was very much aware that my better-known poems had tended toward that terseness, into which I had tried to pack whatever insight and meaning I had received. I was aware of what my "style" was. And now I wished to write a different poem—one through which readers might wander, in the way they do through, say, a Wallace Stevens poem, taking sensory delight in a richness and accumulation of image and phrase. Secondly because I felt I could do it, and wanted to.

So I wanted to see whether it might be possible to sustain, using the normal narrative and rhetorical devices, a symbolic structure throughout the range of the poem. And begin to have, through the recurrence of these more "lyrical" resonances, special meaning. Knowing, by the way, full well—I think I knew—that I would be returning to a method much more evident in my work up until then. This is very much in the spirit of becoming the "man of no title," of not binding oneself, of remaining open to new challenges and problems.

JOHNSON: But your forthcoming collection does represent a return to your more "recognizable" style? That of much of the work beginning with *The Pit and Other Poems?*

STRYK: I think so, very much. No, I think *Bells of Lombardy* was a very special book. But I recall delighting at the time in its difference. And I still do.

JOHNSON: As you know, I'm interested in *haiku*, and I'd like to ask you a couple of questions on the subject. Here is a quote from your introduction to *Zen Poetry:*

The Zen experience is centripetal, the artist's contemplation of subject sometimes referred to as "mind-pointing." The disciple in an early stage of discipline is asked to point the mind at (meditate upon) an object, say a bowl of water. At first he is quite naturally inclined to metaphorize, expand, rise imaginatively from water to lake, sea, clouds, rain. Natural, perhaps, but just the kind of "mentalization" Zen masters caution against. The disciple is instructed to continue until it is possible to remain strictly with the object, penetrating more deeply, no longer looking *at* it but, as the Sixth Patriarch Hui-neng maintained essential, *as* it.

Yet on the previous page you speak also of the finest *haiku* having a "range of association that is at times astonishing." Does metaphorization in the art of *haiku* interfere with or deepen the identification with the object itself? For example, is Basho's "Old Pond," read as symbol of the poet's mind, an obstacle to understanding the poem's transcendent nature, or a signpost pointing the way?

Old pond,
leap-splash—
a frog.

STRYK: I think you might remember that in that introduction I draw the comparison between Pound's "In a Station of the Metro,"

The apparition of these faces in the crowd;
Petals on a wet, black bough.

and a *haiku* by Onitsura,

Autumn wind—
across the fields,
faces.

I point out that in the Onitsura piece there is no metaphor, but rather that it stuns with its immediacy. I think that the greatest *haiku* avoid the kind of symbolization that tends to take place—consciously or not—in most Western poetry. The paragraph you read aloud is as true as anything I've ever written of Zen training or Zen experience. It *is* "centripetal." I have heard Zenists speak constantly of the dangers of mentalization, and they would see the seeking for similes and comparisons as instances of mind-drifting. I think that the most important examples of *haiku* probably come as a result of that *staying* with the object, exploring *it* for all its worth, finding within *it* the imaginative essence. I'm sure there would be exceptions, but if you take, for example, the great Buson *haiku:*

> A sudden chill—
> in our room my dead wife's
> comb, underfoot.

Well, there is no metaphor there. And I think there are very few figurative flights in great *haiku*. The directness, the simplicity, the extraordinary juxtaposition, that in its truest form *cancels* simile.

JOHNSON: But what of the "range of association?"

STRYK: The range of association is precisely the result. For example in the Buson, there is no metaphor to that. The complexity of sentiment that is generated by that act is what I mean by association. It isn't the sort of thing we might mean in speaking of the many different metaphors or images we would be likely to find in a "good" Western poem. There is a very great range of *association* in the Basho poem you mentioned, but not in terms of simile or metaphor.

JOHNSON: Very well, but I believe I speak for many in saying that I have read Basho's "Old Pond" on a symbolic level, where the pond is the *real* pond itself, but also a metaphor for the poet's mind.

STRYK: That is the way it is often read and quite properly. I think that it might be read on both levels, and why not? That profound symbolism is part of its greatness—and I use "symbolism" here in distinction to metaphor. In Western metaphor an image tends to stand for something beyond itself, and often in a subordinate relation to it. In the kind of "symbolization" we find in the Basho poem, there is a profound dissolution of categories; a pure merging of inside and outside.

I think that one has to know, in order to appreciate the poem as much as it should be appreciated, the circumstances of Basho's conversation with the Master Butcho. It is out of that exchange, and the act of the frog's leaping, that his mind was exploded and enlightenment ensued.

JOHNSON: In the way that double reading is made possible, could it be said that *haiku collapse* the expected hierarchies of symbolization? In other words, that while in our tradition the symbol points to an "other," in the *haiku* the "suchness" of experience fully encompasses the symbol?

STRYK: Take, for example, the great poem by Boncho:

Nightingale—
my clogs
stick in the mud.

How much that tells us of Boncho's sensibility. We might say the poem is "symbolic," in a narrative sense; we know here that an unusual man has been stopped in his tracks by a bird's song. And we may well imagine many things about the circumstances surrounding the event. And yet the poem simultaneously shatters the narrative connection, exposing the utter strangeness and mystery of the experience. Again, the range of association becomes infinite.

JOHNSON: Then the challenge would be to penetrate that narrative level?

STRYK: Well, I suppose I might say that great *haiku* ultimately challenge our propensities to make these analytical distinctions! It's curious, I had a meeting with two young poets in Chicago just the other day . . .

JOHNSON: Not Language poets, I suppose?

STRYK: (Laughing) No, though I do hope *they* would understand that my previous comments were made in a modest and non-contentious spirit—perhaps sometime I will have the chance to sit down with one or more of them also, and learn more about their views. But anyway, one of these poets in Chicago was telling me that *haiku* had influenced his work a great deal and that Issa was his favorite poet in the world. And though his own poetry bears no resemblance whatsoever to the *haiku*, he spoke to me of how the work startles him and of the way he receives impressive *haiku*. And he wants, somehow, to bring that spirit into his own work. I mention this, without being more specific, I suppose, because poems by Buson, Issa, Basho, the other great masters, make their impact *through* their method, without recourse to the kinds of elements and practices we seem to feel Western poetry would require. The bareness is the *marrow* of that richness. The Boncho, the Onitsura examples I quoted, make this so clear.

JOHNSON: There is a relatively large and vibrant community of *haiku* poets in the United States and Canada—some of them like Robert Spiess, Marlene Mountain, John Wills, Elizabeth Searle

Lamb, to name only a few, important practitioners of the art. But the *haiku* seems little practiced among "mainstream" poets. In fact, you do not seem to write any yourself! Why?

STRYK: As for myself, I can only answer with the utmost frankness and risk, I suppose, seeming overly dramatic. Because I have worked now for so many years studying the great *haikuists*, I find myself powerless, simply not knowing how to begin. I have tried, I have found myself too much concerned, too self-conscious, in a way that I never am with my other writing. I am too aware of the shadow of Issa and Basho, of what this art has brought into being. It's a confession of which I am not proud. But I have tried from time to time, and always have felt the efforts were laughable in comparison. Perhaps those pieces I have come away with might have been seen by others as "publishable." I don't know, because no one except myself has ever seen them! I *do* think I understand the dynamics of *haiku*, their linguistic structure, their relationship to Zen spirit and principles. But I am afraid I have become too overwhelmed by what has been accomplished to be a true artist in the form. Now, my great hope is that as a translator I am successful in registering the excitement I feel. And I would like to think I have contributed meaningfully in this way.

Another issue is that as a writer of "normal" poems, the world I experience as an American living in Illinois rests, as far as making poems goes, on devices that would have to be seen as more traditional and Western. This is a very odd thing, perhaps. As you know, image and metaphor are very important to my work. The *haiku* on the other hand, certainly must have affected my work—even if unconsciously—when, for example, I composed "Rocks of Sesshu" or "Awakening." So the feeling here is a strange mixture.

JOHNSON: Might that "silence" on your part toward the *haiku* imply you would consider it the highest expression of written art?

STRYK: I believe very strongly that the finest *haiku* are among the most sophisticated expressions of human spirit, yes. No poetry has affected me more profoundly than the *haiku* of the great masters. But I wanted to return to something you said in your question about *haiku* not having found an audience among mainstream poets. And I must say that if that has been true, then things would seem to be undergoing a change. I think there has been a shift toward a new receptiveness.

JOHNSON: You have been involved with Zen for many years now, and a number of your poems have dealt frankly with the difficulties and frustrations of spiritual discipline. (At Johnson's request, Stryk here reads "Willows," see pp. 311–312.)

You have devoted your life to Zen, and yet speak without hesitation about being an "unenlightened man." To conclude this interview, I wanted to ask you: How can we be sure that there really is such a thing as "enlightenment"?

STRYK: We can be sure by meeting those who have experienced it. It has been my great privilege to know intimately people like Taigan Takayhama, Shinkichi Takahashi, and to see how their lives have been affected; to live among them, to hear them talk, observe their interaction with the world, to read their work, that is how we can know.

While "Willows" is, on one level, about disappointment, I want it to be seen equally as a poem of positive values—an expression of an unenlightened man attempting to better his life, who makes an effort to practice *zenkan*, or pure-seeing, so that he might go from one willow to another, without being turned around constantly by inner conflicts and problems. It is a mirror poem in the sense that more than any mirror could show, the trees reveal one after another the degree of my unenlightenment, the distance I would have to travel in order to find awakening. And the poem, I suppose, might be seen in its final stanza as humorous. Maybe it should be! It is in a way amusing that I must lower my sights by "practicing on my bushes." But I'm still involved and hopeful, and this is the most important thing.

And we can be aware of the possibilities of Zen through practice itself. *Zenkan* is difficult, but through it we *can* come to sense, even if we never fully grasp it, that there is something fathomless of which we are a part. I may never become enlightened, but I can say that I am not the man I was when I began. My hope, always, is that the change over the years has been transmitted through the work.

Acknowledgments

The writing of much of this book was made possible by a Fulbright Travel/Research Grant and was partially supported by a grant from the Illinois Arts Council, a state agency.

For permission to use material previously printed in periodicals, thanks are due the editors of *American Poetry Review, American Book Review, Antioch Review, Chicago Review, The Georgia Review, loblolly, Malahat Review, Michigan Quarterly Review, The Mountain Path, New Letters, The North American Review, Ohio Review, The Spirit That Moves Us,* and *TriQuarterly.*

For permission to use material previously printed in books, thanks are due the following publishers: "Making Poems," from *American Poets in 1976,* (c) 1976 by Bobbs-Merrill Co., Inc.; "What? Why This. This Only," from *Singular Voices: American Poetry Today,* Stephen Berg, ed., (c) 1985 by Avon Books. "Let the Spring Breeze Enter," from *Zen: Poems, Prayers, Sermons, Anecdotes, Interviews,* (c) 1965 by Lucien Stryk and Takashi Ikemoto, Doubleday & Co., Inc. "Poetry and Zen," from *Zen Poems of China and Japan: The Crane's Bill,* (c) 1973 by Lucien Stryk, Takashi Ikemoto, and Taigan Takayama, Anchor Press/Doubleday & Co., Inc.; "Buddhism and Modern Man," from *World of the Buddha,* (c) 1968 by Lucien Stryk, Doubleday & Co., Inc.; "Zen Poetry," from *The Penguin Book of Zen Poetry,* (c) 1977 by Lucien Stryk and Takashi Ikemoto, Swallow Press, Inc.

Part I of "The Range of Zen" is edited from a transcript of "Encounter with Lucien Stryk," a videotaped interview, April 18, 1984.

354

KODANSHA GLOBE

International in scope, this series offers distinguished books that explore the lives, customs, and mindsets of peoples and cultures around the world.

INVISIBLE MEN
Life in Baseball's
*   Negro Leagues*
Donn Rogosin
Introduction by
   Monte Irvin
1-56836-085-1

BLACKBERRY WINTER
My Earlier Years
Margaret Mead
New Introduction by
   Nancy Lutkehaus
1-56836-069-X

ELDEST SON
Zhou Enlai and the
*   Making of Modern*
*   China, 1898–1976*
Han Suyin
1-56836-084-3

THE AWAKENED SELF
Encounters with Zen
Lucien Stryk
New Introduction by
   the Author
1-56836-046-0

ALONE
Adm. Richard E. Byrd
Original Illustrations by
   Richard Harrison
Facsimile of the 1938 Edition
Introduction by David Campbell
1-56836-068-1

OF DREAMS AND DEMONS
A Memoir of Modern
*   India*
Patwant Singh
New Introduction by
   the Author
1-56836-086-X

PASSING STRANGE AND
**   WONDERFUL**
Aesthetics, Nature, and
*   Culture*
Yi-Fu Tuan
1-56836-067-3

THE DESERT ROAD TO
**   TURKESTAN**
Owen Lattimore
New Introduction by
   David Lattimore
1-56836-070-3

OPTIMISM
The Biology of Hope
Lionel Tiger
Reintroduction by the
   Author
New Introduction by
   Frederick Turner
1-56836-072-X

THE MOUNTAIN OF NAMES
A History of the
*   Human Family*
Alex Shoumatoff
New Preface by the Author
New Introduction by
   Robin Fox
1-56836-071-1

EMPIRES OF TIME
Calendars, Clocks, and
*   Cultures*
Anthony Aveni
1-56836-073-8

ESSENTIAL SUBSTANCES
A Cultural History of
*   Intoxicants in Society*
Richard Rudgley
1-56836-075-4

To order, contact your local bookseller or call 1-800-788-6262 (mention code G1). For a complete listing of titles, please contact the Kodansha Editorial Department at Kodansha America, Inc., 114 Fifth Avenue, New York, NY 10011.